Desktop Publishing with WordPerfect® 5.0

Jim Tevis

WILEY

John Wiley & Sons, Inc.

New York • Chichester • Brisbane • Toronto • Singapore

Publisher: Stephen Kippur
Editor: Therese A. Zak
Managing Editor: Ruth Greif
Compositor: Line & Tone Typografix Corp.

This publication is designed to provide accurate and authoritative information in regard to the subject matter covered. It is sold with the understanding that the publisher is not engaged in rendering legal, accounting, or other professional service. If legal advice or other expert assistance is required, the services of a competent professional should be sought. FROM A DECLARATION OF PRINCIPLES JOINTLY ADOPTED BY A COMMITTEE OF THE AMERICAN BAR ASSOCIATION AND A COMMITTEE OF PUBLISHERS.

Copyright 1989 by John Wiley & Sons, Inc.

All rights reserved. Published simultaneously in Canada.

Reproduction or translation of any part of this work beyond that permitted by section 107 or 108 of the 1976 United States Copyright Act without the permission of the copyright owner is unlawful. Requests for permission or further information should be addressed to the Permission Department, John Wiley & Sons, Inc.

Library of Congress Cataloging-in-Publication Data
Tevis, Jim.
    Desktop publishing with WordPerfect 5.0 / Jim Tevis.
       p.   cm.
    Bibliography: p.
    ISBN 0-471-61848-9
    1. Desktop publishing.   2. WordPerfect (Computer program)
  I. Title.
Z286.D47T45 1989
686.2'2--dc19   88-30586

Printed in the United States of America

89 90 10 9 8 7 6 5 4 3 2 1

This book is dedicated to my wife Deborah, who heaped on the encouragement and soft drinks when there always seemed to be one too many deadlines and generally kept things running (including me) when I was in absentia with WordPerfect, my computer, and this book.

Trademarks

1-2-3 is a registered trademark of Lotus Development Corp.
2400etc is a trademark of ATI Technologies, Inc.
Adobe Illustrator 88 is a trademark of Adobe Systems, Inc.
Amiga is a trademark of Commodore Business Machines, Inc.
Apple is a registered trademark of Apple Computer, Inc.
AST is a trademark of AST Research, Inc.
AutoCAD and Autoshade are trademarks of Autodesk, Inc.
Bitstream is a registered trademark of Bitstream, Inc.
BubbleJet and CX are trademarks of Canon U. S. A., Inc.
Compaq is a registered trademark of Compaq Computer Corp.
CompuServe is a registered trademark of CompuServe Information Services, an H&R Block Company
DesignCAD 3-D is a trademark of American Small Business Computers, Inc.
Designer is a trademark of Micrografx, Inc.
DESQview is a trademark of Quarterdeck Office Systems
Disk Optimizer is a trademark of SoftLogic Solutions
Document Description Language is a trademark of Imagen
Epson is a registered trademark of Epson America, Inc.
Font Effects and Font Solution Pack are trademarks of SoftCraft, Inc.
Fontware is a trademark of Bitstream, Inc.
Hercules is a registered trademark of Hercules Computer Technology, Inc.
HOTSHOT Graphics is a trademark of Symsoft, Inc.
HyperACCESS is a trademark of Hilgraeve, Inc.
IBM, IBM PC, and IBM AT are registered trademarks of International Business Machines Corp.
Intel is a registered trademark of Intel Corp.
Interleaf is a trademark of Interleaf Inc.
Interpress is a trademark of Xerox Corp.
LP4120 is a trademark of Ricoh Company
Laser Fonts is a registered trademark of SoftCraft, Inc.
LaserJet, LaserJet Series II, ScanJet, and ThinkJet are trademarks of Hewlett-Packard Company
Laserwriter, Laserwriter Plus, and Macintosh are trademarks of Apple Computer, Inc.
Library is a trademark of WordPerfect Corp.
Linotronic and Linotype are trademarks of Allied Corp.
LOTUS is a registered trademark of Lotus Development Corp.
Mace Utilities is a trademark of Paul Mace Software
Micrografx is a trademark of Micrografx, Inc.
MNP is a trademark of Microcom Corp.
MS-DOS is a registered trademark of Microsoft Corp.
MultiSync is a trademark of NEC Home Electronics Corp.
PageMaker is a registered trademark of Aldus Corp.
PC Paintbrush Plus is a registered trademark of ZSoft Corp.
PC Scan 2020 is a trademark of Dest Corp.
PostScript is a registered trademark of Adobe Systems, Inc.
PS/2 is a trademark of International Business Machines Corp.
Publisher's Paintbrush is a trademark of ZSoft Corp.
Quattro and Sidekick Plus are trademarks of Borland International
QMS is a registered trademark of QMS, Inc.
RamFont is a trademark of Hercules Computer Technology, Inc.
Snapshot is a trademark of Aldus Corp.
Sun is a registered trademark of Sun Computer Corp.
SuperVGA HiRes is a registered trademark of Genoa Systems Corp.
Times Roman is a registered trademark of Allied Corp.
Ventura Publisher is a trademark of Ventura Software, Inc.
Video Graphics Array is a trademark of International Business Machines Corp.
Word is a registered trademark of Microsoft Corp.
WordPerfect is a trademark of WordPerfect Corp.
Wordstar is a trademark of Micropro International, Inc.
Wordstar Professional is a trademark of Micropro International, Inc.
Xerox is a registered trademark of Xerox Corp.

Preface

To publish or not to publish? That is the dilemma facing corporations, small businesses, and individuals from Newport, Rhode Island to Newport Beach, California. The question "Can I do it?" is rapidly being replaced with the even more perplexing question "How do I do it?" Aside from the considerations of training, control, and talent, managers and users are being faced with the formidable task of selecting the hardware and software components of their publishing system. Everyone interested in self-publishing is looking for that delicate balance in hardware and software that meets all of their current requirements without overwhelming the user, yet allows for growth and change as the user's requirements evolve. Nowhere are the decisions more difficult than in selecting the right software.

We are at a time when it is becoming increasingly difficult to separate the chaff from the grain in desktop publishing software. Virtually every product advertisement and news release finds the opportunity to tout various features as having an application for desktop publishing. So it comes as no surprise that many users are immediately skeptical of a product that claims to provide a powerful and robust word processor combined with all of the desktop publishing features that most users will require.

The latest incarnation of the market-leading WordPerfect word processor makes those very claims. How well does WordPerfect 5.0 live up to its claims and how can the user get the most desktop publishing from this software? "Desktop Publishing with WordPerfect 5.0" takes a unique approach to answering these questions. The bookstore shelves are crammed with

WordPerfect books, each providing step-by-step instructions on how to use the software. That's all very good, but fails to shed any light on the pivotal question of how a job is done, start to finish, using the new publishing features of WordPerfect 5.0.

As you read each chapter in this book, you will probably be struck by something that may seem odd if you are used to reading other "hints and how-to" books. This book assumes that you are familiar with the basic operation of WordPerfect and your concerns are not in how to load a file or perform a search-and-replace operation. This book will show you, instead, how to build a complete desktop publishing system around Word-Perfect 5.0 and how to milk every drop of desktop publishing performance from both the hardware and the software. In that respect, this book will take you not only into the depths of Word-Perfect 5.0, but to the heights of desktop publishing itself. From page design and layout, through the desktop publishing features of WordPerfect 5.0, to finally getting the most from your printer, this book puts it all together for you.

Acknowledgments

As with every major effort in the publishing industry, the people behind the scenes are to be thanked for their efforts in bringing this book to market. Among those that I am most deeply indebted to are Teri Zak (John Wiley & Sons), one of the industry's great motivators, Ruth Greif (John Wiley & Sons), who kept her humor through it all, Joe Dec (Line & Tone), who kept the printing schedules in spite of me, and Bill Gladstone (Waterside Productions), my agent who got my proposal noticed.

I cannot overlook the efforts of those companies who participated in the preparation of this book by graciously providing advice and evaluation units of their products. Deepest thanks to the following companies and the people behind them.

American Small Business Computers, Incorporated
Bitstream, Incorporated
Borland International
Genoa Systems Corporation
Hayes Microcomputer Products, Incorporated
Hercules Computer Technology, Incorporated
Micro Display System, Incorporated
Micrografx, Incorporated
Quarterdeck Office Systems
Relay Communications, Incorporated
RIX SoftWorks, Incorporated
SoftCraft, Incorporated
SymSoft, Incorporated
WordPerfect Corporation
ZSoft Corporation

And a special thanks to my loving parents for all they have done.

Contents

Introduction   1

Chapter 1 - The State of Desktop Publishing   7
    The Lines Are Drawn—Obliquely   7
    The Paperless Office?   8
    The Evolution of Desktop Publishing   9
        Publishing System Software   10
        Page Composition Systems   11
    Hardware Comes of Age   15
        Word Processors Move Up   17
    Document Processors   18
        Jobs for Document Processors   20

Chapter 2 - Document Processors and WordPerfect 5.0   21
    What Makes a Document Processor?   21
        Using Multiple Typefaces   22
        Eliminating Cut-and-Paste   24
        Typographic Controls   25
        Document Management   30
        Stylesheets   32
        WYSIWYG Display   35
        Printer Controls   37
    Doing the Dirty Work   39

Chapter 3 - What's in a Word?   47
    No Word Is an Island   47
        The Convert Program   48
        The Text In/Out Function   49
        Importing ASCII Files   51

Importing DIF Files	52
Fonts Make the Page	55
What Is a Soft Font?	56
Public Bulletin Board Systems	58
Trojan Horses and Program Viruses	60
Modems	61
Communications Software	61
Where to Start?	62
Making the Newsletter Fonts	63
Selecting the Fonts	64
Making a Newsletter Printer	65
Cutting the WPRINT1.ALL File Down to Size	67
Creating the Printer Resource File	68
Cartridges and Fonts	70
Initial Font	72
Path for Downloadable Fonts and Printer Command Files	72
Completing the Printer Resource File	73
Exploring the Printer Resource File	73
Typeface Description	76
Orientations	77
Character Map	78
Sizing and Spacing Information	80
Load and Select Strings	83
Groups	84
Resources	85
Automatic Font Changes	86
Substitute Fonts	86
Quality	87
Miscellaneous Font Features	87
WordPerfect Sure Is Nosy	88
Tying Up Loose Ends	88
Simplification Is the Key	89
Doing It in Styles	90
Redefining the Keyboard	95

Chapter 4 - A Picture Perfect Document — 99

- Get the Picture? — 99
  - Bit-Mapped versus Vector — 99
- Bit-Mapped Graphics — 103
  - Paint Programs — 104
  - Clip Art — 106
  - Image Scanners — 106
  - Screen Capture Software — 109
  - Back to the Boards — 114
- Vector Graphics — 115
  - Bringing in the Vector Files — 116
  - HPGL Format — 116
  - DXF Format — 117
  - Capturing Vector Graphics — 118
  - Colorful Graphics — 118
- Styles Revisited — 119
  - The Banner Style — 120
  - Entering the Banner Text — 121
  - The Misplaced Line — 124
  - Completing the Banner Text — 125
  - Pointing a Finger — 127
  - Advance—WordPerfect's "Mr. Fixit" — 131
    - Aligning Text — 131
    - Line Drawing with Proportional Fonts — 134
  - Creating the Other Hand — 135
- How about Those Macros! — 142

Chapter 5 - Satisfaction through Composition — 143

- The Foundation Is Laid — 143
  - Setting Up for Composition — 144
  - Entering the Newsletter Basics — 144
  - Calling All Styles — 145
- Using Master Documents — 147
- Composing the First Page — 148

Creating the Table of Contents Frame	149
Putting in the First Graphic	152
Placing The First Story	155
Saving Our Work	161
Onward to Page 2	161
Laying in NEWS2.WP5	163
Separating the Stories	164
Over the Hump with Page 3	171
Finishing Up with Page 4	180
Generating the Table of Contents	180

Chapter 6 - Start the Presses! — 189

Putting It On Paper	189
Saving the Best for Last	189
Raster Printers	190
Dot Matrix Printers	190
Ink Jet Printers	191
Thermal Printers	193
Laser Printers	195
Typesetters	198
The Mathematics of Print—Vector Printers	199
WordPerfect and Printers	200
What Do You Need?	200
The Right Printer for the Job	202
Cheating on Resolution	205
Printing the Newsletter	205
First Things First	206
Initializing the Printer	206
Sending the Newsletter to the Printer	208
Printing to a Typesetter	209

Chapter 7 - The Complete System — 213

Laying Out the Basics	213
Buy or Upgrade?	214
Aces and Spaces	214

The Big Three	216
Speed	216
Speed Reading	218
Speed Writing	219
Storage	221
Resolution	222
A Mouse for All Systems	224
Backing Up Those Words	224
The Economy System	225
Economy Hardware	226
The Economy Computer	226
Economy Display Groups	229
Major Brand PC Compatibles	230
Economy Printers	231
Economy Software	232
A System for the Masses	232
The Standard Computer	233
The Display Group	234
Standard Peripherals	236
The Scanner	236
The Modem	238
The Standard Printer	239
The Standard Software	241
Bit-Mapped Graphics	241
Vector Graphics	243
Font Management	244
The Power System	248
The Power Computer	249
The Power Display Group	250
The Power Peripherals	251
The Scanner	251
The Power Modem	253
The Power Printer	253
Power Software	256

Bit-Mapped Graphics	256
Power Vectors	257
Communications Software	258
Operating System Enhancements	259
Other Utilities	261

Appendix - Newsletter Source Files   **263**

Index   **273**

Introduction

This book was written to help you get a head start on desktop publishing with WordPerfect™ 5.0. Features such as sophisticated page layout and direct importation of graphics have taken WordPerfect out of the "word processor" category of applications software. For the first time, WordPerfect users have the power, in a single package, to produce a document complete with complex page formats and integrated graphics.

Because of the amount of material that needed to be covered by this book, a basic understanding of both personal computers and previous versions of WordPerfect is assumed. Before beginning the exercises in the following chapters, you should familiarize yourself with WordPerfect's own documentation. Considering the state of some software documentation, WordPerfect's manuals are marvels of clarity and completeness.

Presented here, then, is a brief description of the contents of this book. I hope that by the time you finish reading each chapter, you will be able to apply the techniques described to your own desktop publishing requirements.

Chapter 1 - The State of Desktop Publishing

Chapter 1 provides a brief history of desktop publishing and brings you up-to-date with the current crop of hardware and software products available for desktop publishing. Such topics as applications suitable for desktop publishing, and the capabilities and limitations of desktop publishing in general, are discussed. After reading Chapter 1, you will be in a more informed position to evaluate your requirements for a desktop publishing system.

Chapter 2 - Document Processors and WordPerfect 5.0

Chapter 2 introduces the document processor, a new breed of application software that cuts across the traditional lines that have separated word processors and page composition software. The functional requirements of document processors are described and the publishing features of WordPerfect 5.0 are examined as elements of the document processor. Other areas covered include the design process for page formats, font and type selection capabilities, typographic controls, drawing functions for the creation of simple graphics, and graphics importation. The types of publications best suited to WordPerfect are also described.

Chapter 3 - What's in a Word?

Chapter 3 begins a composition and printing exercise for a sample newsletter that is continued throughout the remainder of the book, with each chapter building on the foundation laid by the previous chapters. Although this book is not an in-depth tutorial for using WordPerfect, Chapter 3 describes the text editing and manipulation features of WordPerfect. Emphasis is placed on those areas of text editing requiring special attention and consideration from a desktop publishing standpoint.

WordPerfect operations significant to document composition are explored in-depth. The steps required to define and select fonts and typeface groups are also described in detail. This chapter also provides a look at importing text from other word processors and scanners into WordPerfect and tips for making the importation as clean as possible.

Chapter 4 - A Picture Perfect Document

Chapter 4 describes the types of graphic images supported by WordPerfect (bit-mapped, vector, ASCII text, scanned bit-map, etc.) and the methods for bringing these images into a document. Such topics as page placement, sizing, scaling, and rotation are covered. The special considerations for the type of graphics to be used and the hardware requirements for producing and printing each type are discussed.

The exercise for Chapter 4 illustrates the use of both bit-mapped and vector graphics to enhance the sample newsletter. The compatibility and use of imported graphics from each type is discussed. The examples used are taken from popular software packages such as Publisher's Paintbrush™ (bit-mapped) and Lotus 1-2-3® (vector).

Chapter 5 - Satisfaction through Composition

Chapter 5 looks at WordPerfect's page composition features in detail. This chapter examines some of the most dramatic changes to WordPerfect introduced with the 5.0 release. Topics include spacing (letter, line, and paragraph), kerning, and paragraph alignment. The methods for combining text with graphics to produce page designs are explained in detail.

The exercise for Chapter 5 brings together the text and graphics from previous chapters into the completed newsletter. The methods for positioning of graphics in the text are also demonstrated. The graphics are sized, scaled, and rotated.

Chapter 6 - Start the Presses!

Special considerations and tips for using output devices with WordPerfect 5.0 are discussed in Chapter 6. A look at current printer technology is provided, as well as techniques for maximizing the output quality of matrix, laser, and typeset printers. The required interconnections and WordPerfect printer setups are explained in detail for each type of output device.

The exercise for Chapter 6 describes how to print the newsletter to a matrix printer for a rough draft review. The completed newsletter can then be printed with a laser printer for proofing, and finally printed with a typesetter for camera-ready output. The options available for transmission to typesetters (direct connection, in-house print shop, service houses, etc.) are explained in detail.

Chapter 7 - The Complete System

Chapter 7 concludes this book with a description of typical low-end, mid-range, and high-end desktop publishing systems. The trade-offs involved in acquiring and implementing each system are discussed. The considerations made in selecting the components of each system are thoroughly discussed. Hints on how to shop for your perfect system and recommendations on specific hardware and software designed to provide satisfying and professional results for years to come are provided. The advantages and disadvantages of pre-packaged or "turnkey" systems are explored. Each system uses WordPerfect for text editing and page composition with other parts of the system selected with this in mind.

Assumptions

Before you begin reading this book and working through the preparation of the sample newsletter, there are some assumptions that must be made about your software. First, you should have a copy of WordPerfect 5.0 dated July 15, 1988 or later. You can check the date of your software release by pressing F3 (Help). The release date is show in the upper right-hand corner of the first screen. Releases of WordPerfect 5.0 dated prior to July 15 will not work properly with the fonts we will use in the newsletter as created and installed with the Bitstream Fontware™ program. If your software has an earlier date, contact WordPerfect's Customer Support and ask for the latest set of maintenance disks.

Also, you should have the Bitstream Fontware Installation Kit. This is provided free to all registered users of WordPerfect 5.0. As with most things that are free, you have to ask that this software be sent to you. Call WordPerfect at (800) 222-9409. The kit comes with the Dutch (Bitstream's version of Times Roman) font that is used in the examples throughout this book.

Finally, the illustrations in this book are based on a "clean" copy of WordPerfect. Chances are good that you have been using the software for a while and have already defined at least one printer with the fonts you require. If this is true, bear in mind as you progress through the tutorial that your screens may look slightly different than those presented in this book. However, the tutorial will still work and you need only be aware that these differences exist.

Conventions Used in This Book

As you work through the tutorial in this book, you will be asked to perform the tasks required to produce a sample newsletter. These tasks are presented in the following manner.

> Press   **Key** (Function or Option)

Press the key or key combination indicated in bold type.

> Type   Text

Type the text as shown.

Italicized text may appear in some steps. This is supplemental information that is given to clarify the operation. The following examples illustrate this convention.

> Press   **Return** (*twice*)

Press the **Return** key twice.

> Type   NAME (*your name*)

Type your name and press **Return**.

1 | The State of Desktop Publishing

The Lines Are Drawn—Obliquely

By the time you have completed reading this book, *Desktop Publishing with WordPerfect 5.0*, we will have covered a lot of desktop publishing ground using WordPerfect 5.0. But there has been so much hype said and written about the wonders of desktop publishing that you may be wondering what you are getting into. In this book, the first thing that we will try to sort out has little to do with WordPerfect 5.0, and everything to do with desktop publishing. As the lines drawn between different types of desktop publishing software (e.g., word processors, page makeup, page composition, document processors) become less clear, the decisions necessary to implement a desktop publishing system become more difficult.

In later chapters, some recommendations will be made on how you should spend some of your hard-fought dollars. Will you get your money's worth? Can the system you purchase perform all the publishing functions you require? Will you be satisfied with the results? By the time you finish this chapter, we will have cut through some of the mumbo jumbo and you will have a better understanding of the possibilities and limitations of any kind of desktop publishing. Whatever the product, hardware or software, you won't feel like you got your money's worth if it doesn't live up to your expectations or do what you need it to do.

So let's get on with a bit of history and hopefully a better understanding of exactly what desktop publishing is. And most important, don't be overwhelmed by the possibilities, even seasoned computer jockeys get the jitters when asked to recommend a complete desktop publishing system.

The Paperless Office?

When the IBM PC® was introduced to the public in 1981, the term paperless office sprang into our vocabulary. Predictions of massive networks for sharing data and electronic mail for sending and receiving information abounded. Every computer and business tabloid touted these new marvels as the road to the paperless office, ending the paper shuffle that was strangling the productivity and profitability of the modern workplace. The new wonder machines were destined to make an impact on the way large corporations handled the massive amounts of information that they generated every day.

As it has turned out, most of these predictions came true. However, a funny thing happened on the road to that paperless office. We, the users of these personal computers, got sidetracked on the way to the paperless office. One of the first things we did with our new computers was generate paper with them. From word processing to database reports, from short memos to documents of several hundred pages in length, we cranked it out. By the reams and rolls and boxes of paper, we cranked it out. And so ended the myth of the paperless office.

For a time, we were satisfied with the output provided by dot matrix and daisy wheel printers. Dot matrix printers were fast, produced legible documents good enough for rough drafts, and could even print some graphics. Daisy wheel printers were slow and noisy, but met our needs for business correspondence and other documents that required a "typed" look. It has been said that the ultimate oxymoron was buying a computer, word processing software, and a daisy wheel printer for thousands of dollars so that letters could look like they came out of a $300 typewriter using technology several decades old. Could it be that we had all been duped? Not only were we still producing as much paper as ever, the computer made it possible to produce more paper faster and at less cost. And the computer-generated material looked the same as what we had been churning out with our electric typewriters. We were also using the same old cut-and-paste methods to put complex documents together, the art department was as busy as ever, and the typesetting machines never saw an idle moment.

The Evolution of Desktop Publishing

The personal computer (PC) enabled the writer to change text to suit his or her needs, save the file in an electronic format, and transmit it across telephone lines to others using a modem. This was all very good and indeed saved time and money, but something was missing. This, after all, was a computer sitting here on the desk. There had to be more to it than this.

Just as the PC was beginning to look to writers like a solution in search of a problem, some very forward-thinking people realized that if a dot matrix printer could print graphics, it could just as easily consider text as just another graphic form. So these bright entrepreneurs set about producing software that could add different type styles and sizes to our plain memos and reports. The earliest of these software packages merely allowed a writer to use multiple fonts in a single document. Still it was better than we had before, but the appearance of the text printed with a dot matrix printer left much to be desired. Thus, while other bright entrepreneurs were busying themselves inventing the desktop laser printer, there was another attempt going on at providing quality output from existing word processing packages—publishing system software.

Publishing System Software

Publishing system software designed to run on PCs was first available in the early 1980s. This software emulated the dedicated front-end terminals required by large and expensive typesetting machines. These terminals are used to send instructions to the typesetter on the makeup of the document to be printed. Information, such as the fonts to be used, the typographic controls required, and the actual text and graphics files, is entered at the terminal for each page. This is a very complex and painstaking process that demands the operator have special training and an extensive background in typography. Needless to say, before this process could become available to the PC user, a simpler user interface had to be designed.

This new PC-based publishing system software simplified the process, allowing the writer more power over the appearance of the final document. For example, text format commands for font types and styles, setting text in multiple columns, adding ruling lines to separate text or graphics from surrounding page elements, and boxes around text where available using Wordstar™-like dot commands. The commands were inserted directly into the text by the writer during its creation. This was an improvement, however, it had a major drawback. It still required that the user have more than just a general knowledge of typography, since the software did not allow the writer to see, prior to the actual printing, what the page would look like. Therefore, the insertion of typesetting commands was often left to a second person that had typographic expertise. The hardware and software capable of providing the so-called

WYSIWYG (what-you-see-is-what-you-get) display was yet to be invented for the personal computer. Page composition systems capable of approximating the appearance of the printed page for the writer would be the next step in the evolution of desktop publishing.

Page Composition Systems

Complete page composition systems began to appear as the price of dedicated workstations based on high-end minicomputers such as those made by Sun™ and Apollo™ began to fall (see Figure 1-1). Although priced in the $10,000 to $30,000 range, these systems have found widespread acceptance in

Figure 1-1. The Interleaf® publishing system offers a total publishing environment for those users with power publishing requirements.

large corporations and are still preferred over microcomputer-based systems for users with heavy publishing demands. These workstations are normally networked within a large group of writers, editors, and graphic artists.

Overall, these page composition systems offer more control over the appearance of the final page than had been previously available on microcomputers. This increased control is also offered with a better user interface, a much-improved level of reliability, and more extensive support for third-party software such as computer-aided design and manufacturing (CAD/CAM), spreadsheet, graphics, and word processor packages. And to allow flexibility in implementing the systems, they are often designed for modular implementation and operation. That is, the text entry and editing software, the graphics design software, and the page layout software are offered as separate options that can be purchased by each individual work group or upgraded separately as the user's requirements grow.

Page composition software for the PC began to appear in the mid-1980s and is still quite popular today. This software allows the writer to compose complete pages, integrating text and graphics. Most offer some form of WYSIWYG display of the page, but many of the editing features that writers have come to expect from word processing software is not yet available in page composition software. Page composition software differs from earlier print enhancement packages in that the text and graphics can be imported from several different sources.

They also allow the writer to do something that had previously been unavailable—the capability to print completely composed pages on the new laser printers. Laser printers had just begun to arrive on the scene and since their arrival have become the ideal printing solution for thousands of writers. Small and fast, these new laser printers had what it took to take the market by storm. While these printers were not inexpensive for the individual user, ranging from $5000 to $8000, they were cheap enough to be seen as a viable alternative to typesetting machines costing ten times as much and more.

The early page composition systems were not without faults. They were expensive, more than $7000. And the user could expect to pay extreme consequences when a wrong code or command was entered. Often the entire computer came to a halt at the first instance of operator error. This not only made these packages less than desirable to the writer, but could significantly decrease the systems' productivity when work was lost due to computer crashes. And since productivity was the name of the game, the search went on for the more perfect page composition system.

The introduction of the Macintosh® computer and the LaserWriter™ laser printer from Apple Computer put a lot of pressure on the IBM®-standard computer industry. Nowhere was this more apparent than in the area of desktop publishing. The Macintosh offered an intuitive user interface, powerful page composition software packages, and a very attractive price. When connected to the LaserWriter, this system offered the writer most of the tools necessary for producing professional publications. Often purchased by the writer as a complete system, sometimes referred to as a turnkey approach, the number of hardware and software decisions facing the prospective purchaser were all but nonexistent. The Apple® system shown in Figure 1-2 was a complete plug-and-play approach to desktop publishing.

Apple made a tidy sum of money selling their system to writers with visions of instant desktop publishing gratification. But all too soon, buyers that had enthusiastically ripped open all those boxes and connected all those cables came to realize the shortcomings of buying a turnkey system. In the case of the original Macintosh, the turnkey system was a double-edged sword. The elimination of the hardware and software decisions created a sense of security for the first-time computer user, but

Figure 1-2. The Apple Macintosh computer offers a complete plug-and-play approach to desktop publishing.

denied the experienced user the capability of making any decisions, even if the user were so inclined. This meant that there was no upgrade or expansion path. What you saw was what you got. Need a better monitor? Tough luck. What about more hard disk storage space? Sorry about that. What about adding some memory? You couldn't even open the case. In designing the Macintosh, Apple had abandoned the idea that users should be allowed access to the inside of the machine. Needless to say, there were some unhappy people around.

However, Apple® had done something that might have taken years to do had IBM been left without competition in the desktop computer market—they had awakened the DOS world to the possibilities of full-fledged desktop publishing for the common user. When IBM set about designing the PC, they understood the importance to the user of being able to modify an off-the-shelf computer. In a most uncharacteristic move for IBM, they not only capitalized on another company's idea (Apple's), but they offered a design which not only allowed but encouraged the owners' participation in how their computer would be configured. With the open architecture of the IBM PC standard, the possibilities seemed unlimited. But few things in life are really unlimited. And such was the case of the IBM PC.

Hardware Comes of Age

The original, first-issue IBM PC was a wonderful machine for those who had cut their hacker's teeth on small, temperamental home-brew computers. These computers generally had 4000 bytes of random access memory (RAM), a very slow 8-bit data bus, and required programming with either wires or switches each time they were turned on. On the other hand, the IBM PC provided 64,000 bytes of RAM (referred to as 64K of RAM), a much faster 16-bit data bus, and the capability of writing a program and storing it either on an audiocassette or floppy disk for later reloading into the computer.

The IBM PC was a giant leap ahead in desktop computer technology, but its shortcomings soon became apparent. For many applications, it was still too slow and limited in the size of a program that could be loaded. Programs were beginning to grow in size as well, and the only mass storage available for the PC was a small 10-megabyte hard disk. In its current state, desktop publishing was simply not feasible with the IBM PC. Gradually the PC's RAM would grow from 64K to 640K and hard disks of 20 to 32 megabytes would become readily available at an affordable price, but it was still limited to a speed of 4.77 Mhz.

In 1985, IBM introduced a new line of PCs that would change the way software developers viewed the capabilities of desktop computing. The IBM AT® offered the user more speed, more RAM, and more disk storage space. The original AT ran at 6 Mhz, but users were quick to find a way to bring these machines up to 8 Mhz. The price of RAM began to fall, thus encouraging AT owners to pack up to 2 megabytes of RAM into their new computers. And IBM had upgraded the monitors and video boards used with the AT line. The Enhanced Graphic Adapter™ (EGA) supplemented the original Color Graphics Adapter™ (CGA), offering an increase from the CGA's 320 by 200 dot resolution to 640 by 350 dot resolution. Combined with the introduction the year before of the $3500 Hewlett-Packard LaserJet® laser printer (Figure 1-3) designed specifically for use with the new generation of word processors and page composition systems being developed for the PC, the hardware was finally in place to unleash a desktop publishing explosion on DOS-based computers.

The first round of DOS programs to appear were PageMaker®from Aldus Corporation, Ventura Publisher™ from Xerox Corporation, and The Office Publisher® from Laser Friendly. These programs offer the user a very simple and interactive user interface, an extensive set of typographic controls, and a WYSIWYG display that allows the writer to edit both text and graphics on the same page. The prices of these software packages place them within the financial reach of most PC users. These new page composition software packages can

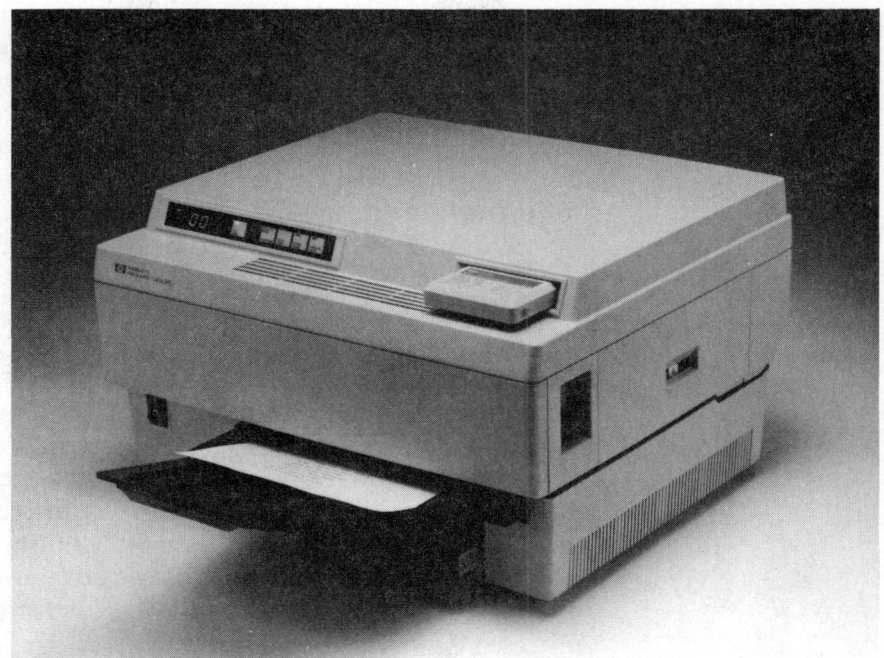

Figure 1-3. The Hewlett-Packard LaserJet laser printer enabled DOS-based computers to realize their desktop publishing potential.

read text files generated with a number of popular word processors, as well as graphic images from the leading computer-aided design and drafting programs, paint programs, and scanners.

Word Processors Move Up

The competitive pricing and versatility of page composition software for the PC made them immediately popular with professional writers and publishers. However, they still required the use of separate word processing software for the generation of text to be loaded into them. Thus, before the first page could be printed, the price of desktop publishing with these software packages began to grow. In addition, the compatibility between the word processing software and the page composition software has never been quite what writers wanted. Although the page composition software could readily import the text from a writer's favorite word processor, most of the format and attribute commands were lost in the translation. Format commands such as margins, headers, footers, and page numbering scheme had to be reentered with the page composition software's own set of commands for these things.

The first attempt by a word processor to incorporate some desktop publishing capabilities was Microsoft Word®. Microsoft Word allowed the formation of more sophisticated page layouts than had been previously available in a word processor. It also allowed text and graphics to be combined in the same document, although the graphics could not be viewed. As Microsoft Word has evolved through the current version 4.0, others have joined the battle. Among them are WordStar Professional® from MicroPro International and Byline® by Ashton-Tate. WordPerfect Corporation, always a keen observer of its competition and responsive to the needs of the user, has produced a first-rate word processor with extensive desktop publishing capabilities in WordPerfect 5.0 (see Figure 1-4). For the sake of brevity, we will coin a new phrase for these programs—the document processor.

Document Processors

As discussed, document processors are those programs that have their roots in word processing, but have evolved or have been created to incorporate some desktop publishing capabilities. Document processors are not desktop publishing or page composition programs. As Andre Peterson, Executive Director of IBM Products Marketing for WordPerfect Corporation states, "We're touting [WordPerfect 5.0] as a high-level word

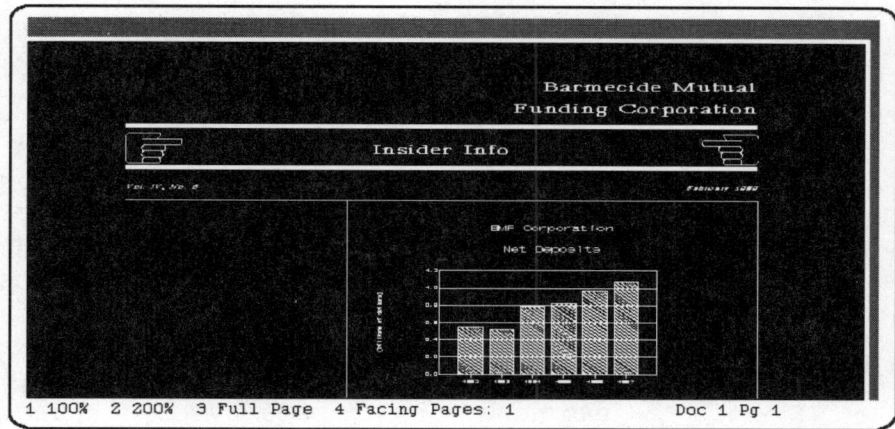

Figure 1-4. WordPerfect 5.0 is a powerful, full-fledged document processor that provides both character-oriented and graphic interfaces.

processing package rather than a low-end desktop publishing program." The document processor's page format, typographic, and text/graphics integration capabilities are more limited than its more expensive and full-bodied counterpart. Where the distinction of capabilities begin to blur between high-end word processors and low-end desktop publishing (page composition) packages is the domain of the new document processors. They do have the important advantage that no separate word processor is required. Everything is in one package, just a few keystrokes away. Once you have learned how to use the document processor, you have actually learned at least two applications. You need not buy and learn separate word processor and page composition packages. And for most of our needs, this is just fine. In most cases, some form of graphics editing capability is also provided, possibly eliminating the requirement for a graphics editing package.

Jobs for Document Processors

What sort of jobs are suited for these new document processors? As a simple rule of thumb, any document of 8 pages or less can be handled easily by document processors. Longer documents can certainly be attempted, but the time required and the inherent limitations of document processors would justify your investment in a more complete page composition package. Of course, you will probably find longer documents with simple formats that document processors can make quick work of (WordPerfect has added several features that assist in managing large documents) and shorter documents with extremely complex page layouts that required the additional power of page composition software. However, for the sake of consistency, we will limit our examples to 8 pages.

As an example of the type of documents best suited for document processors, we will be putting together a whimsical company newsletter in the chapters that follow. We will begin by laying out the format of the newsletter, then bring the text and graphics together, and finally print the finished job. Along the way, you will probably want to experiment a bit with our little newsletter and you are encouraged to do so. However, before you continue on to subsequent exercises using our newsletter, put everything back the way it is described so that we all get the same end results as we move through the book.

2 | Document Processors and WordPerfect 5.0

What Makes a Document Processor?

The document processor occupies a unique niche among software products designed to produce professional documentation. With more functionality than a word processor but with limitations on page composition, the document processor must strive to be many things to many people. This is not an easy task to perform. Therefore, before we consider attempting document processing with any software package, we should look at what functions a true document processor must be able to perform. Although each vendor's document processor may vary in the degree and innovativeness of the implementation of these features, we can readily identify seven functions that are a "must have" for any document processor.

1. It should allow the use of multiple fonts and typefaces on the same page.

2. It should eliminate cut-and-paste methods to the greatest possible extent.

3. It should offer a healthy set of typographic controls.

4. It should provide a set of tools for document management.

5. It should provide a convenient method for implementing stylesheets.

6. It should provide some WYSIWYG capability, either in the edit or preview mode of operation.

7. It should provide extensive user control of the printer and its capabilities.

These functions are the basics, the starting point for defining a document processor. Other functions offered by a document processor that enhance the usefulness and ease of use of the program are those subjective points which either sell the software or relegate it to the "I think I remember that one" category. Let's look at each of the basic functions closer and see how well WordPerfect 5.0 stacks up.

Using Multiple Typefaces

As illustrated in Chapter 1, the capability for using multiple typefaces on a single page has been around for quite a while in one form or another. Therefore, rather than simply classifying a word processor as a document processor because it can manipulate fonts, we must look deeper into how the font manipulation function is implemented.

The criteria used to determine the implementation of this function must be narrowed to focus on the way in which the document processor allows the user to install, select, and display multiple fonts and typefaces. Is the installation of a font easy and straightforward? What are the limitations on the number of fonts that can be installed and used?

The automation of typographic changes required by a font change must also be considered. Is the spacing between lines (referred to as the leading) automatically changed for the new font? And will the user be required to manually change existing margins, tabs, and multiple column definitions be required when a different font is selected?

A "font" is a specific combination of a typeface (e.g., Times Roman®), the typeface's size (e.g., 10-point, 12-point, etc.), and appearance attributes (e.g., bold, italic, etc.). Therefore, a Times Roman font in WordPerfect might be described as Times Roman 12-point bold. The installation of fonts in WordPerfect 5.0 would be a rather complex and tedious process if WordPerfect's Printer Program was the only means available. Fortunately, there are several programs available that will ease the font installation task. These programs isolate the user from the complexities of the Printer Program and automatically update the printer resource file to make selected fonts available for document processing. These programs will be described in more detail in Chapter 3.

If you are forced to deal directly with the Printer Program to modify a printer definition file, there is help in the Printer Program Users Guide available from WordPerfect. This guide provides indepth information on every aspect of the Printer Program. There is also a description of each Printer Program function required for font definition in Chapter 3. These font functions include describing a particular font in terms of appearance and typographic attributes, as well as declaring alternate and substitute fonts for that font.

An alternate font is the font that WordPerfect will use when it encounters an attribute change in your document. For instance, if you are composing your text with a base font of Dutch 12-point and mark a block of text to be printed with the italic font, WordPerfect automatically picks the Dutch 12-point italic font. The substitute font is selected for use by WordPerfect if it encounters a font request in your document that does not have a font definition. This is especially useful if you use special characters in your document. Both the alternate fonts and substitute fonts for a specific font are automatically generated by WordPerfect during the installation of the font, unless you override the automatic generation by specifying your own alternate and substitute fonts.

Eliminating Cut-and-Paste

The elimination of cut-and-paste methods of document production is the core of any document processor. This capability encompasses such diverse tasks as the integration of text and graphics, laying in ruling lines, combining several separate different blocks of text on the same page, and easily modifying the completed page to accommodate last-minute changes in the document. While every software product that claims to have desktop publishing capabilities offers some functions that reduce the cut-and-paste process, only a few provide a richness of desktop publishing features so as to warrant serious consideration.

As with all document processors, WordPerfect 5.0 has the capability of mixing text and graphics on the same page. A frame is placed in the document where the graphic is to appear. This frame defines the size and location of the image. A frame may contain either a separate text file or a graphic image. A frame that contains text may be edited within the frame using many of the same controls that WordPerfect provides for text on the page (e.g., tab settings, line spacing, font selection, etc.).

These frame capabilities are very useful when the frame contains text such as a table of contents frame that requires a different font and tab settings than the body of the document. The frame may be placed at a specific location on the page, attached (anchored) to a paragraph, or inserted in the middle of a sentence in the same way as any other character. Anchoring a frame to a paragraph is useful during text editing. If the figure, text, or table within a frame is referenced in a paragraph, the frame should remain with the paragraph as the paragraph moves due to the insertion or deletion of text before that paragraph.

WordPerfect also offers a variety of ruling line functions. Lines may be placed horizontally, vertically, between text columns, and around text and graphics frames. The line width may be varied and the density of the line may be set so as to provide a shaded line rather that a solid one. Most ruling lines are placed in the document by indicating an absolute position for the line on the page rather than a positional relationship to another element on that page. Therefore, as with most of WordPerfect's document processing capabilities, a good pencil and paper layout of the finished page is essential before actually starting the composition process.

Typographic Controls

Before we can fully appreciate the necessity of typographic controls, a bit more history is necessary. Back in the good old days (i.e., before electronic typesetting), a skilled and experienced typographer was required to make the on-the-spot decisions needed to produce legible printed matter. Type was first set by hand, one letter and one space at a time, into a box or "chase" that was the exact size of the page to be printed. The final printed page looked very good because each letter had been cast with a specific width according to the space required by that letter. The space that an "i" needs, for instance, is much less than the space an "m" requires. The text was said to be proportionally spaced which resulted in a page of text that had a compactness that provided a high degree of readability. As you can imagine, however, setting type by this method was not only time-consuming and mentally demanding, it was also very

Figure 2-1. The Monotype machine was the first evidence of automation in the typesetting process.

physcially laborious. Each character and space had to be manually placed in the chase and, if that weren't enough, each letter and space had to be returned to the master set of letters and spaces by the printer after the page was printed.

Things began to look up for that tired typographer in the 1880s when two products of the Industrial Revolution enabled text to be mechanically composed. The Monotype® machine shown in Figure 2-1 provided a means of composing text one character at a time while the machine from Linotype® shown in Figure 2-2 could compose a complete line at one time. The typographer had a kind of typewriter for entering the text and both these

Figure 2-2. The Linotype machine was capable of setting an entire line of type in a single operation.

machines cast the required character (Monotype) or line (Linotype) on the spot. When printing of the page was completed, the type was melted back down for reuse. This accounted for an immense savings in time and cost, a necessary by-product of any successful invention. However, there was one more capability that these two machines brought to the typographer—the ability to end lines evenly at the right margin, or "justify" a line of text. By adjusting the space between words (word spacing) and the space between letters (letter spacing), a line of justified text can be made to start at the left margin of the page or column and end evenly at the right margin of the page or column, resulting in a balanced appearance. Taken all together, these typographic elements allowed the typographer to control the layout of text on the page, thus the term typographic controls.

With all of the time and effort that went into creating typographic controls, we can understand why a complete set of typographic controls is essential for fine-tuning the finished appearance of your document. The most basic of these controls include the ability to adjust leading (the space between lines of text) and provide line justification. Further, if you are using a proportionally spaced font, kerning (the space between two specific letters pairs) should also be adjustable (see Figure 2-3). If you choose to use line justification in your document, the

This is a kerned letter pair
of a proportionally spaced font.

This letter pair has only
the proportional values applied.

Figure 2-3. Adjustable kerning allows the user to increase or decrease the space between specific letter pairs.

document processor should allow the use of several typographic functions including adjustment of the space between words (word spacing), the space between letters (letter spacing), and the use of hyphenation. Note that if you are not using justification in your document, the use of word spacing becomes a moot point; the width of a standard space is used to separate words until no more words will fit on the line. Hyphenation may be used to somewhat even out the ragged right margin, but no attempt is made to make the words end exactly on the right margin.

WordPerfect offers all of these controls, and most are within easy reach of the writer. For instance, adjusting the leading of a paragraph is as simple as selecting the line spacing function and entering the desired value. You can enable and disable justification with just a couple of keystrokes. Word spacing takes a bit more thought, because WordPerfect implements that function as a minimum and maximum allowable space between words. Therefore, in setting the word spacing, you have to be careful not to set the minimum to small or the maximum to large. The result will be a very unsatisfactory line. The minimum should be no less than the space required for a capital "M" (referred to as an em space) and no larger than 1.5 em space. (See Chapter 3 for more about word spacing.) Kerning two letters takes a bit more effort because it requires the use of WordPerfect's printer program to examine and change the character width table of the font you are using. This may sound intimidating, but it really isn't. (See Chapter 3 for a discussion of this process.)

Hyphenation is probably where you will first see a document processor's completeness or weakness of typographic controls. Does the document processor merely run the words to the end of the line and then ask you to supply the hyphenation or is the process automated? If it is automatic hyphenation, how complete is its implementation? The size of the document processor's hyphenation dictionary is one key to how well automatic hyphenation will perform. But aside from the "brute force" method of looking up words in a hyphenation dictionary, the more complete document processors have a set of hyphenation rules that are applied to words not in the hyphenation dictionary.

WordPerfect has reversed this process. The hyphenation rules are applied to a word first. If the word cannot be hyphenated according to these rules, you are prompted for a hyphen position. If this is too troublesome or you want more complete hyphenation ability, you may order an extensive 115,000 word hyphenation dictionary directly from WordPerfect Corporation. The result is the elimination of most manual hyphenation decisions.

Additionally, WordPerfect allows you to set a "hyphenation zone." This is an area on each side of the right margin that determines whether the word is to be hyphenated or wrapped to the next line. The hyphenation zone is measured as a percentage of the line's total length. If a word starts prior to the start of the zone and extends past the end of the zone, WordPerfect will try to hyphenate it. Otherwise, the word will be wrapped to the next line. By adjusting the width of the hyphenation zone, you can control the degree to which words are examined for hyphenation. A large zone width will wrap words that would normally be hyphenated; a very small zone width will try to hyphenate virtually every word that falls at the end of a line.

Document Management

Document management is probably one of those things that receives the same amount of attention from writers as tax preparation does from most people—you don't give it a second thought until you are required to, and then you desperately need all the help you can get.

Any document processor worth its salt should implement some method for easily tracking document revisions and review comments. It should also allow the writer to combine several different text files into a master document file. This capability is extremely useful if you work with longer documents composed of several different text files. For instance, you may be writing a book with several chapters, the table of contents, and the index. The "book" file would keep track of which text files make up the book and the order in which the text files should be printed. The book file of the more powerful document processors also provides functions that operate on all the text files associated with the book file. For instance, if you are building an index by marking words in each text file, you do not want to have to generate an index for each file and then manually combine all the indexes into a single index file. The document processor should allow you to generate an index from all the files in the book file, creating just one index file.

WordPerfect offers several tools for document management. For tracking changes to a file, WordPerfect provides a file comparison function that will mark changed, added, or deleted text in either file with a redline code. Review comments may be added to the document at any point and either displayed or hidden from the text entry screen.

WordPerfect has also implemented a powerful master document feature that provides a convenient means of tracking, manipulating, editing, and generating lists from all of the subdocuments associated with a master document. Suppose you are writing a book that will have a table of contents, six chapters, and an index. With the traditional word processor, the first task would be to write the six chapters, marking the appropriate text for inclusion into the table of contents and index, and then save the chapters as individual files. This process is unchanged by WordPerfect 5.0. However, the generation of the table of contents and index for the entire book is now a single operation for each. You may recall that the old method for generating a table of contents involved marking the text in each chapter file for list generation, then cutting the generated list from each chapter and saving each into a table of contents file. Not a very efficient way to do business. With the master document feature, a single file is opened and a code indicating the insertion point for each chapter file is placed in the file. The table of contents and index are then generated from all six files at once, resulting in a finished book. As if that weren't enough, the files included in the master document file can be expanded, edited, and then saved when the file is condensed. If you choose to edit each subdocument file outside of the master document file, the files in the master document file will be current at all times.

Stylesheets

A stylesheet is a set of specifications that control the appearance of a particular element. Does that sound sufficiently complex? Well, it's not if we consider each part of that definition separately. First, the element in question could be any part of the printed page that can be treated as a single, complete item. This could include the header of a newsletter, the table of contents, or even an entire page. Page specifications include such things as margins, line spacing, headers and footers, and figure and text frame defaults. The set of specifications is just the various attributes that the element will have when the style is evoked.

Perhaps you are producing a brochure that requires one-half inch left and right margins, a one inch top margin, and a three-quarter inch bottom margin. The page will be printed in three columns with the company name centered at the top of the page immediately below a one-tenth inch wide rule running from the left to the right margin. Further, page one of the brochure always has a two column wide by three inch box in the right hand corner reserved for your company's address and telephone number. All of these design elements are part of the page specification that will be incorporated into the final document. It would be very helpful if a way existed to auotmate setting up these specifications.

Stylesheets (or styles as they are called in WordPerfect) are powerful tools of the desktop publishing trade and easy to define and use with WordPerfect 5.0. There are two types of styles that you can define: the open style and the paired style. An open style is a set of specifications that is applied once to your document and operates on the entire document unless changed by insertion of another open style. Paired styles are turned on and off between the elements that the style applies to. In our previous example, the page specification would be contained in an open style. We insert the style at the beginning of our document and forget it. If, however, you want to set a particular piece of text apart from the paragraph it is in, you might want to change to a large, bold font before typing the text. In this case, you could create a paired style for the new font,

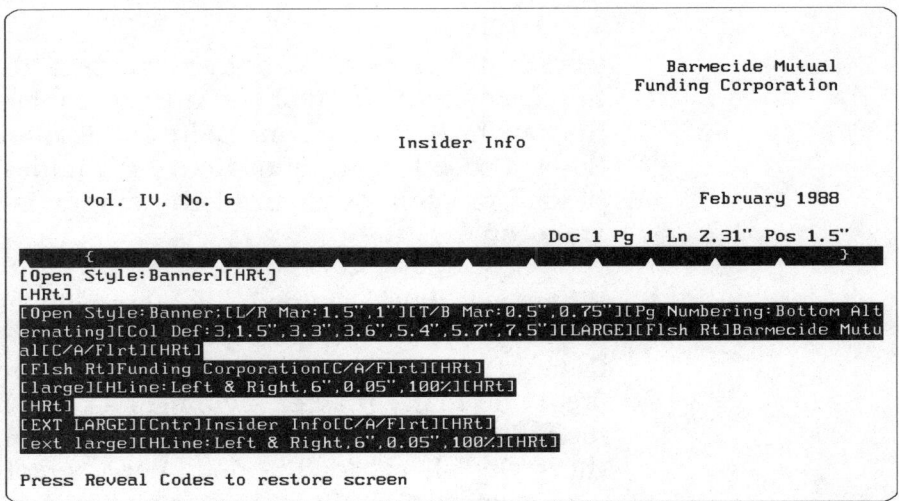

Figure 2-4. WordPerfect's "open" style in collapsed and expanded views.

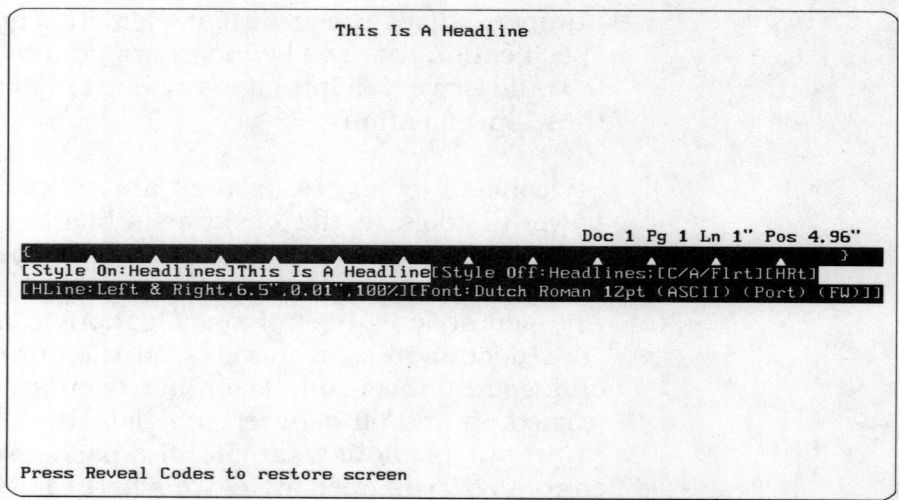

Figure 2-5. WordPerfect's "paired" style in collapsed and expanded views.

turn on the new style and type the text, then turn off the style to return to our normal text attributes. Figures 2-4 and 2-5 illustrate how the open and paired styles look with WordPerfect's Reveal Codes feature activated. Also notice that the styles are hidden or "collapsed" until the cursor is positioned over the style code.

When you have defined all of the styles required by your brochure, you save the styles to a single file. This file can be thought of as a master style file for your brochure and you may create as many master style files as you have different document formats. Thus, the master style file may be thought of as the style "sheet" for the document, which brings us back to where we started. We will be using WordPerfect's style function extensively in Chapter 3 when we begin to set up our sample newsletter.

WYSIWYG Display

The WYSIWYG display of text and graphics prior to printing the page is probably the single most important development in desktop publishing. Advances in hardware and software have enabled writers to compose the entire page completely before sending the page to the printer. Adjustments to the placement and appearance of the elements on the page are easily accomplished in "realtime," thus eliminating the seemingly endless loop of composition, printing, editing, composition, printing, editing, and so on. Some of the improvements in hardware necessary to produce a WYSIWYG display were more speed, more memory, larger storage capacities, and higher resolution monitors. Once the hardware was in place, the software needed only to take advantage of the hardware's capabilities.

Each document processor provides some capability to display a relatively close representation of how the printed page will appear. The degree to which each document processor is able to achieve this "relatively close" appearance is the ruler by which

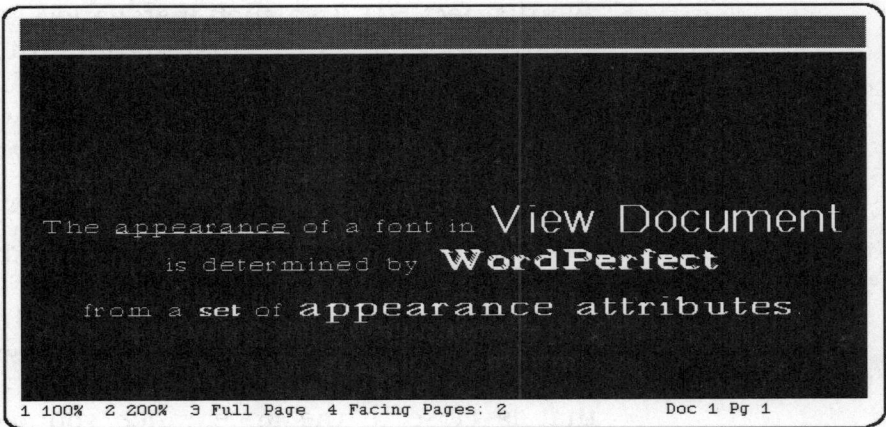

Figure 2-6. WordPerfect's typeface appearance capabilities provide control of its WYSIWYG display.

the WYSIWYG capabilities are measured in each document processor. WordPerfect gets high marks for its WYSIWYG capabilities as shown in Figure 2-6.

WordPerfect has implemented a unique approach to the manner in which the WYSIWYG display is constructed. Each font and typeface has a set of appearance attributes assigned to it. These attributes are located in the printer definition file that contains the fonts being used in the document.

For instance, we will specify that a Dutch 14-point italic font is available for use in composing our newsletter. We will do this from within WordPerfect and WordPerfect will modify the printer definition file accordingly. If we look at the printer definition file with the Printer Program, we will be able to examine (and change if desired) the various appearance attributes assigned to this font.

Each typeface's appearance description (appearance/style, attributes, serifs, shape, stress, weight, and proportions) is automatically set for the font definitions supplied by WordPerfect, or a font installation kit specifically designed for WordPerfect 5.0. Two such installation kits are available. The Bitstream Fontware™ Installation Kit from Bitstream is provided free to purchasers of WordPerfect 5.0. However, the Bistream Fontware Installation Kit will only work with Bitstream or Bitstream-compatible typefaces.

Another installation kit, Laser Fonts® by SoftCraft, uses Bitstream's font technology to produce fonts having the same high quality, but it is also capable of installing fonts from other manufacturers. If you want to use a font that neither of these installation programs can recognize (a custom font file that you have created, for instance), you can copy one of the definitions that is close to the appearance you need and modify the attributes as necessary to approximate the appearance of the new font.

Before you begin to change the appearance attributes of a font, there is one consideration to bear in mind. WordPerfect uses a font's appearance attributes not only for screen display, but for matching your font selection to the fonts that are available at your printer. In the example, we are using a Dutch 14-point italic font for our text. When we have completed our file and saved it on a floppy disk, we give the disk to a reviewer for editing and printing. However, our editor doesn't own the extensive font library that we have at our disposal. When the editor sends the document to a laser printer that only has a few standard fonts, WordPerfect automatically selects the closest font in appearance to our Dutch font. How does WordPerfect do this? Based on the appearance attributes of all the fonts known to WordPerfect (and the list seems virtually endless) and the appearance attributes assigned to the Dutch font, WordPerfect selects an alternate font that is available and as close in appearance as possible to the requested font. In this case, we would probably get our document back from the editor printed in Dutch bold italic. You also have the capability of specifying a particular alternate font for WordPerfect to select if the font you want is not available. (Printer and font manipulation is discussed further in Chapter 3.)

Printer Controls

The output of a document processor is the only thing that your reader will see. It is the reason you invested in your document processing software in the first place. The degree to which you can control the actions of your printer will help you accomplish the fine-tuning necessary for professional quality publications. And because printer control is so closely associated with all of the other functions necessary for document processing, a weakness here will manifest itself throughout the software.

Fortunately, printer control is among WordPerfect's most powerful and vastly improved functions. As a matter of fact, the limitations on what you can print with WordPerfect are more a reflection on the slow pace of laser printer development than on WordPerfect's implementation of printer control. And because of WordPerfect's new graphics and printer control features, it would be almost criminal to strap anything less than a laser printer to your computer for final output. But since their introduction more than three years ago, laser printer technology has crept along at a snail's pace when compared to the dramatic advances in other computer hardware. WordPerfect will, however, milk every drop of performance from even the most modest printers. WordPerfect has even anticipated new laser printer features by including text color manipulation. Presently, this feature will only be useful for printing with some thermal and ink jet printers capable of producing color output. Until an economical color laser printer is introduced, the usefulness of thermal and ink jet printers to professional writers is limited because of the extremely slow print speeds required.

To maximize the quality of your output, WordPerfect provides controls for advancing the print up or down in fractions of an inch, enabling/disabling of letter kerning, word and letter spacing adjustment, word spacing justification limits, and direct entry of printer commands. Most of these adjustments are made to the default values assigned to the font in the WordPerfect's printer resource (.PRS) file for your printer. Taken together, these controls allow an almost infinite amount of fine-tuning to the final appearance of your printed document.

Other capabilities of current laser printers can be tapped by WordPerfect to initialize the printer with selected downloadable fonts, select form types and paper bins, and adjust the order of documents in the print que. The print "que" is the list of files that have been sent to the print in the order in which they were sent. When several long documents are in the print que, it is often convenient to put a small print job at the front of the que. WordPerfect allows you to "rush" a job, thereby placing it at the front of the que.

Doing the Dirty Work

As stated earlier, WordPerfect requires that most elements making up a page be specified by entering the absolute measurements of the element. At first this may seem a hindrance to productivity, but this restriction may actually help you save time and frustration by forcing you to make a paper and pencil layout of the finished page before you begin the layout process within WordPerfect. The paper and pencil layout can be changed as necessary until a satisfactory layout is achieved far easier than making the same changes within Word-Perfect.

The layout will show where the different elements (stories, pictures, ruling lines, page numbers, etc.) will appear on the page. A well-balanced layout is essential for the finished document to be attractive and readable. There are several books available from your local library or bookstore that will give you advice and guidance on the correct techniques for good page design. The most powerful and complete document processor can not overcome a weak page design, the results of which will become painfully obvious when the first page is printed.

Another source of page design ideas is as close as your coffee table. Pick up some of those magazines and newspapers and find a page layout that you like and fits your requirements. Then copy it—that's right, copy it. There has yet to be a page layout that is copyrighted, so don't worry about any infringement. After all, the name of the game is to avoid re-inventing the wheel. So get out some paper and a pencil and let's design our example newsletter.

The first task is to assemble all the elements that will go into the newsletter. You will probably have several text files and graphic images, as well as the standard files that make up every newsletter (e.g., the banner text, a table of contents, etc.). For our example, we will use the text files listed in Appendix A, a few of WPG graphics files supplied with WordPerfect, and one graphics file that we will create from a spreadsheet program such as LOTUS 1-2-3 or Borland International's Quattro™. If you do not own any spreadsheet program capable of producing graphics files in the PIC format, you may use one of the WordPerfect graphic images.

Now that we know which files we are going to use, we must base our first pass at a page layout on the size of these files. Very long files will probably need to run from one page to another, so space on a subsequent page must be left for this runover. In addition, most newsletters have some elements that are constant from one newsletter to the next (e.g., header, table of contents, masthead, etc.). These elements are always located in the same place on the page, and use the same space and font. On the first page, for example, the table of contents always goes at the bottom right corner, so we can assign a space for this element. The header of the newsletter always goes at the top of the first page, so we block this out as well. The other elements assigned to the first page are laid out in the remaining space.

Not to be overlooked in the first pass at our page layout process is font selection. The font we select for use in headlines and body copy will have a definite impact on the amount of space that will be required for each item. For this sample newsletter, we have chosen an 18-point Dutch (Bitstream's version of Times Roman) font for the headlines and a 12-point Dutch font for body copy. These may not be very imaginative font selections, but they are fairly safe and we don't want to get to carried away on our first newsletter. As you develop your own unique newsletter style, you will no doubt find more exotic fonts with which to express yourself and give your newsletter its own identity. Other fonts will be required for the standard elements, but they are predefined for those elements and need not be considered during the first pass at our page layout. We will also need a 14-point italic Dutch font for the pull quotes that we will use. Pull quotes are short extracts from the story that are placed between the columns of the body text to draw attention to the story. During the latter stages of actual page composition, we can adjust the type sizes of these elements as necessary to achieve the desired page balance. An example of the first page of our newsletter page layout appears in Figure 2-7.

As you can see, the page contains all of the constant elements and stories we have chosen to appear on page 1. There is also space left for the graphic images and the pull quote. We continue the page layout process for the other three pages of our newsletter as shown in Figures 2-8 through 2-10. Notice that there are several stories that run across multiple pages. These will require a break in the text file, but the exact place of the break is not yet known, so we will have to load the file into its initial position to see where the break will occur. This will be done in Chapter 5 when we really get into composing the page.

Admittedly, we have abandoned most of the rules for good page design in laying out the sample newsletter. You might even go so far as to say that our newsletter represents the epitome of dreadful page design—too many fonts are used, too many ruling lines are being drawn, shading is being overused, and on and on. But before we really begin to have our sensibilities impinged on, let's make a justification for this page design. It illustrates two points better than any other method. First, its intended purpose is to demonstrate the majority of WordPerfect's document processing capabilities. As such, this page design will fit our purpose nicely. Second, and probably more important, it demonstrates just how awful a newsletter **you** can make if you don't keep your head about you. The temptation will be great to use all of the tools that WordPerfect supplies you when you create your first document. But we would advise that you take the "Jack Benny" approach to page design—be greedy with what you have.

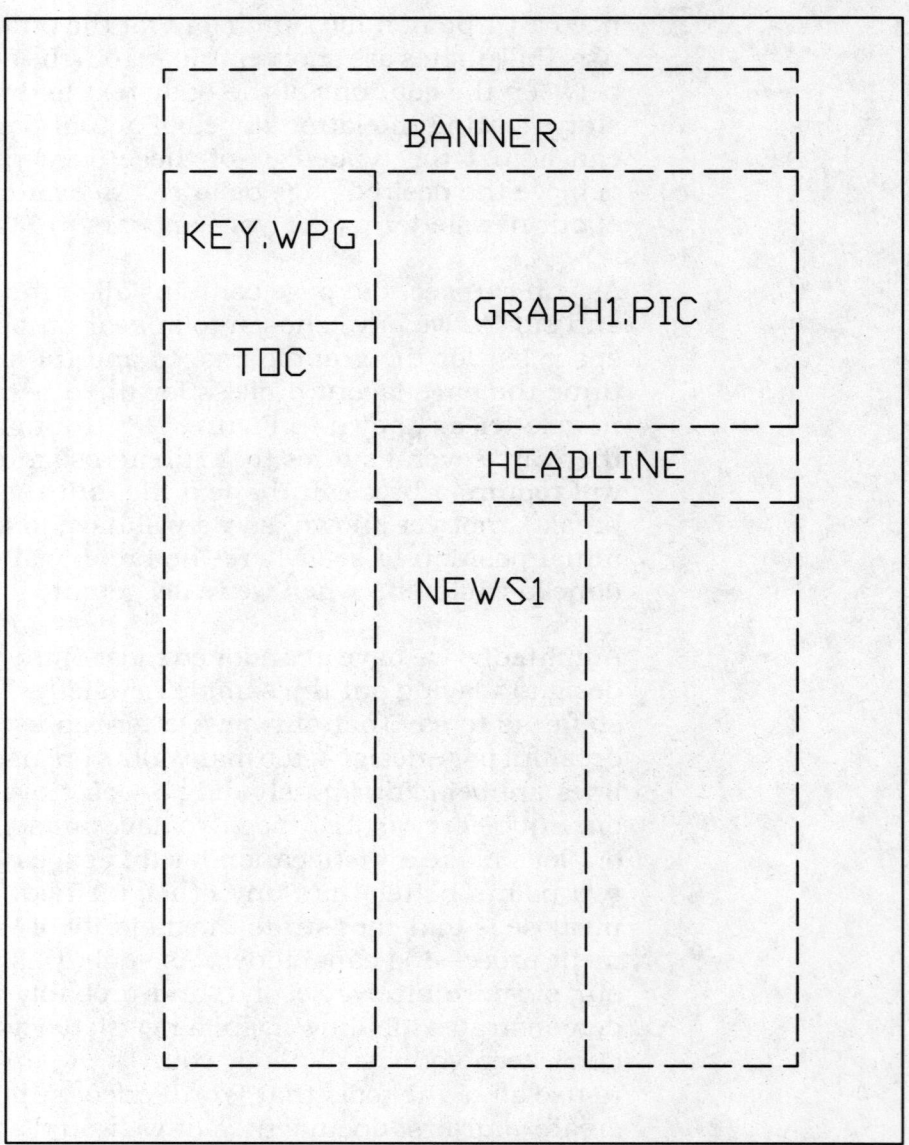

Figure 2-7. The page layout for page 1 of the sample newsletter.

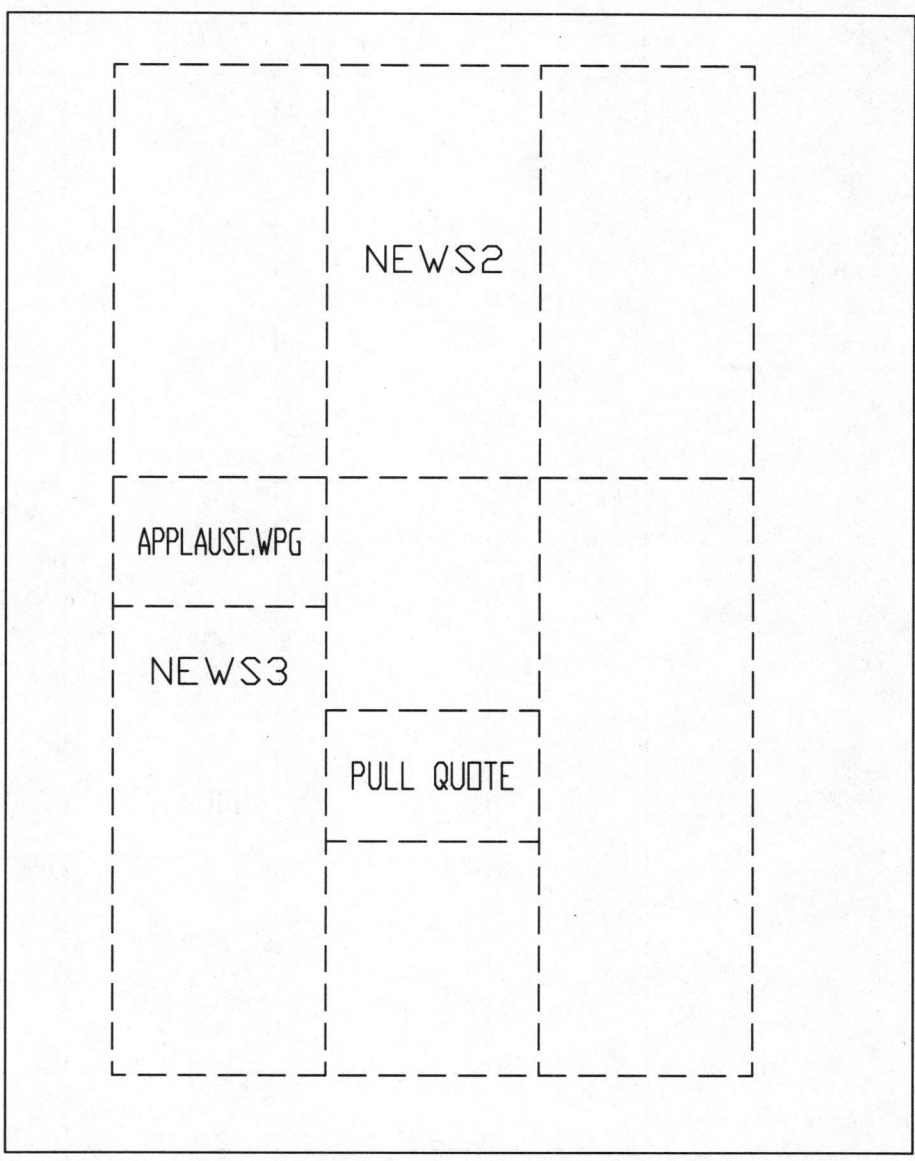

Figure 2-8. The page layout for page 2 of the sample newsletter.

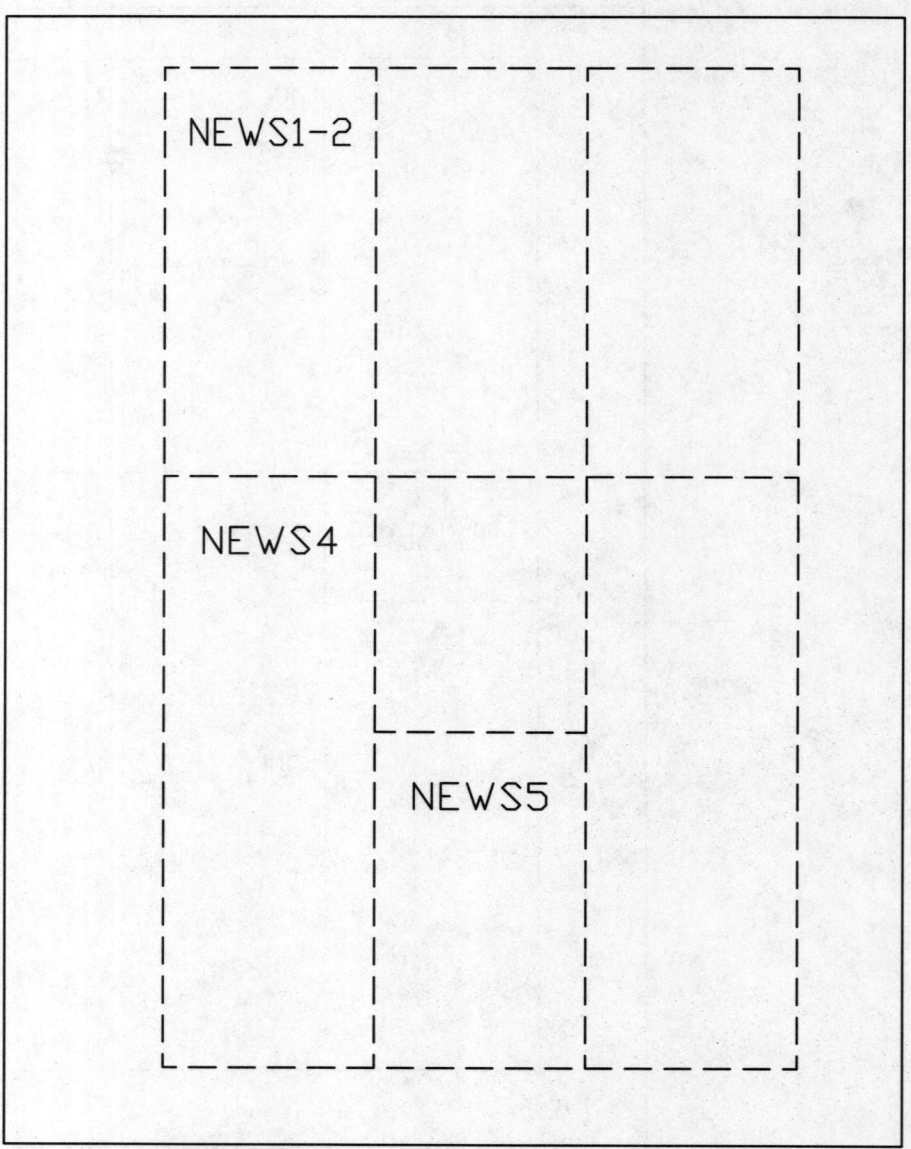

Figure 2-9. The page layout for page 3 of the sample newsletter.

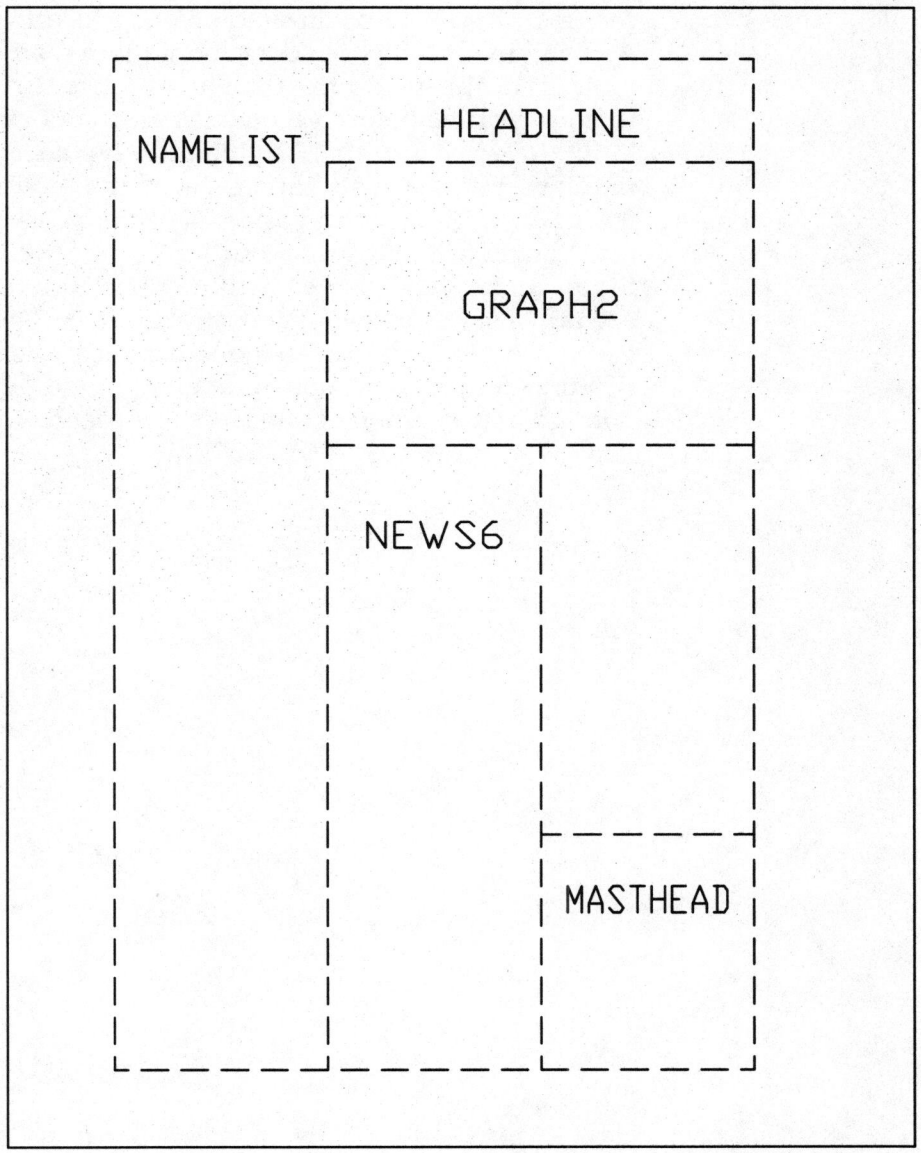

Figure 2-10. The page layout for page 4 of the sample newsletter.

At most, you should limit typefaces to one per text element. Aside from making your document more readable, you may save a bit of thumb-twiddling time if you have to download the fonts to your printer before you can print the document. If possible, limit the total number of different typefaces even further by using variations in size and style of one typeface for several different elements. For instance, if you have headlines, body text, and figure captions, limit your font usage to a maximum of three fonts. Make good use of "white space," areas of the page that are purposely left void of text and artwork. The less white space, the more cluttered the page will appear. And remember that when in doubt, copy someone else's page design. You will seldom go astray when taking this approach.

3 | What's in a Word?

No Word Is an Island

The document processing capabilities of WordPerfect 5.0 were thoroughly explored in Chapter 2. Now it's time to put this power to work. Of course, your first task is to get your text files together. These may be files you have typed in WordPerfect or files from other people working on the newsletter in either WordPerfect 4.2 or another popular word processor. In both cases, you can easily import these files into WordPerfect 5.0 using either WordPerfect's Convert Program or the Text In/Out function within WordPerfect.

The text files for our newsletter are printed in Appendix A. These files include NEWS1.WP5, NEWS2.WP5, NEWS3.WP5, NEWS4.WP5, PULQUOTE.WP5, NEWS6.WP5, NEWS5.TXT, and NAMELIST.DIF. The last two files are not WordPerfect 5.0 files and will therefore require conversion into WordPerfect's format. The file NEWS5.TXT is a file that was produced by another word processor and saved as an ASCII text file. The NAMELIST.DIF file is a Lotus® 1-2-3® file that was saved in the Lotus WKS file format and then converted to a DIF (data interchange format) file with Lotus' translation utility. If you do not own 1-2-3 or some other spreadsheet capable of producing DIF files, you can simply type the text in WordPerfect in the format shown to simulate the DIF format.

The Convert Program

The Convert Program supplied with WordPerfect 5.0 can convert documents to and from the formats shown in Figure 3-1. Operation of the Convert Program is simple and straightforward. To convert a document to or from one of the formats shown, type CONVERT at the DOS prompt. You are asked to provide the input file name and output file name. The Convert Program then presents the menu shown in Figure 3-1. (Note that Figure 3-1 is a composite of two separate screens, combined here for brevity.) Most of these choices (except option **9**) provide conversion from the formats indicated to WordPerfect. We will use the spreadsheet DIF conversion later to import a list of new hires, terminations, and retiring employees into our sample newsletter. If option **1** is selected, the translation options in Figure 3-1 are displayed. These options include

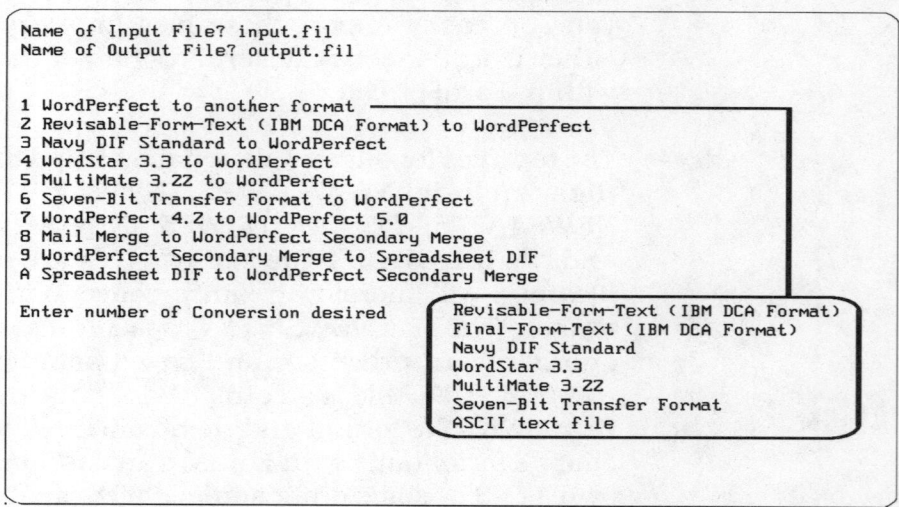

Figure 3-1. The Convert Program provides the door to the outside world.

conversions of the WordPerfect file to the formats indicated.

The Text In/Out Function

You can perform some text conversions directly from within WordPerfect. The Text In/Out function provides options for saving and retrieving files in DOS text format and saving files in WordPerfect 4.2 format. The distinction between a DOS text file and an ASCII text file (as produced by the Convert Program) is a small but important one to understand if you will be using these formats. The DOS text file retains the appearance of the WordPerfect file by inserting spaces where required to maintain the document's appearance.

Consider the instance of a line of centered text. When either conversion is applied to the centered text, the WordPerfect code for centered text is removed. But the DOS text file will have spaces inserted from the left margin so that the text remains centered. The same line of centered text that is converted to ASCII text with the Convert Program will not have spaces inserted and thus will be flush with the left margin.

The method of saving the WordPerfect file (convert to ASCII or save as DOS text with the Text In/Out function) will depend on your plans for the file after it is saved. If the file will at some point be imported back into WordPerfect, it is wiser to use ASCII text conversion and re-enter the WordPerfect code to center the text. The centered text will then remain centered if the margins require adjustment. Otherwise, it is more convenient to the DOS text save option in the Text In/Out function.

There is one other option for saving text that is offered by the Text In/Out function—the Generic format. The Generic format is similar to the DOS text format in that WordPerfect codes for text format (e.g., center, indent, etc.) are saved as spaces to maintain the format of the document. The only difference is the treatment of the tab code, which is retained when the file is saved with the Generic option. Most word processors have standardized on a specific ASCII character to represent a tab, so this option may save a bit of cleanup work when the file is retrieved into a word processor other than WordPerfect.

If you choose to import text with the DOS text option, you will also be given the opportunity to choose the type of CR/LF (carriage return/line feed) character conversion to use. The CR/LF combination is required by DOS at the end of each line of text. Think of the file you are creating as a piece of paper and DOS as the printer. The carriage return tells DOS that the end-of-line has been reached and the line feed tells DOS to start the next line at the left margin one line below the one just completed. Your selection when importing DOS text into WordPerfect determines how these CR/LF character combinations are converted. Option **2** (CR/LF to [HRt]) will create a WordPerfect file in which each line ends with a hard return (HRt). In essence, each line will be treated by WordPerfect as a separate paragraph.

On the other hand, option **3** (CR/LF to [SRt] in HZone) will convert a CR/LF to a soft return (SRt) if the CR/LF occurs in the hyphenation zone (HZone). (The hyphenation zone is an area at the end of each line of text that determines if the last word in the line is to be hyphenated or wrapped to the next line.) Selecting option **3** protects two consecutive hard returns from being mistakenly converted to a soft return and hard return, thus ensuring that paragraphs are properly separated. If your WordPerfect margins are set close to the margins of the file being imported, the file conversion will result in a WordPerfect document that is very close to the way the original document was entered.

For our sample newsletter, we will be importing two files that are not in WordPerfect format. The first file is an ASCII text file called NEWS5.TXT. We may have received this file by a modem transfer from a remote office or produced by a word processor not supported by WordPerfect's Convert Program and saved by that word processor as an ASCII text file (most word processors have this capability). We will also be importing a DIF file into WordPerfect via the spreadsheet DIF-to-WordPerfect Secondary Merge conversion option in the Convert Program. The NEWS5.TXT file is listed in Appendix A and should be created with any word processor capable of saving the file in ASCII text format (such as WordPerfect). The contents of the NAMELIST.DIF file are also listed in Appendix A. If you have a spreadsheet program that can either save files in the DIF format or translate spreadsheet files into DIF format (and most do), enter the names in the spreadsheet and save as a DIF file with the file name NAMELIST.DIF. Otherwise, just type these names into a WordPerfect 5.0 file and save it as NAMELIST. You will still get a lot from following along with the DIF importation process, though. So let's begin with the ASCII text file.

Importing ASCII Files

The file NEWS5.TXT is an ASCII text file that we need to convert to WordPerfect's format and then clean up a bit. First, we need to perform the conversion. Since this is an ASCII text file, we will use WordPerfect's Text In/Out function. As explained earlier, ASCII text and DOS text are closely related, so we can use the DOS text function of WordPerfect on ASCII text files with the caveats explained. But before we do the actual conversion, there is one thing we need to do in order to get the best conversion. As mentioned earlier, we intend to convert the ASCII file with option **3** (CR/LF to [SRt] in HZone) in the Text In/Out function. Thus, we need to set our hyphenation zone to cover the widest possible area.

    Press   **Shift+F8** (Format)

    Press   **1** (Line)

Press   **2** (Hyphenation Zone)

Set the left and right hyphenation zones to 99 percent and exit the Format menu. To convert the text:

Press   **Ctrl+F5** (Text In/Out)

Press   **1** (DOS Text)

Press   **3** (Retrieve (CR/LF to [SRt] in HZone))

Type   NEWS5.TXT

After the document is imported, delete the hyphenation zone code that you just inserted. If you leave the hyphenation zone set to 99 percent left and right, you will be very busy answering hyphenation questions! You may need to clean up the document a bit before you save it as a WordPerfect file. Most, if not all, of this cleanup work will be replacing spaces with the appropriate WordPerfect code (the centered text, for instance). When you have completed the cleanup, save the file as a WordPerfect file under the name NEWS5.WP5.

Importing DIF Files

The DIF file format is another form of ASCII file that is produced by most spreadsheet programs. This format has a specific form that defines where the column and row values are placed in the file (see Figure 3-2). When WordPerfect imports a DIF file into its secondary merge format, rows in the spreadsheet become records and cells within each row in the spreadsheet become fields within the record. The data in A1 (the first cell in the first row) becomes the first field in the first record, the data in B1 (the second cell in the first row) becomes the second field in the first record, the data in A2 (the first cell in the second row) becomes the first field in the second record, and so on until

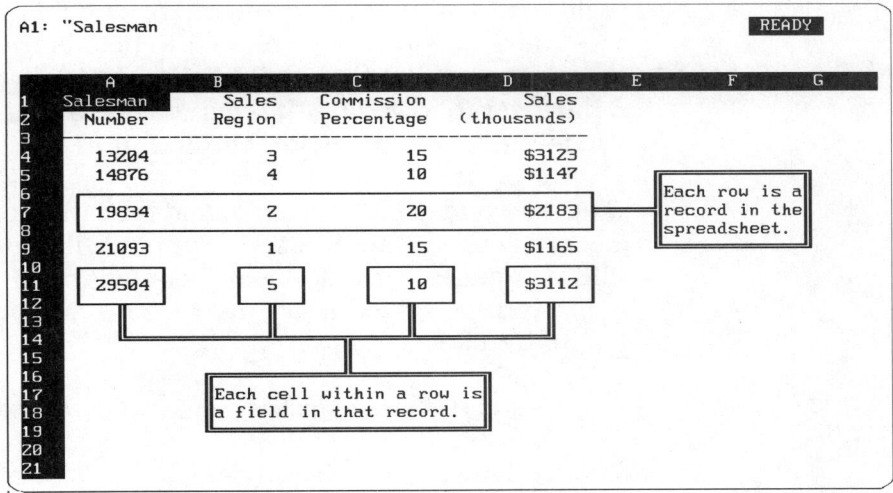

Figure 3-2. A Lotus 1-2-3 spreadsheet is converted to the DIF file format as indicated.

the entire spreadsheet has been converted. The file NAMELIST.DIF is a file in this format that we will use to create a list of names for our newsletter. When we import the file NAMELIST.DIF, the names, status, and dates will be placed in the secondary merge file as NAME in field 1, STATUS in field 2, and DATE in field 3. Fields 1, 2, and 3 comprise a complete record. After we import the DIF file into a secondary merge file, we can define the primary merge file and then combine the two to produce our list of names and dates.

The primary merge file contains the WordPerfect merge commands for each field and record within the secondary merge file. A record is one complete set of information (e.g., name, status, and date). Each field within a record contains a single piece of information (e.g., the name). For our list of names, we will need commands to insert three fields in each record. The first field is the name, the second field is the status (hire or terminate), and the third field is the date. WordPerfect uses the ^ character followed by the merge code and a closing ^ character to define a field insertion command in the primary file.

The secondary file has each field terminated with a ^R and each record is terminated by a ^E. For our DIF file, the primary merge file will contain the following codes and the Convert Program will produce a secondary merge file with the fields and records formatted accordingly.

The Primary Merge File	The Secondary Merge File
Codes	**Data**
^F1^	John Smith^R
^F2^	New Hire^R
^F3^	March 10^R
	^E

To complete the merge procedure and create our names file, first start WordPerfect and enter the merge commands above in a blank document as follows:

    Press **Shift+F9** (Merge Codes)

    Press **F** (*the field code*)

    Press **1** (*code for field 1*)

    Press **Return** (*twice*)

Repeat this process three times until you have created the primary merge file that was shown earlier. Save the file as

NAMELIST.PRI. Then create the secondary merge file using the WordPerfect Convert Program or, if you do not have a spreadsheet program that converts files to DIF format, enter the data in a WordPerfect file in the format shown above using **Ctrl+R** to end each field and **Ctrl+E** to end each record and save the file. In either case, the resulting file should be named NAMELIST.SEC.

Now start from a blank WordPerfect document screen and press **Ctrl+F9**. You will be asked to supply file names for the primary and secondary merge files. Enter NAMELIST.PRI for the primary merge file and NAMELIST.SEC for the secondary merge file. WordPerfect will then complete the merge operation, writing each complete record on a separate page. The last thing we need to do is perform a search and replace operation replacing each hard page break with a space. When this is done, save the file as NAMELIST.WP5. We now have all of our text files in WordPerfect format and we are ready to continue composing our sample newsletter.

Fonts Make the Page

The next step in producing the newsletter is selecting the fonts that we will use for each text element. However, before we can select the fonts, we need to know which fonts are available for selection. For the purposes of this exercise, we will be using the Hewlett-Packard LaserJet Series II™ as our printer. The process for using any other printer supported by WordPerfect is the same as described here for the LaserJet Series II. Therefore, if you have a printer other than a LaserJet Series II, just substitute the name of your printer wherever you read "LaserJet Series II."

The standard LaserJet Series II has capacity for two font cartridges and 512 kilobytes of RAM. However, only about 350 kilobytes is available for soft font usage. The practical limit on the amount of RAM available for downloading soft fonts should be kept even lower (around 300 kilobytes) to allow space for the composition of complex page layouts. (Of course, if you add more RAM to your printer, these numbers will change accordingly.)

The majority of Hewlett-Packard's font cartridges are different combinations of Times Roman® and Helvetica®. These are extremely versatile fonts and do not require any effort on our part to use them other than putting the cartridge in the cartridge slot and telling WordPerfect of its presence. In fact, they are so easy to use that they would not provide a good example of how the Printer Program is used. It is also impossible to assume that everyone reading this book owns the same font cartridge. So we will concentrate on how to get the most from the soft fonts available from Hewlett-Packard and third-party suppliers.

What Is a Soft Font?

Soft fonts are essentially a type of software that is downloaded to the printer and stored in the printer's memory until the printer is reset or turned off. The size and style of the font will determine how many different fonts your printer will hold at one time. There are two types of soft fonts—outline and bitmapped. Actually, there is no such thing as an "outline font." As described in Chapter 2, a font is a combination of a specific typeface and attributes (including size) that are assigned to that typeface. Outline fonts are supplied by a vendor in a maximum of four files that describe the appearance of the typeface in mathematical terms. The four files comprise the normal-weight upright typeface, the normal-weight italic typeface, the bold upright typeface, and the bold italic typeface.

With the appropriate companion program (normally an installation program), the mathematical expressions for each of these four typeface types can be read and manipulated to produce a bit-mapped font of the typeface in whatever size we prefer. Hence, there is no real outline font, only an outline typeface with appearance attributes. We don't have a font until we generate a specific size of one of the four typefaces. The Bitstream Fontware program and accompanying soft fonts are examples of an installation program and outline typefaces. Fontware will read any of Bitstream's outline typefaces, generate fonts in the sizes you specify, and install the fonts' descriptive information into WordPerfect's printer definition file. When the font is created from the outline typeface, it is saved to a file in bit-mapped form. With this in mind, we will adhere to the normal convention of calling outline typefaces outline fonts.

Bit-map fonts are true, complete fonts. Each font file contains only one typeface in a specific size with specific appearance attributes. Thus the bit-map font file contains "pictures" of each character. If you purchase bit-map font files, you will have less flexibility in creating new fonts from them because what you see is what you get. There are a few very good utility programs, however, that can add some special effects to bit-mapped fonts to create variations of the basic font. These variations can range from simple shadow effects and font outlines to complex letter hatching and slanting. One of the best such utility packages is the Font Effects™ program from SoftCraft. Font Effects can manipulate any Hewlett-Packard compatible bit-mapped font in an almost infinite number of ways.

When using Font Effects, it is quite possible that your eyes could become bigger than your hard disk, so be careful. A preview function is provided within the program that enables you to view the results of your modification on screen, thus allowing you to abort the creation of a really awful font before you make it, install it in WordPerfect, download it to the printer, and print the atrocity. SoftCraft also has a companion program called Laser Fonts that will read the font files that you create with Font Effects (or any bit-mapped font that adheres to the Hewlett-Packard font format) and install the fonts' descriptive information in WordPerfect's printer definition file, complete with character width table and kerning information. The new font is then accessible from within WordPerfect just like any other font.

For the cost-conscious, there are some Hewlett-Packard compatible bit-mapped fonts to be found on many of the bulletin board systems dedicated to desktop publishing. These fonts can be downloaded from the bulletin board and installed with an installation kit for bit-mapped fonts. Alternatively, the descriptive information for these fonts can be installed manually in the printer definition file. This is a tedious job and quite time-consuming, but it can be done. Additionally, these font files normally do not contain any kerning information.

Again, there are some public domain programs that can assist with this task. FONTINFO and SOFTREAD are two such programs. Either of these programs will read a Hewlett-Packard compatible bit-mapped font file and generate information such as the character set being used by the font and the character width table for the font. This information can be entered into the printer definition file with WordPerfect's Printer Program.

Public Bulletin Board Systems

Public bulletin board systems are a veritable treasure trove of information and software for all of your desktop publishing needs. A computer bulletin board is the electronic equivalent of a community bulletin board where messages and requests are posted for reading and copying via your telephone. Some computer and publishing companies run bulletin boards for advertising and selling their services in addition to providing a source of information and software. But most bulletin boards are run by private individuals called system operators

(SYSOPs). The majority of these bulletin boards provide free access in exchange for your participation, but a few require a modest donation to help them maintain and expand the system.

Whether a particular bulletin board is fee based or free has little to do with the quality of the board itself. Some of the largest and best run bulletin boards are free while some of the fee-based bulletin boards offer little that cannot be obtained elsewhere. However, for the free bulletin boards to remain free, you are strongly encouraged to donate your ideas and non-copyrighted programs to the system. Once a bulletin board has gained a national reputation for its quality, a bulletin board SYSOP can sometimes obtain sponsorship to continue the bulletin board's expansion.

Other SYSOPs, either out of a love for the "stuff" or some form of computerized insanity, or both, operate and maintain free bulletin boards in their own time and out of their own pockets. Therefore, before you get involved with a bulletin board, consider the SYSOP on the other end. If you can't donate software, a small donation would certainly be accepted with humble appreciation. In this way, the board can continue to expand and prosper without charging each user a fee.

However, there is another price to be paid for free access to all of this information. As with any human endeavor founded and maintained on wires and chips and bits and bytes, these system may be "off-the-air" from time to time. Most bulletin boards run 24 hours a day, 7 days a week with only short periods of down time required for maintenance and enhancement. If you should call one of these boards and get no answer, wait a day or two and try again. On the more popular bulletin boards, you may also have to try calling several times before the line is open for you to get on. Some bulletin boards are trying to alleviate this problem by installing several telephone lines (called nodes). These alternate nodes often require a small subscription fee for access, but the time saved by being able to access the system immediately may well be worth it.

Trojan Horses and Program Viruses
We would be remiss if you were not warned of a very real threat in using public domain software. You have probably read or heard about trojan horses and program viruses. These programs are designed by individuals to destroy programs and data on your computer for no more apparent reason than any thug has for destroying a stranger's personal property.

The trojan horse program is nothing more than a program written to erase files or format disks under the guise of being a useful and innocent program. A program called READ-TYPE.EXE may be described as a program to display a typeface file's characters. Instead, it may erase all the files in its directory. Most reputable SYSOPs try to test programs they receive before making them available to others via the bulletin board. However, the best protection against a trojan horse program is to run the program yourself from a floppy disk with a write protect tab. If the program does indeed do what it says it will do, chances are its safe to use elsewhere.

Program viruses, on the other hand, are the most serious threat to users of public domain software. A program with a virus may behave exactly as it is described, but sends out a small piece of code that attaches itself to other uninfected software in your system. If you then send a different file to a bulletin board that has been infected by the originally infected program, the virus can spread like wild fire throughout the bulletin board community. The ultimate purpose of viruses range from a benign message such as "All Your Files Are Infected! Gotcha!" to creating catastrophic hardware failures and lost data.

Bulletin board SYSOPs are virtually helpless against program viruses because of their ability to attach themselves to any program. The best protection against these programs can be found in a new breed of commercial software—the vaccine program. These programs are continually updated to protect your system against known viruses. Most vaccine programs look at your files when the vaccine is first run (this assumes your system is not already infected) to make a record of the program's file structure and to check for known viruses. If a virus is found, you are immediately notified. Each time the vaccine program is run thereafter, the programs are examined again. If any changes to the file structure are noted or a virus is found, the program warns you that your computer may have been infected by a virus. Since these vaccine programs are continually being released and updated, check with your local software dealer for the latest software availability.

Modems
Once you are protected against those software demons, you are ready to start bulletin board roving. Before you can take advantage of bulletin boards, however, you must have the proper hardware and software installed in your system. The hardware in this case is a modem (MOdulator/DEModulator). A modem's capability is measured by the rate at which it can send and receive data. Early modems transferred data at a rate of 300 bits per second, or 300 baud. These modems were rapidly replaced by ones operating at 1200 baud. And the 1200 baud modems were upstaged by 2400 baud modems. Currently, the highest speed modem affordable by the average user is 9600 baud, although the majority of modems in use by individuals are still 2400 baud. Most bulletin boards will support data transmissions of 300, 1200, and 2400 baud. As the 9600 baud modem drops in price and hence becomes more popular, more and more bulletin boards will offer compatibility with this higher rate.

Communications Software
The software required is called, not surprisingly, communications software. The communications software will provide the protocol, or language, with which your modem will talk to the

bulletin board's modem. The communication parameters for most bulletin boards is eight data bits, one stop bit, and no parity. Don't be concerned with what these communication parameters mean, just be aware that they exist so that you can set your communications software accordingly. If all you want to do is read and post messages on the bulletin board, this is all you need to know. However, if you want to upload and/or download files, there is one other parameter that your communications software needs to know—the transfer protocol.

The transfer protocol not only sets up the type of file transfer, but also tells the bulletin board software what type of error-checking you wish to use. Each file transfer consists of blocks of data. Depending on the transfer protocol you select, the block is encoded such that your software can double check the block to ensure that there were no transmission errors along the way.

The standard transfer protocol recognized by all bulletin boards is called XMODEM, although most boards offer other protocols as well. You may set your communications software for this protocol, or select another one that is supported by both your communications software and the bulletin board that you have called.

Where to Start?
An excellent place to start your search for desktop publishing programs and information is the Eastern Publisher's Exchange based in Tampa, Florida (813-989-3375). The Eastern Publisher's Exchange is the charter bulletin board of the National Publisher's Exchange (NPE). NPE was founded by Ed Aborn to promote the exchange of ideas and software for all aspects of desktop publishing. The closing credits that are displayed when you disconnect from the Eastern Publisher's Exchange include a list of other NPE member bulletin boards which are spread across the country. Try all of these member bulletin boards. You may find some duplicate files among them, but each is unique enough to offer some real treasures.

If you need assistance purchasing fonts, clip art graphics, hardware, software, or other desktop publishing services, contact Publisher Information Service (312-342-6919). This bulletin board is a commercial operation established by George M. Weinert V in Chicago, Illinois. Though directed primarily at commercial accounts, this bulletin board has over 5000 public domain files devoted to desktop publishing available for downloading.

The two bulletin boards mentioned here only scratch the surface of what is available to the desktop publisher. The rule of getting the most from bulletin boards is be nosey! Look around the system. Often a bulletin board will post a list of related bulletin boards. If you call each of the bulletin boards listed, they in turn will usually have lists of bulletin boards posted. In a short time, you can turn this "pyramid" of bulletin boards into an almost unlimited source of not only fonts and font-related software, but for all your desktop publishing requirements.

Making the Newsletter Fonts

For our example newsletter, we will be using the Bitstream Fontware Installation Kit that WordPerfect gives free to any registered WordPerfect 5.0 user that requests one. Accompanying the Installation kit are three Bitstream typeface packages with the kit including the upright typeface for Bitstream Charter, and all four typefaces (upright, italic, bold, and bold italic) for Dutch (Bitstream's version of Times Roman) and Swiss (Bitstream's version of Helvetica). The Dutch typeface will be used for our sample newsletter, not because it is the best typeface for the job (it's not), but because as a WordPerfect 5.0 owner, it is a safe bet that you will have this typeface package (since you get it free). This single typeface will probably not be sufficient for "real world" newsletters, but by restricting ourselves to bit-mapped fonts created from the Dutch typeface it is certain that you will have the same fonts available that we are using for the newsletter. Also note that these fonts adhere to the Hewlett-Packard font file format standard, although Bitstream uses a different file naming convention.

Selecting the Fonts

We will need a font created from the Dutch typeface for each text element in our newsletter. The newsletter title and header information will require two fonts, two more for the body text and body text quotes, one more for supplementary text, and a final one for headlines. That's six fonts and more than enough to start the ball rolling. Any other text elements should use one of these six in order to adhere to the good page layout practices that were discussed in Chapter 2. We will make an 18-point bold font for the title, a 14-point bold italic font for the headlines, a 12-point normal font and 12-point italic font for the body text and body text quotes, a 10-point normal font for the header, and an 8-point italic font for the supplementary text.

Before we begin to make the fonts, we need to install the Fontware program and the Dutch roman (upright), italic, black (bold), and black italic typefaces on our hard disk. Follow the directions in the Bitstream Installation Kit User's Guide to accomplish this. Next copy the files on the Bitstream Dutch font disk to the directory containing the Fontware files. You are now ready to make the desired fonts. To start Fontware, enter the directory containing the Fontware files and type FONTWARE. Follow the directions given on screen and in the User's Guide. We will only be using portrait text and none of the characters found in the extended character sets, so select only portrait and ASCII when prompted for orientation and character set, respectively. Fontware will create the fonts and install their definitions in the WPRINT1.ALL printer definition file. The time required to produce and install the bit-mapped font files will thus be greatly reduced.

Making a Newsletter Printer

Have you ever had the urge to make your own printer? Well this is your chance, although it will be only a software printer. We will make a printer definition specifically for printing newsletters. If you intend to produce a number of different types of documents, each having their own set of fonts, then you will probably grow tired of marking and unmarking fonts for each type of document. There is a better way—make your own printer for each type of document. This is easily accomplished by simply copying the printer definition for the HP LaserJet Series II (or whatever printer you have) to a printer named whatever you like. Creating your own printer definitions has the advantage of allowing you to configure each definition (e.g., which fonts are available and how they are handled) for each type of document you produce. Therefore, you won't be continuously changing a single printer resource file for the fonts used for each job. Instead, you will only need to select the printer created for the job. In this example we will create a printer called Newsletters. We could create other printers called Flyers, Bulletins, and so on using the same procedures described here.

To create our printer, we will call upon WordPerfect's Printer Program. The Printer Program allows us to examine and change the definitions for all of the printers supported by WordPerfect. Prior to starting the Printer Program, you must ensure that you have no other programs present in you computer's memory. This includes running the Printer Program from within WordPerfect's own Library™ program. The Printer Program lives up to the truest definition of "memory hog" and all of your memory resident programs must be removed before loading the Printer program. Further, if you added a lot of fonts to your printer definition, you may not be able to load the Printer program even if your computer has 640K of RAM and nothing but DOS resident. There is another approach we can take if this situation occurs, but we will cover that later.

To start the Printer Program, make sure you are in the directory containing the WordPerfect files and start the program by typing PTR WPRINT1.ALL. This will start the program and automatically load the WPRINT1.ALL printer file, displaying the screen shown in Figure 3-3. Conversely, if you start the Printer program by typing just PTR, a blank screen will be displayed and you will have to load the WPRINT1.ALL file in the usual WordPerfect manner (by pressing **Shift+F10**).

To begin the process, we will instruct the Printer Program to add a new printer.

    Press   **1** (Add)

All of the new fonts just created are in the HP LaserJet Series II printer definition, so we will use this printer as the pattern.

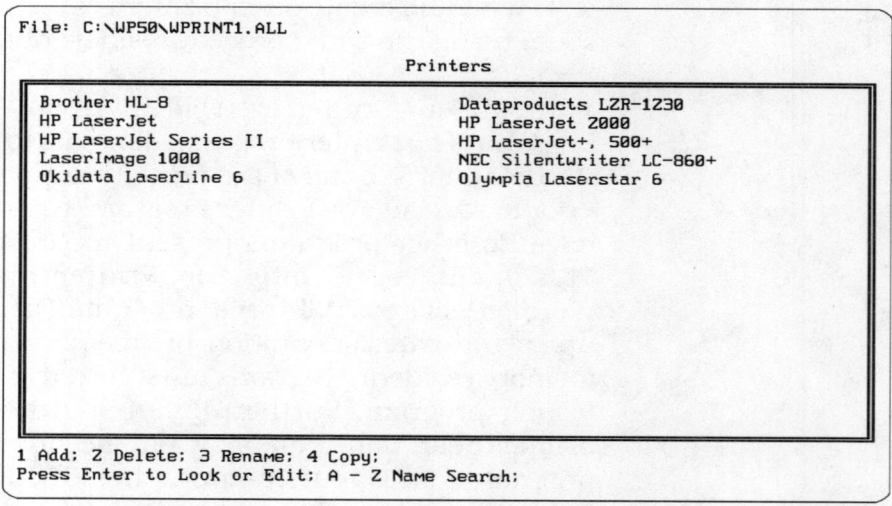

Figure 3-3. The Printer Program opening screen with the WPRINT1.ALL file loaded.

Highlight	HP LaserJet Series II
Press	**Return**
Type	Newsletters

The Newsletters printer definition is created and highlighted. Press **F7** (Exit) and you will be asked if you want to save the file. If you answer yes, all of your changes will be saved. This will take several minutes because the printer definitions for all printers defined in the WPRINT1.ALL file are saved. This completes our use Printer Program, so type Y when asked if you want to exit. You have just created your first printer! Remember to set your printer to Newsletters in the Fontware control panel if you later need to create more fonts for this printer.

Cutting the WPRINT1.ALL File Down to Size

WordPerfect does not use the entire WPRINT1.ALL file for processing your documents. Instead, it produces a printer resource file that contains just the information about the resources you use from a single printer (such as soft fonts and font cartridges available). Remember that the WPRINT1.ALL file defines several different printers. There is no reason for WordPerfect to try to keep track of all these printers and the fonts associated with each one if you are only using the Newsletters printer. Further, there is no reason for WordPerfect to bother with the more than 100 fonts defined for the Newsletters printer if you are only going to use the six Bitstream Dutch fonts that we have created. For this reason, WordPerfect creates a printer resource (.PRS) file when you first select the Newsletters printer from the printer list in WordPerfect. This file will contain the information for only those resources that you will be using. But you must tell WordPerfect what those resources are (e.g., the printer you are using, the amount of printer memory, etc.).

Creating the Printer Resource File

We have created a Newsletters printer and filled it with information about fonts, escape sequences, kerning information, and so on. However, to this point WordPerfect knows nothing about our new printer. All of this information has been kept in the WPRINT1.ALL file. Our final task to be completed before we can start using our printer is to tell WordPerfect about it.

The process of actually creating the printer resource file is so easy that if you blink, you'll miss it. If you have not already done so, start WordPerfect.

> Press **Shift+F7** (Print)
>
> Press **S** (Select Printer)

A blank screen is displayed since no printers have yet been selected.

> Press **2** (Additional Printers)

The printers in the WPRINT1.ALL file are listed, including the Newsletter printer that we created.

> Highlight Newsletters
>
> Press **Return**

You will be asked if you want to create a file called NEWSLETT.PRS. WordPerfect constructed this name from the first eight letters of the printer name and the .PRS extension. Press **Y** and wait until WordPerfect updates the printer resource file with the fonts that are resident in the printer at all times. Press **F7** (Exit) after reading the printer helps and hints screen. We have just created the printer resource file—almost. The only thing left for us to do is configure the printer.

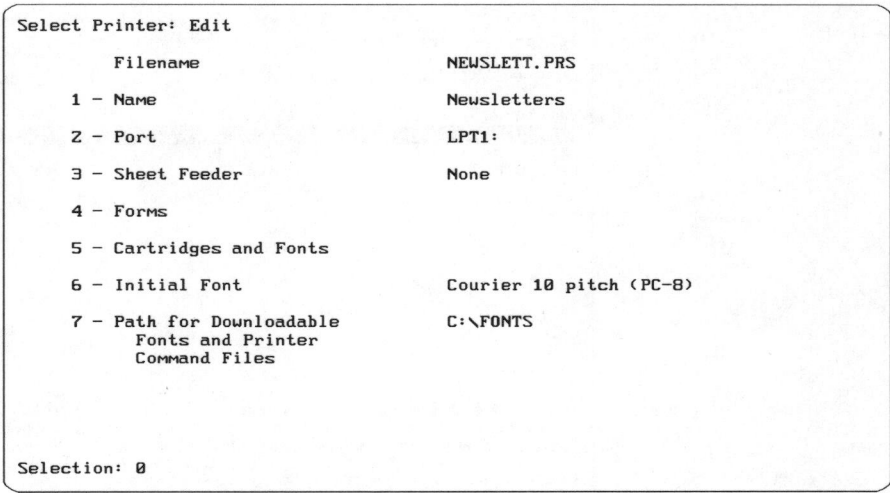

Figure 3-4. The printer definition screen in WordPerfect.

The Select Printer: Edit screen (Figure 3-4) should now be displayed. Option **1** (Name) may be changed, but this is not required. Option **2** (Port) allows you to select your printer port. Your printer will be connected to either a serial (COM) or parallel (LPT) port. Choose the appropriate port type and number. If a COM port is selected, WordPerfect displays the serial port configuration screen. These are the preset defaults and should not be changed. Press **Return** to exit this screen and select the default values. Option **3** (Sheet Feeder) allows selection of a sheet feeder. Unless you have an unusual circumstance, the HP LaserJet sheet feeder should be selected, and then press **F7** (Exit).

Option **4** (Forms) requires a bit of explanation. WordPerfect determines what form you wish to use during printing by the paper size and type you specify with the **Shift+F8** (Format) command. However, you must also define the paper size and type in the printer resource file so that WordPerfect can match the command to the forms available. If we want to print single-wide

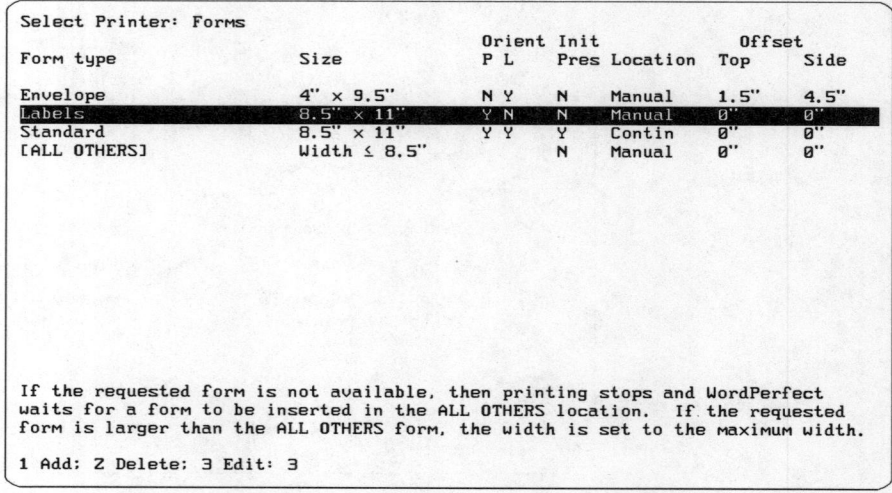

Figure 3-5. The forms definition screen with a label form defined.

mailing labels for our newsletter that are 3 inches wide and 1 inch high, we must select option **4** (Forms) to define the size and type of form that the mailing label will require. Perform the steps provided in the WordPerfect user's manual to define the mailing label form. The form screen with the completed mailing label form is shown in Figure 3-5. There is one trap set along the way that you should be aware of. If you specify a form's height or width larger than the margins would allow (as in our 1 inch long mailing label on a page with 1 inch top and bottom margins), you must reduce the margin sufficiently for text to fit on the form. Otherwise, you will never be able to select the form.

Cartridges and Fonts

Finally we come to the point that we've been anticipating—telling WordPerfect that our Bitstream Dutch fonts are available for use. However, before we do, we have one more decision to make. When you specify a font is available for use, you must choose to either have the font downloaded when the printer is initialized or downloaded when you print the job. The way that you choose to have the fonts downloaded will depend on your work situation. If you use the same fonts consistently throughout your work day, you will probably choose to initialize the printer once and forget about it.

On the other hand, if you work with different documents that have different font requirements, you will likely prefer to have the fonts for each print job downloaded with the job. Be aware, however, that downloading fonts takes time, time that your computer will not be available for other work. With this in mind, let's select the new fonts by first selecting option **5** (Cartridges and Fonts) from the printer edit menu.

The first screen shows the available resources in the LaserJet Series II; two font cartridges and 350K of RAM. If you change the amount of RAM in the WPRINT1.ALL file during the printer definition process, that change will be reflected here. To install our new Bitstream Dutch soft fonts, highlight the Soft fonts option and press **Return**. After a few moments, the list of all the fonts defined in the NEWSLETT.PRS file is displayed. Perform a search operation on the (FW) character string. When the search is complete, press any cursor key to stop the search. Depending on how you decided to download your fonts, each Bitstream Dutch font can be marked with either a * (download upon printer initialization) or + (download with print job).

For our sample newsletter, mark each Bitstream font with an *. When you have completed marking the Bitstream fonts (your screen should look like the one in Figure 3-6), press **F7** (Exit). If you want to select a font cartridge, highlight the Cartridge Fonts option, press **Return**, and mark the cartridge with an * (cartridges in the LaserJet Series II are not swappable, so you cannot mark the cartridge with both * and +), and press **F7** (Exit). If you are satisfied with your selections, press **F7** (Exit) again. You will see WordPerfect update its internal list of available fonts with your selections.

```
Select Printer: Cartridges and Fonts
                                       Total Quantity:   350 K
                                   Available Quantity:   262 K

Soft Fonts                                           Quantity Used

    (EA) Prestige Elite 10pt Italic 12 pitch (Land)        25 K
    (EA) Prestige Elite 10pt Italic 12 pitch (Legal)       12 K
    (EA) Prestige Elite 10pt Italic 12 pitch (Legal) (Land) 12 K
*   (FW) Dutch Bold 14pt (ASCII) (Port)                    17 K
*   (FW) Dutch Bold 18pt (ASCII) (Port)                    25 K
*   (FW) Dutch Italic 12pt (ASCII) (Port)                  14 K
*   (FW) Dutch Italic 8pt (ASCII) (Port)                    8 K
*   (FW) Dutch Roman 10pt (ASCII) (Port)                   11 K
*   (FW) Dutch Roman 12pt (ASCII) (Port)                   13 K
    (SA) Century Schoolbook 06pt                            8 K
    (SA) Century Schoolbook 06pt Bold                       8 K
    (SA) Century Schoolbook 06pt Italic                     8 K
    (SA) Century Schoolbook 07pt                            8 K
    (SA) Century Schoolbook 07pt Bold                       9 K
    (SA) Century Schoolbook 07pt Italic                     8 K

Mark Fonts:  * Present when print job begins      Press Exit to save
             + Can be loaded during print job     Press Cancel to cancel
```

Figure 3-6. The Bitstream fonts marked for downloading when the printer is initialized.

Initial Font

The Initial Font option **(6)** displays a list of available fonts and asks you to select one as the initial font. It is usually good practice to specify the font assigned to body text as the initial font. Highlight the Dutch Roman 12pt (ASCII) (Port) (FW) font and press **Return**.

Path for Downloadable Fonts and Printer Command Files

This option is really the simplest of the entire printer edit menu. Simply select option **7** and enter the path where your soft fonts and printer command files are located. For the Bitstream fonts, this path will be C:\FONTS if you did not change Fontware's defaults during its installation. Note that any printer command files that you create should also go in this directory.

Completing the Printer Resource File

You have now completed defining your new Newsletters printer and you have told (either directly or indirectly) everything it needs to know to get the most from it. The only task left is to select the printer so it can be used to print our newsletter. To complete the printer resource file definition process, press **Return** to exit the Select Printer: Edit screen. The Print: Select Printer screen is displayed with the Select (1) option set by default. The Newsletters printer is already highlighted, so press **Return** to select the new printer. When the Print screen is displayed, press **Return** to get back to the document editing screen. We are going on an exploration of the printer resource file we just created before we continue, so exit WordPerfect and return to the DOS prompt.

Exploring the Printer Resource File

Let's take a look at exactly what WordPerfect knows about your fonts and what it will do with this information. The key to our exploration is the Printer Program that is included in the WordPerfect 5.0 package. This program has little in common with versions that accompanied earlier versions of WordPerfect.

The Printer Program includes brief help screens for each item in the program. These help screens are accessed by pressing the **F1** key. The first help screen is global help for the program's function key usage. Pressing **Ctrl+F3** with this screen displayed will provide help for the function category you are in. Alternatively, pressing **Alt+F3** will provide help for the item within the category that is currently highlighted.

The help screens provide only a modest amount of information about the functions of the Printer Program. Since we are writers and/or publishers and probably not printer technicians, we will

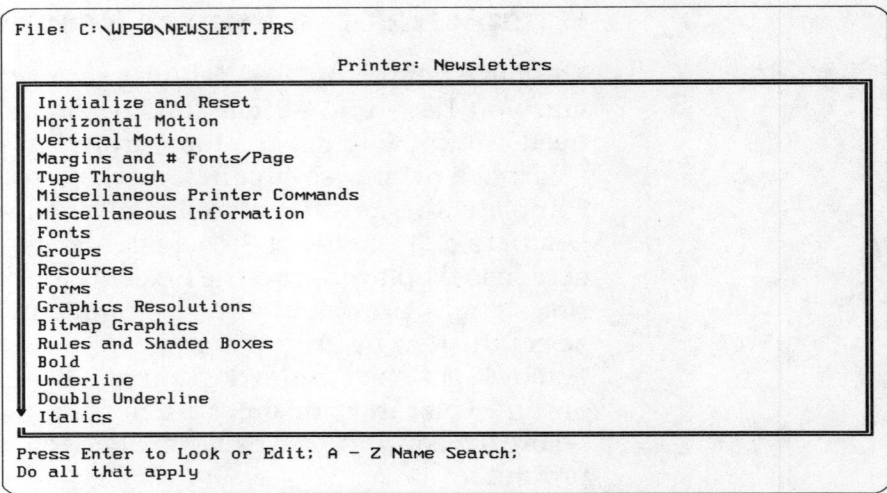

Figure 3-7. The Printer Program printer definition menu.

look only at each item in the font category in detail. Other categories deal with how the printer interacts with WordPerfect. Remember that once inside the Printer Program, you can exit from any screen by pressing **F7** (Exit).

The Newsletters printer resource file is the only file available and will thus be highlighted. Press **Return** to display the printer definition screen shown in Figure 3-7.

| BEFORE DOING ANYTHING ELSE!! |

    Press   **Shift+F1** (Setup Options)

    Press   **2** (Sorting Off)

If this setup option is not selected, every list will be sorted before it is displayed. The lists in our small Newsletters printer doesn't take long to sort, but font lists containing 100+ fonts will take several minutes to sort on a PC-class computer. Turning the

```
File: C:\WP50\NEWSLETT.PRS
                    Printer: Newsletters
                          Fonts
┌────────────────────────────────────────────────┐
│ Courier 10 pitch (PC-8)                        │
│ Courier 10 pitch (PC-8) (Land)                 │
│ Courier 10 pitch (Roman-8/ECMA)                │
│ Courier 10 pitch (Roman-8/ECMA) (Land)         │
│ Courier Bold 10 pitch (PC-8)                   │
│ Courier Bold 10 pitch (PC-8) (Land)            │
│ Courier Bold 10 pitch (Roman-8/ECMA)           │
│ Courier Bold 10 pitch (Roman-8/ECMA) (Land)    │
│ Line Draw 10 pitch                             │
│ Line Draw 10 pitch (Land)                      │
│ Line Printer 16.66 pitch (PC-8)                │
│ Line Printer 16.66 pitch (PC-8) (Land)         │
│ Line Printer 16.66 pitch (Roman-8/ECMA)        │
│ Line Printer 16.66 pitch (Roman-8/ECMA) (Land) │
│ Solid Line Draw 10 pitch                       │
│ Solid Line Draw 10 pitch (Land)                │
│▼(FW) Dutch Bold 18pt (ASCII) (Port)            │
└────────────────────────────────────────────────┘
1 Add; 2 Delete; 3 Rename;
Press Enter to Look or Edit; A - Z Name Search;
```

Figure 3-8. The list of fonts that are currently defined in the Newsletters printer resource file.

sort option off will speed up the program's operation considerably and is a good practice to get into the habit of doing.

Most of the items listed in the printer controls screen deal with how the printer operates. The selection that we are interested in is named Fonts. This is where all of the font definitions are for the Bitstream fonts that we just created and those fonts that are built into the printer by the manufacturer. So choose the Fonts selection and press **Return**. The list of fonts currently defined for the Newsletters printer is displayed as shown in Figure 3-8.

Those fonts that are not built into the printer have their names' prefaced by a two-character identifier in parentheses. These identifiers represent the manner by which Hewlett-Packard identifies each typeface package (or typefaces that belong to one group). For instance, the first font listed (assuming you haven't done anything to the WPRINT1.ALL file except add the

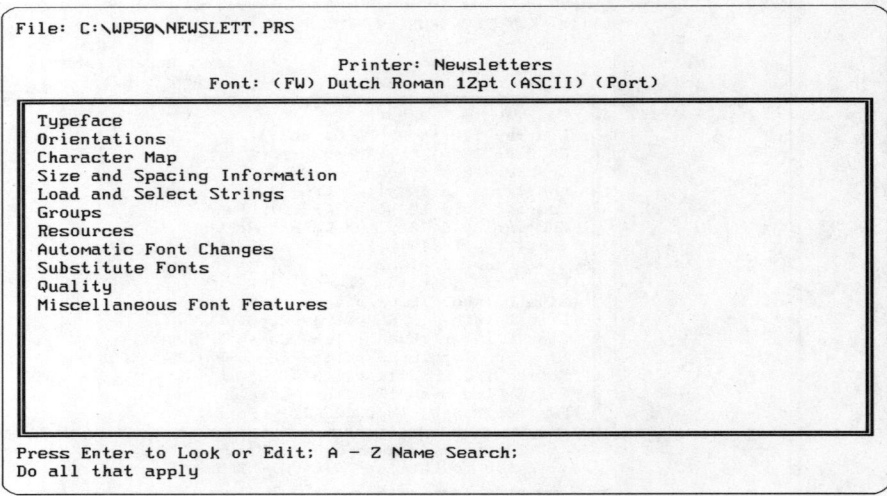

Figure 3-9. The appearance categories that define each font are shown in the printer description screen.

Bitstream fonts) is Courier 10 pitch (PC-8). This is a font built into the LaserJet Series II. These built-in fonts do not have a font group identifier prefix as do all other fonts. Newly added fonts will always be at the end of the font list because we turned off the sort operation. Therefore, for the list of Bitstream fonts we added, press **Home,Home,2** (WordPerfect's Goto end-of-file command) on the cursor keypad. Notice that Bitstream's font group identifier is (FW) for Fontware. Other font makers should state what their identifier is in their user documentation. If we highlight the (FW) Dutch Roman 12pt (ASCII) (Port) font and press **Return**, the font description screen shown in Figure 3-9 is displayed.

Typeface Description
If we select the Typeface item and press **Return**, the list of typefaces defined for the Newsletters printer shown in Figure 3-10 is displayed. The Dutch (Roman) selection is marked with an asterisk indicating that this typeface description is assigned to

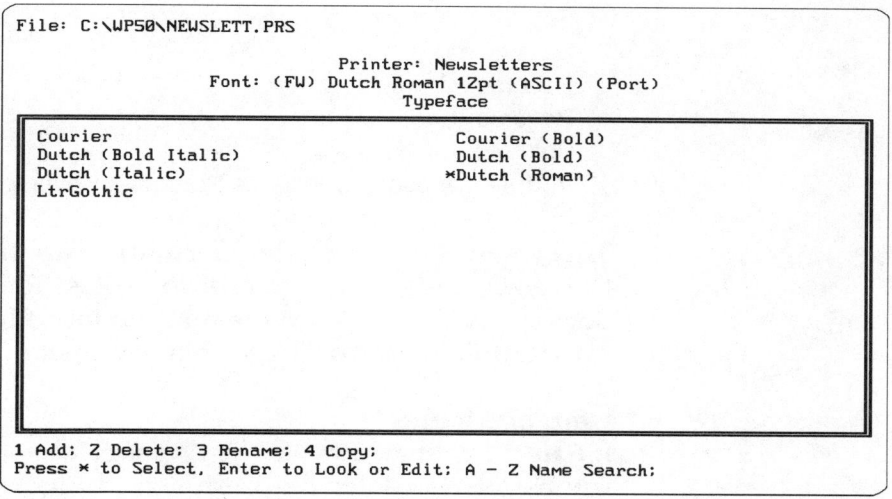

Figure 3-10. The typefaces desribed in the printer resource file.

the (FW) Dutch Roman 12pt (ASCII) (Port) font. Press **Return** again to display the following list of typeface attributes.

  Appearance/Style
  Attributes
  Serifs
  Shape
  Stress (Line Thickness)
  Weight
  Proportions

For a brief explanation of each of these typeface attributes, use the Printer Program's help function. Note that an asterisk by any selection indicates that the selection is active and that only one selection may be active at one time.

Orientations
Pressing the **Return** key while the Orientations option is selected displays the following list of possible orientations:

Portrait
Landscape
Reverse Portrait
Reverse Landscape
Portrait & Landscape
Portrait, Landscape, Reverse Portrait, & Reverse Landscape

These selections provide information about the orientation of the characters in the current font files. Reverse means upside down. Hewlett-Packard compatible font files only contain one orientation (either portrait or landscape).

Character Map

If **Return** is pressed while the Character Map option is highlighted, the list of character maps shown in Figure 3-11 is displayed. This screen lists all the character maps for the font groups currently defined for the Newsletters printer. The character map is exactly what the name implies; it contains a list of all the characters that WordPerfect is capable of composing (more

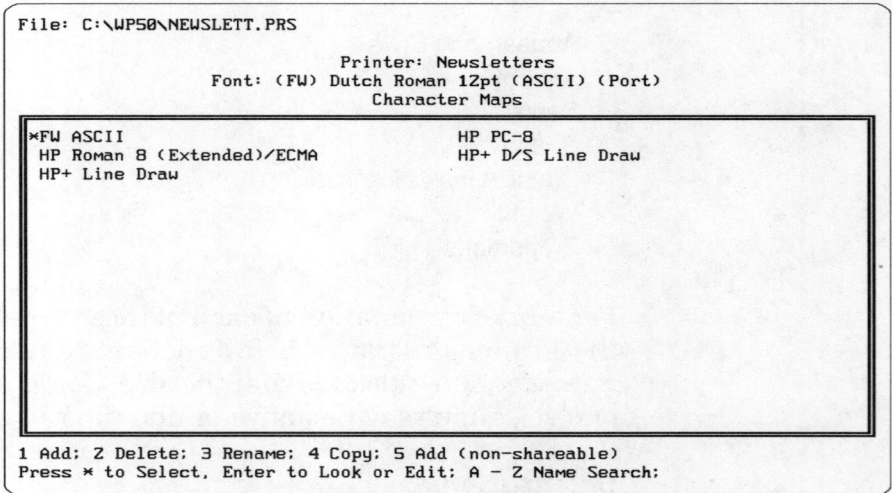

Figure 3-11. The character maps for each of the typefaces defined in the printer resource file.

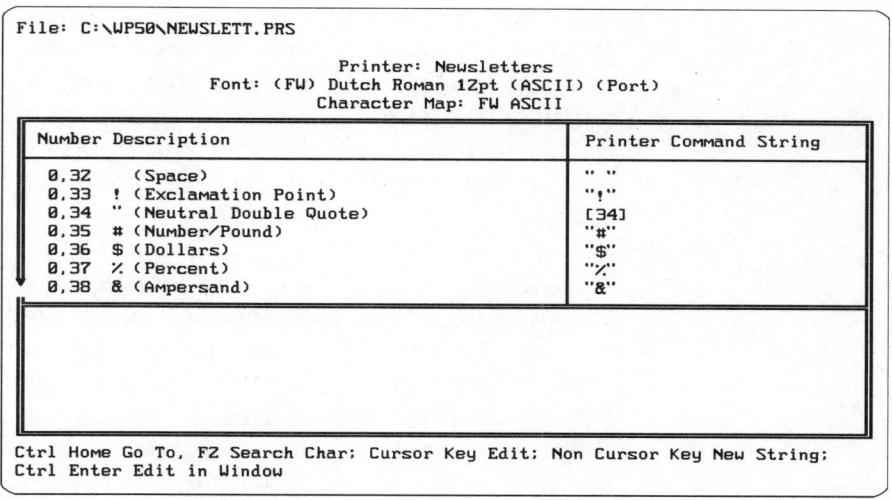

Figure 3-12. The contents of the character map for the (FW) Dutch Roman 12pt (ASCII) (Port) *font.*

about composing characters follows) and the corresponding characters in the selected font. The character map associated with the font we are examining is marked with an asterisk. Pressing **Return** with this character map highlighted will display the character map shown in Figure 3-12. The left column lists the compose combinations provided by WordPerfect. Since the ASCII character set was specified when the font was created, only the first 126 characters have a corresponding printable character in the right column.

Notice the left column lists each character as a two-number combination (such as 0,32). This combination corresponds to how the character is selected using WordPerfect's compose function. Compose is one of WordPerfect's more versatile functions. The first number indicates the WordPerfect character set in which the character is located. The second number indicates the position of the character within the character set. While typing a document, you can press either **Ctrl+V** or **Ctrl+2** to start the compose function. The **Ctrl+V** method displays a prompt at the bottom of the screen and thus provides positive feedback that you are indeed using the compose function. The **Ctrl+2** method is a "blind" entry method without any prompts, but using this method is required in some situations. By entering the appropriate two-number combination (such as 4,56), you can access the characters not provided by direct keyboard entry.

Why would you need to examine the character map for a font? Suppose you want to compose a character but you are uncertain if the font you have selected can print that character. Perhaps you have examined the character sets in the WordPerfect manual and found the same character appears two different character sets (characters 4,2 and 6,94 for instance) and you are wondering which character is supported by your font.

If you examine the font's character map, you can immediately see which characters are supported. While examining the character map, use the up and down cursor keys to stay within one character set and the **PgUp** and **PgDn** keys to jump from one character set to another.

Sizing and Spacing Information
If **Return** is pressed while the Sizing and Spacing Information option is highlighted, the screen shown in Figure 3-13 is displayed. The data in this screen provides WordPerfect with information about the dimensional characteristics of the selected font. Of most importance to us is the proportional spacing table being used. Use the up and down arrow keys on the cursor pad to highlight the entry and press **Return**. A list of all currently defined proportional spacing tables is listed with an asterisk marking the currently selected table. In this case the FW ASCII table created by the Fontware program when the font was created is selected and highlighted. Press **Return** again to display the proportional values for each character displayed. Use WordPerfect's search operation (**F2**) to locate the hyphen

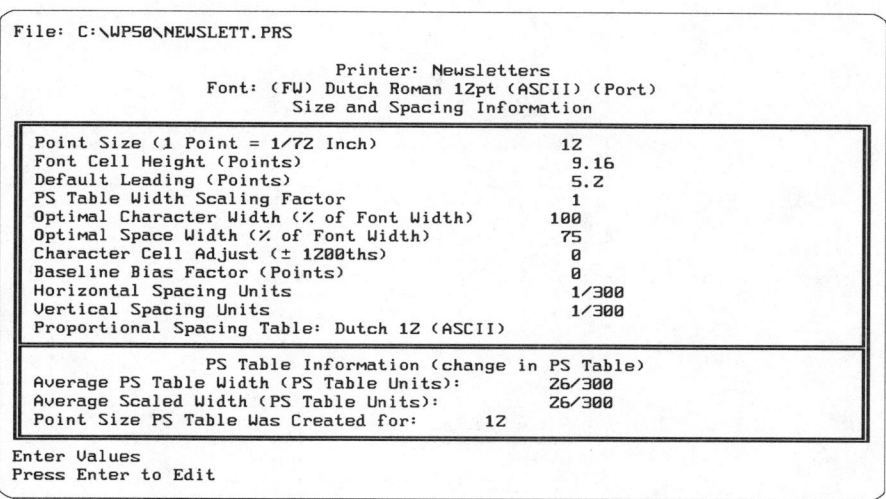

Figure 3-13. The sizing and spacing information for the currently selected font.

character. (Note that search can only be used to find a character, not a compose combination.) Your screen should look like Figure 3-14. Use the right arrow on the cursor keypad to highlight the ⌐ symbol in the right column. This symbol indicates that kerning information has been entered for this character.

To examine which characters are kerned with the hyphen character, press **Return**. Since we are using only the ASCII character set, we need only examine the characters in the 0,XX character set. If we use the down arrow on the cursor keypad to scroll down to the 0,84 character (T), we will see an entry of -6 as shown in Figure 3-15. This indicates that the character will be printed 6 printer units to the left of its normal print position. The printer unit value is shown in inches at the lower left-hand corner of the screen. Other characters that are kerned with the hyphen include the V and W characters.

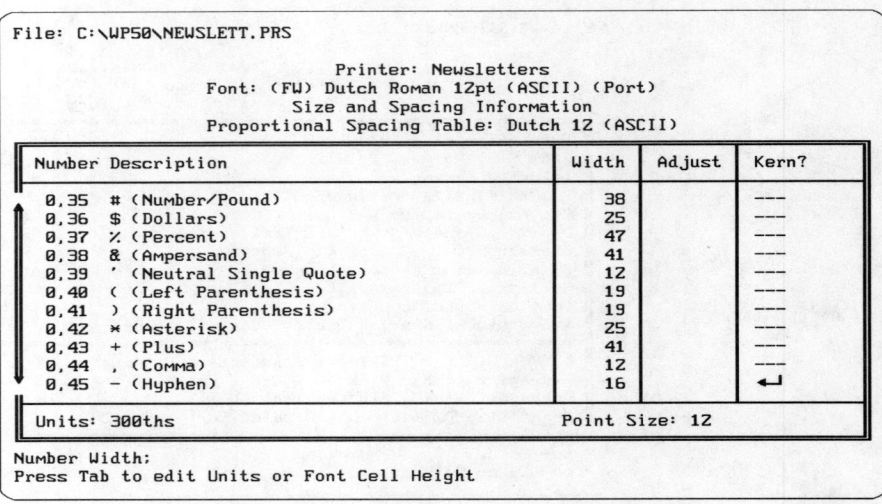

Figure 3-14. The Printer Program indicates that the hyphen character is kerned with at least one other character.

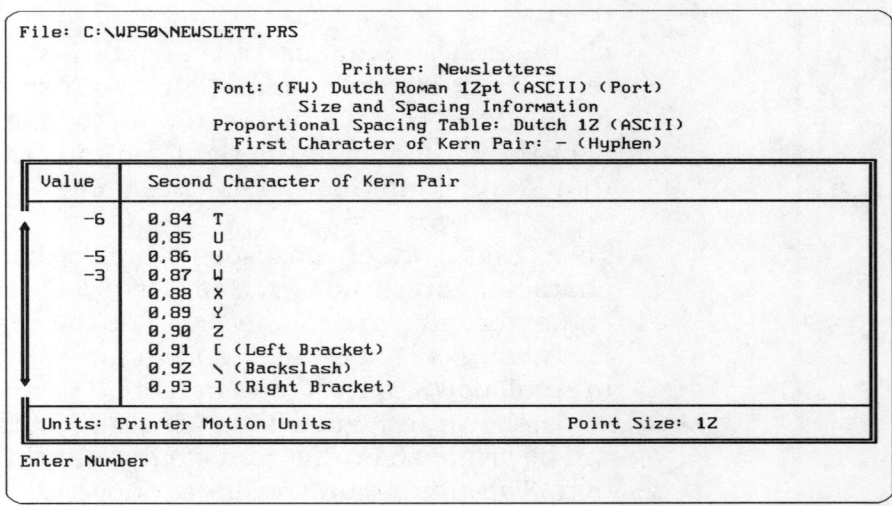

Figure 3-15. Kerning information is displayed for the characters that are kerned with the hyphen characters.

Load and Select Strings

The load and select strings are sent to the printer when the font is downloaded during initialization or with the print job. These codes are comprised of a series of escape sequences (the character [27] followed by a value) that include information on the font's point size, weight, orientation, and so on. If we look at the font load and select sequences for the (FW) Dutch Roman 12pt (ASCII) (Port) font, we can see the long line of codes necessary to load and select this font as shown in Figure 3-16. For instance, the code [27]"0U" indicates that the font is comprised of characters in the ASCII character set.

These codes are difficult to remember at best and almost always require a trip to the printer's technical reference manual for information on escape sequences. Fortunately, Bitstream has provided this information for the fonts we created, but suppose we are defining a font that the Bitstream installation kit cannot install for us? WordPerfect has simplified the creation of these escape sequences by hiding them under an English label.

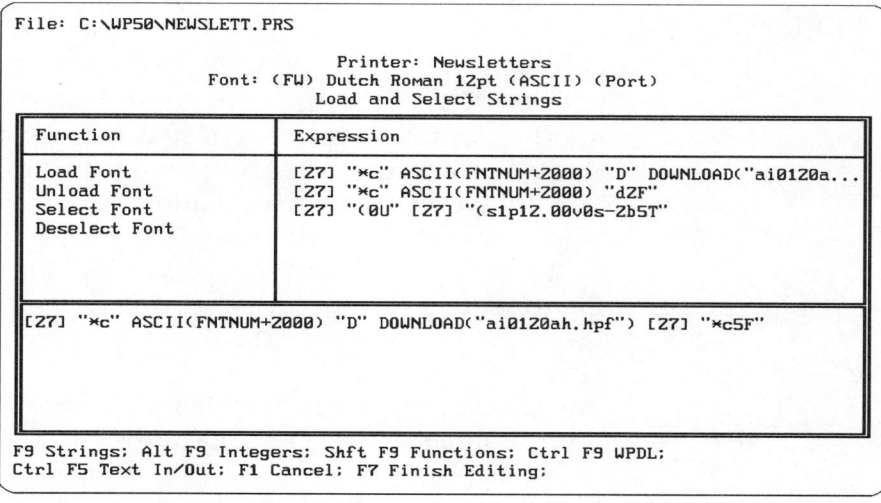

Figure 3-16. *The font load and select strings for the* (FW) Dutch Roman 12pt (ASCII) (Port) *font.*

For instance, the WordPerfect code for the [27]"0U" escape sequence is reduced to a "US" code. The result is a much simplified user interface for creating these escape sequences. Compare the following two lines required to load the (FW) Dutch Roman 12pt (ASCII) (Port) font:

Bitstream's load font printer command string:

[27] "*c" ASCII(FNTNUM+2000) "D" DOWNLOAD("ai0120ah.hpf") [27] "*c5F"

WordPerfect's load font printer command string:

font DOWNLOAD("ah0120ah.hpf")perm

Each command string tells the printer exactly the same information, and since Bitstream automatically created its load string we really don't mind all the extra characters. However, if you were creating your own load string for a font that could not be installed by an installation program, which would you rather write? The English equivalents to the required escape sequences are available with **F9, Alt+F9, Shift+F9,** and **Ctrl+F9**.

One other option available is the Text In/Out function available with **Ctrl+F5**. If you have written a load or select sequence for another font, you can save it in a file with the Text Out option. Then if you require the same sequence for another font, use the Text In option to read the sequence from the file into the string being created. You will probably have to make minor changes to the string, however, to change the font file name or the font identification number.

Groups
The Groups item is used to allocate a series of fonts to a specific group name. This is a convenience feature of the Printer Program. For example, we could assign all of the Bitstream Dutch fonts we have created to a group named (FW) Dutch (Newsletter). Later when we wanted to select these fonts as

available for use, we would only have to mark the font named (FW) Dutch (Newsletter). All of the fonts assigned to that group would then be available for either downloading to the printer during printer initialization or when the print job was sent to the printer, depending on the option we had selected for the group within WordPerfect. These two options will be discussed in more detail later in this chapter.

Resources

The Resources item is used to change the number of cartridges or amount of RAM available at the printer (see Figure 3-17). The number of font cartridges available are determined by the physical limitations of the printer (the number of cartridge slots provided by the printer). However, if you upgrade the amount of memory in your printer by installing an expansion board, you will need to change to amount of RAM that the printer definition file indicates. Highlight the current value and enter the new value.

```
File: C:\WP50\NEWSLETT.PRS
                         Printer: Newsletters
                Font: (FW) Dutch Roman 12pt (ASCII) (Port)
                              Resources
```

Resource Name	Font or Group Type	Quantity	Units	ID	Type/Order	I
Font Cartridge Slot	Cartridge Fonts	2		1	Fixed	N
*Memory available for	Soft Fonts	350	K	2	Load/Any	N

I=Intervention Required?

```
1 Add; 2 Delete; 3 Rename;
* Select; Backspace Unmark; Enter Look or Edit; A - Z Name Search;
```

Figure 3-17. The resources available to the Newsletters printer (actually a copy of the Hewlett-Packard LaserJet Series II printer).

Automatic Font Changes

> Ordinarily, WordPerfect generates Automatic Font Changes (AFCs) when the printer resource (.PRS) file is created or updated from within WordPerfect with the Select Printer or Edit Printer functions. If *any* AFCs are entered in the printer definition (.ALL) file manually, WordPerfect's generation of AFCs *and* substitute fonts will be inhibited for all fonts.

The Automatic Font Change item is used to change or examine the fonts used when WordPerfect encounters an appearance command such as bold, italic, and so on. These AFCs are automatically generated by WordPerfect when the printer resource file is created. If the **Return** is pressed when this item is highlighted, the screen shown in Figure 3-18 is displayed. Normally you will not need to change anything here. We will be using the AFCs extensively during the creation of our newsletter, so note the AFCs that WordPerfect has assigned to the Bitstream Dutch Roman 12-point font. We will use this information later.

Substitute Fonts

> Ordinarily, WordPerfect generates substitute fonts when the printer resource (.PRS) file is created or updated from within WordPerfect with the Select Printer or Edit Printer functions. If *any* substitute fonts are entered in the printer definition (.ALL) file manually, WordPerfect's generation of AFCs *and* substitute fonts will be inhibited for all fonts.

Substitute fonts are those fonts that the printer switches to if a character to be printed is not in the currently selected font's character set. A maximum of nine fonts may be defined as substitutes for a given font, with each assigned a priority of from one to nine. If a substitute font is required to print a character, WordPerfect looks for the character in each of the substitute fonts for the character starting with the highest priority font (1) and proceeding to the lowest priority font (9). All of the fonts to

```
File: C:\WP50\NEWSLETT.PRS
                         Printer: Newsletters
                Font: (FW) Dutch Roman 12pt (ASCII) (Port)
                       Automatic Font Changes For
                   (FW) Dutch Roman 12pt (ASCII) (Port)

   Feature            Font Name

   Extra Large Print  (FW) Dutch Bold 18pt (ASCII) (Port)
   Very Large Print   (FW) Dutch Bold 18pt (ASCII) (Port)
   Large Print        (FW) Dutch Bold 18pt (ASCII) (Port)
   Small Print        (FW) Dutch Roman 10pt (ASCII) (Port)
   Fine Print         (FW) Dutch Italic 8pt (ASCII) (Port)
   Superscript        (FW) Dutch Italic 8pt (ASCII) (Port)
   Subscript          (FW) Dutch Italic 8pt (ASCII) (Port)
   Outline
   Italics            (FW) Dutch Italic 12pt (ASCII) (Port)
   Shadow
   Redline
   Double Underline
   Bold

 Enter Select Automatic Font Change;
 Switch Cross Reference List:
```

Figure 3-18. The automatic font changes (AFCs) assigned to the (FW) Dutch Roman 12pt (ASCII) (Port) *font by WordPerfect when the printer resource file is created.*

be defined should be completed before assigning any substitute fonts.

Quality
The Quality item provides for three levels of available text print quality for the selected font. A font may be defined as capable of printing in one or all of the available print qualities (draft, medium, and high). The lower the quality, the less time is required to print the text. This information is used in WordPerfect when selecting the text print quality as a print option.

Miscellaneous Font Features
The Miscellaneous Font Features provides selection of everything not previously defined about the font selected. The two items of most interest are the second and third selections. The second, Send Font Load String when Group is Loaded, should be marked with an asterisk if you have defined this font as belonging to a group with the Groups option. The third, Use Font Only for Automatic Font

Changes, should be marked with an asterisk if you do not want this font to be selectable from within WordPerfect.

WordPerfect Sure Is Nosy

You may be wondering why all this fuss and bother about fonts. Why, for instance, does WordPerfect need to know what a font looks like? Most word processors just load a font and then use that font when directed to use it for printing. But WordPerfect 5.0 is not a word processor, it is a document processor. The first thing that WordPerfect uses the font's appearance description for may be obvious—the View Document feature. With a general idea of what the font looks like, WordPerfect can provide a much more accurate preview of what the printed page will look like. In this respect, WordPerfect is actually "printing" the document to the screen, using the font descriptions in the printer resource file as its fonts.

However, WordPerfect also uses a font's appearance information in another, much more subtle way. As described in Chapter 2, the font's appearance is used to match the font you have specified in your document with what is actually available at the printer. You might consider this to be WordPerfect's own substitute font routine. So even if you have not implicitly selected a substitute font, don't be surprised if WordPerfect uses the closest font in appearance to what you have specified.

Tying Up Loose Ends

We are about finished with our font exercise, but there are a few things left to be done. First, since we have seen that kerning information has been given to WordPerfect via the NEWSLETT.PRS file, we need to ensure that WordPerfect uses this information.

Press   **Shift+F8** (Format)

Press   **4** (Other)

Press   **6** (Printer Functions)

WordPerfect allows you to turn kerning on and off, but verify that it is on by pressing Y. We can also adjust the spacing between words and letters to one of four values. These values are defined in the WordPerfect user's manual. Additionally, the word spacing justification limits may be adjusted to provide the best balance between word spacing and letter spacing in order to justify text.

Under most circumstances, all of these settings may be left in their default values. However, these options provide those additional fine-tuning tools that are sometimes required to produce a document attaining that extra degree of professional appearance. These are the typographic controls that set WordPerfect apart and help us produce the high quality output that we all strive for.

Simplification Is the Key

Now that we have all our text in files and created and installed the fonts we want to use in our newsletter, we can sit back for a moment and try to get a handle on the big picture. What functions does WordPerfect offer to not only produce terrific looking documents, but to simplify the process? Are there things that we can set up now that will save time latter on? Well of course there are. Four such things come immediately to mind: defining styles that can be used repeatedly; redefining the keyboard; providing automatic references within our document; and creating a master document file for generating tables, lists, and indexes on several documents at one time. The latter two are actually done as part of the page composition task, so we will save these for Chapter 5. But let's look closer at the first two. Although we may not use both of them in our sample newsletter, these techniques can be applied to any job we have.

Doing It in Styles

As described in Chapter 2, WordPerfect offers two types of styles—open and paired. As we look over the layout of our newsletter we can see some consistencies that would lend themselves to the creation of a style. The first style would be for the page format itself. The newsletter is to be a newspaper style three-column layout with 0.3-inch gutters, 1.5-inch left margin and 1-inch right margin, 1/2-inch top margin, and 3/4-inch bottom margin. Also, we also want page numbers on the outside margins.

We can thus create a style for the page format that contains this information. And since the page format will not change throughout the newsletter, we can turn it on at the very beginning of the newsletter and forget about it. Therefore, we will create an open style.

    Press   **Alt+F8** (Styles)

The list of currently defined styles is displayed. Since we just started, there are none to select. However, we will create one and after it is saved, it will appear here.

    Press   **3** (Create)

The Styles Edit screen is displayed.

    Press   **1** (Name)

    Type   Newsletter

Press	**2** (Type)
Press	**2** (Open)
Press	**3** (Description)
Type	Newsletter Page Format
Press	**4** (Codes)

The blank codes entry screen is displayed. Most of the WordPerfect codes available in text editing are available for insertion into the style, with the exception of graphics. These codes are incorporated into a style in the same way you would define them in the text editing mode.

We need to define the margins first because we want the column widths for the three-column format and the placement of the page numbers to be automatically calculated based on the new margins.

Press	**Shift+F8** (Format)
Press	**1** (Line)
Press	**7** (Margins - Left, Right)

Set the left margin to 1.5 inches. The default for the right margin is 1 inch, so we can accept the default.

Now we need to set the top margin, bottom margin, and the page numbering type and format. Press **Return** to exit back to the Format menu.

Press	**2** (Page)
Press	**5** (Margins - Top, Bottom)

Set the top margin to 0.5 inches and the bottom margin to 0.75 inches.

Press	**7** (Page Numbering)
Press	**8** (*alternating numbers, bottom outside margin*)

This completes the margin and page number settings, so press **F7** (Exit) twice to return to the Styles: Edit codes screen. We will define our three-column format next.

Press	**Alt+F7** (Math/Columns)
Press	**4** (Column Def)

The default type is Newspaper, so do not change this option. However, the default number of columns and the distance between columns will need to be changed.

Press	**2** (Columns)
Type	**3** (*the number of columns*)
Press	**3** (Distance Between Columns)
Type	**0.3** (*the gutter size between each column*)
Press	**F7** (Exit)

After the page format codes have been entered, the open style will look like Figure 3-19. Now press **Return**, press **F7** (Exit), and then **Return** again to get back to the Styles screen. The style we just created can now be used any time we need the newsletter page format. We will also create an open style for the banner of the newsletter, but since this style incorporates many of WordPerfect's new graphic line features, we will save it for Chapter 4.

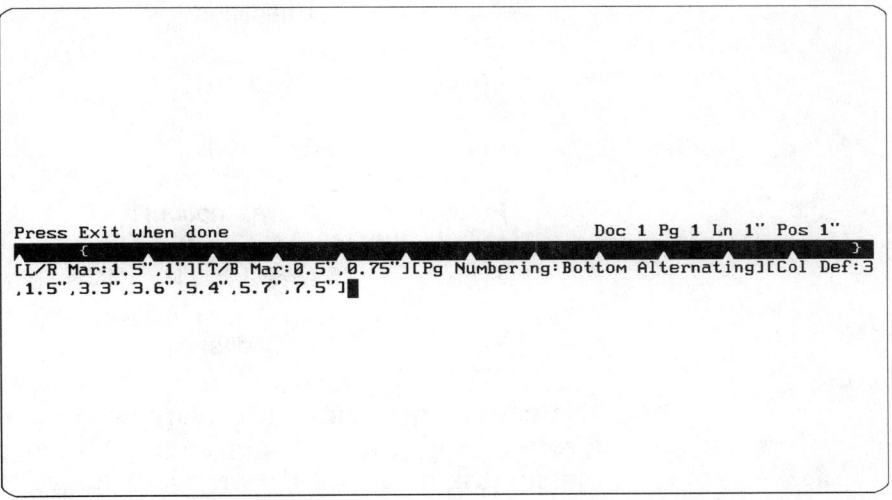

Figure 3-19. The page format for the newsletter is placed in an open style.

Next on our list of styles to create is the one for headlines. This style will be the "on and off" type called a paired style. The definition of a paired style follows the same path as that for an open style except we will specify two sets of codes: a set for when the style is turned on and a set for when the style is turned off.

Actually, we don't need the second set of codes if we want to just pick up where we left off when the style code was turned on. WordPerfect remembers codes that were in effect when we evoked the paired style, and when the off code is inserted, WordPerfect sets everything back the way it was. However, if you want to perform some explicit text or graphics formatting, you will need the off codes.

   Press   **3** (Create)

   Press   **1** (Name)

Type	Headlines
Press	**2** (Type)
Press	**1** (Paired)
Press	**3** (Description)
Type	Newsletter Headlines Font Change
Press	**4** (Codes)

The codes entry screen is displayed. However, there is a difference this time. A comment box separates the screen instructing us to put the on codes above the comment and the off codes below the comment.

To define the on codes for the headline style, we will make a font change to the Dutch Bold Italic 14pt (ASCII) (Port) (FW) headline font. Then we need to center the text. After we have finished typing the headline, we need a hard return, a horizontal line, and a font change back to our body text font. After we have inserted these on and off codes, the codes entry screen looks like Figure 3-20. To save the styles:

Press	**F7** (Exit)
Type	NEWSLTR.STY

If we create other styles, we can recall the NEWSLTR.STY file, create the new style, and save the NEWSLTR.STY file again. The NEWSLTR.STY file is in fact a style library.

The style library enables us to have all of our newsletter styles in one place. This is a very convenient feature for writing groups where consistency in the style and appearance of the documents being created is paramount. As each new style library is

```
┌─────────────────────────────────────────────────────────────────┐
│ ┌─────────────────────────────────────────────────────────────┐ │
│ │ Place Style On Codes above, and Style Off Codes below.      │ │
│ └─────────────────────────────────────────────────────────────┘ │
│ {                                                             } │
│                                                                 │
│                                                                 │
│                                                                 │
│                                                                 │
│ Press Exit when done                    Doc 1 Pg 1 Ln 1" Pos 1" │
│ {                                                             } │
│ [Font:Dutch Bold Italic 14pt (ASCII) (Port) (FW)][Cntr][Comment][C/A/Flrt][HRt]
│ [HLine:Left & Right,6.5",0.01",100%][Font:Dutch Roman 12pt (ASCII) (Port) (FW)]█
│                                                                 │
│                                                                 │
│                                                                 │
└─────────────────────────────────────────────────────────────────┘
```

Figure 3-20. The commands required to make a headline are entered as a paired style named Headlines.

created, it can be shared among all the writers in the group by simply copying the NEWSLTR.STY file to the computers of each writer.

Redefining the Keyboard

WordPerfect includes the capability of redefining keys on the keyboard to suit a particular task and save the keyboard definition file for later reuse. This function would allow us to compose special characters for specific fonts in use and provide remapping of the keyboard for foreign languages, for instance. To define a new keyboard:

    Press   **Shift+F1** (Setup)

    Press   **6** (Keyboard Layout)

Press   4 (Create)

Type   MYBOARD (*with no file extension*)

Press   **Return**

Your keyboard definition will be saved to the file name you supplied with the extension .WPK. The Keyboard Edit screen is then displayed.

Press   4 (Create)

WordPerfect will prompt you to enter the key to be redefined. The key being redefined can be any regular key or any key in combination with the **Ctrl**, **Alt**, and **Shift** keys. (Remember, though, about possible conflicts between the key combinations you define and key combinations used by other programs.) When you complete the entry, WordPerfect displays the Key Edit screen.

Suppose we had created one of our Bitstream fonts as the Roman-8 character set. We would have access to true typographic quotes with the compose function. If we look at WordPerfect's list of character sets, we find that the typographic quotes we need are in character set 4, characters 32 (open quote) and 31 (close quote). We can thus compose a key to insert the composed characters for us. In this case, we will use **Alt+O** for the open quote and **Alt+C** for the close quote.

Press   **Alt+O**

WordPerfect displays the Key: Edit screen. We can now put a name to our key combination as a reminder of its function.

Press   1 (Description)

Type   Open Quotation Mark

Press	**2** (Action)
Delete	{^O} from the edit window

We have to use the **Ctrl+2** key combination here, which will force us to type the two-number combination that specifies the open quotation mark "in the blind." You will not see any response from WordPerfect that you are entering anything until you press **Return**. When you press **Return**, you will see a small dot. This symbol (or a small solid box) is used by WordPerfect for any character that cannot be displayed on your display hardware (such as the typographic quotation mark).

Press	**Ctrl+2** (Compose)
Type	4,32

Did you get the small dot? If you did, repeat this process for the **Alt+C** key combination, substituting Close Quotation Mark for the Description and 4,31 for the Compose function. Then press **F7** (Exit) to return to the Keyboard Layout list. Highlight your new keyboard name and press **Return**. Now test your newly defined key combinations by pressing **Alt+O** and **Alt+C**. The compose code is placed in your document by WordPerfect. Use **Alt+F3** (Reveal Codes) to make sure. This process can be expanded and combined with other functions to make a very complex yet useful keyboard definition.

4 | A Picture Perfect Document

Get the Picture?

One of the most powerful and useful enhancements of WordPerfect 5.0 is its ability to integrate text and graphics into the finished document. With this capability, you can put emphasis and clarity into your documents with pictures and graphs that can explain, persuade, highlight, and entertain. But the word "graphics" is as broad as the term desktop publishing itself. Thus before you can begin using WordPerfect's graphics functions to add life and visual impact to your documents, you should be aware of what graphics really are and, more importantly, what they are not.

Bit-Mapped versus Vector

Graphic images are grouped into two separate and distinct categories: bit-mapped (sometimes called raster) images and vector (also called object-oriented) drawings. At first, there doesn't seem to be much distinction between an "image" and a "drawing," but the difference is substantial and worth consideration. A bit-mapped image is exactly what the name implies. The image is composed of many bits (or dots) placed on a map (or grid) that, taken as a whole, define the appearance of the image. For a black and white image, each bit (the smallest unit of data that the computer can manipulate) is set to either "on" or "off." Thus the resolution of an image is dependent on the number of dots per inch (DPI). For example, a 1-square-inch image with a resolution of 300 dots per inch would contain 90,000 dots. This is the maximum printable resolution of most of today's laser printers.

However, because the bit-mapped image is resolution dependent, even the high-resolution typesetters will not print the image at any greater resolution than the original 300 DPI. Figure 4-1 is a very crude bit-mapped image of a rocket. The vertical and horizontal lines are smooth and continuous. These lines will print very nicely. However, notice that the diagonal lines are not smooth but have a stair-stepped effect, often referred to as the "jaggies." This is one of the major drawbacks to bit-mapped images. The consequence of the jaggies is a printed image that

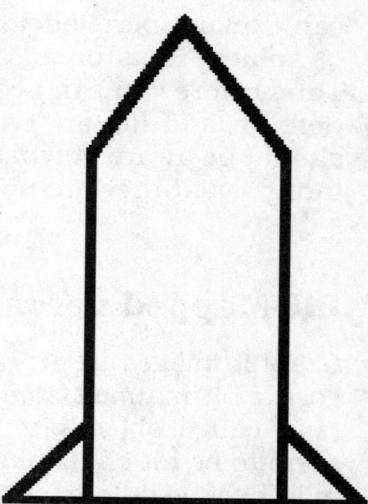

Figure 4-1. Bit-mapped images are composed of dots that are arranged in a "map" to make the desired image.

looks rough and uneven. The other drawback of bit-mapped images is the amount of memory (either RAM or disk) that is required to store the image. An image that is a full 8 1/2-inch by 11-inch page will require approximately 1 megabyte of storage space. If you are working with a color image, this requirement will increase exponentially! WordPerfect's graphic editing functions for bit-mapped images is restricted to moving, scaling, and inverting the image. An inverted image has its colors reversed much like a photographic negative (black becomes white and white becomes black).

A vector drawing, on the other hand, is composed not of dots and spaces, but lines, curves, and shapes. These drawings are mathematic representations of the elements that make up the drawing and thus are independent of resolution restrictions. Figure 4-2 represents our rocket in vector format. Notice that the rocket is composed of lines that have a relationship to the entire drawing. So rather than many dots defining a line, only two points are required. Since vector drawings are based on mathematical relationships of all the objects in a drawing to one another, the space requirements are greatly reduced, regardless of whether the drawing is black and white or color.

Another benefit of vector drawings is the aforementioned resolution independence. Regardless of the output device, the drawing will be printed at the maximum resolution of that device. Vector graphics may also be manipulated in a variety of ways (scaled, stretched, inverted, etc.) with the proper software without losing any of the "apparent" resolution in the drawing. WordPerfect's graphic editing functions for vector drawings is restricted to moving, scaling, and rotating the image once it has been inserted into a frame.

With all of these benefits, why aren't vector drawings used for all graphics? Because nature is not comprised of merely lines, curves, and shapes. A beautiful sunset over a mountain range or the pretty face of a child cannot be represented with the

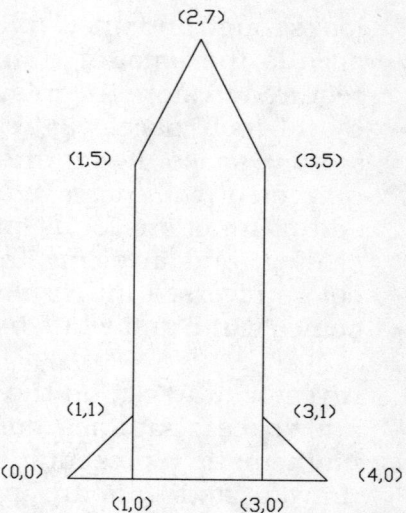

Figure 4-2. Vector drawings are composed of lines defined by beginning and ending points in a two-dimensional plane.

limited drawing entities available in vector drawings. Of course, as all things change, this limitation on vector drawings will certainly be overcome.

One such program for the Macintosh, Adobe Illustrator 88™, is already trying to eliminate this drawback. Adobe Illustrator 88 will produce a vector outline of a bit-mapped image. Snapshot™ from Aldus will trace an image captured from a video source (e.g., video camera or VCR) to produce a bit-mapped outline rendition of the image that can then be traced over with a program such as Micrografx's Designer™ to produce a vector version of the image. The results of these processes are time-consuming and still leave a lot to be desired, but the writing is on the wall. It's only a matter of time before high quality vector graphics can be automatically generated from either a scanned or captured image.

You may recall from Chapter 3 that one of the considerations for font selection and usage was based on whether the font was a bit-map font or a vector typeface. And as mentioned in Chapter 1, many software developers recognized that a character could be treated as any other graphic image. So it stands to reason that the development of fonts and typefaces for desktop publishing has taken a path similar to both bit-mapped images and vector drawings. This comparison will become important later in the book when we begin matching hardware and software components.

Bit-Mapped Graphics

Bit-mapped images are still the most popular and widely available type of images for DOS-based desktop publishing systems. WordPerfect can directly import most of the image file formats produced by the leading makers of software for creating bit-mapped images. ZSoft Corporation's PCX format used in its line of bit-mapped graphics editing programs has become the "standard" bit-mapped format. As is so often the case in this business, the standard was not arrived at by a group of software manufacturers sitting down and working out a format that had benefits across a broad spectrum of applications. Rather, the software users themselves were left to produce the standard by the popularity of the software and, hence, acceptance of its format. In most instances, this standard selection process results in a mishmash of confusion and uncertainty. However, the PCX format is a very good one and has become an almost universal format for bit-mapped graphics input to document processor and page composition software packages. Therefore, if the software you are using is not directly supported by WordPerfect, check to see if the software provides a conversion to the PCX format.

The PCX standard is restricted to DOS-based applications, however. There are other bit-mapped formats that cross the boundary into other machine types as well. One such format is

Compuserve's Graphic Interchange Format™ (GIF). This graphics file format provides a bridge between differing machine types for graphics created on one to be viewed on another. For instance, with a GIF converter program, an image created on a Macintosh with Adobe Illustrator 88 may be converted to a GIF file, transferred to an IBM PC, and viewed with a GIF viewer program. Both the converter and the viewer programs are available on Compuserve. Independent software developers have taken the GIF format to heart and graciously provided software to the public domain that provides more capabilities than just viewing.

One such program, VGIF by Bob Montgomery, will display GIF files on either an EGA or VGA display and convert the file on the spot to one of several popular graphic file formats. Other public domain viewer programs will display Macintosh MacPaint™ files directly on your PC without any external conversion being required. We will learn how to obtain these and other public domain programs later in a discussion of bulletin board systems. When combined with a screen capture program, these bridge formats and viewer programs provide a huge selection of free graphic image resources for the DOS software user. With all of this in mind, let's look at some sources of bit-mapped images and how they can be incorporated into a WordPerfect document.

Paint Programs

Obviously, the most widespread source of bit-mapped images is the venerable paint program. These programs allow you to paint a picture, much as an artist would, using electronic versions of the artist's tools of the trade. A few of the more sophisticated paint programs also extend these artistic capabilities with the ability to create different fill patterns, cut and paste one part of an image into another area, fill an area with either a paint brush or spray, and fill entire areas of an

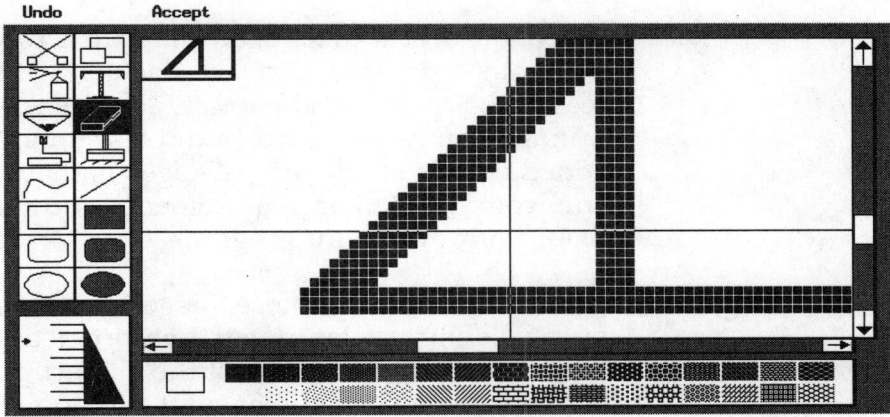

Figure 4-3. Publisher's Paintbrush provides a complete set of artist's tools for image creation.

image with a selected pattern in one operation. Figure 4-3 shows how the rocket in Figure 4-1 was created using Publisher's Paintbrush®. Note that the image in Figure 4-1 was "zoomed" out to show the entire screen, whereas Figure 4-3 is zoomed in to show only a portion of the canvas to allow editing of the image at the 300 dots per inch resolution of the laser printer. The zoomed in image is sometimes referred to as a "fat bit" mode because the individual dots that make up the image are extremely exaggerated to allow you to edit the image at the bit level.

As you can see, paint programs can create images limited mostly by your imagination and artistic talent. However, if you are like most desktop publishers who are long on writing talent and short on artistic ability (this writer included), you will need outside help in putting a good-looking graphic image into your document. There is help available, and from some very unexpected sources. Let's take a look at a few of these sources and see how we can put them to work in our document.

Clip Art

One of the best sources of bit-mapped artwork comes from commercially available clip art packages. These packages are reasonably priced and contain anywhere from a few to several hundred images created by professional graphics artists. An added benefit of clip art packages is that they can be made to suit your particular requirements with minor modifications using your own paint program.

The ability to modify these images assumes, however, that you purchase clip art files in the same format as your paint program. So be aware of the format of the clip art package before laying out your hard-earned money. If you do not need to modify the images, you are less restricted to the formats available to you. In this case, you need only be concerned that the format of the clip art package is supported by WordPerfect. These formats include PCX, PPIC, IMG, TIFF, and MSP, all of which are explained more thoroughly in the WordPerfect user's manual.

Image Scanners

If you have a piece of artwork that needs to be incorporated into your document but you would prefer to import it directly into the document rather than relying on the old cut-and-paste methods, the image scanner is the answer to your dreams. Scanner technology has become very sophisticated during the past two years and prices have dropped accordingly. The scanner package actually consists of two products: the hardware and the software. In most cases, the hardware from one vendor to another is pretty much equal. The software that comes with the scanner is what separates the good scanners from the mediocre.

There are two considerations to be made when selecting a scanner. Is the artwork being scanned line art or continuous tone (halftone) photographs? And what file format does the software produce when the scanning is complete? In answering each of these questions, you will be able to obtain the desired output with the least amount of risk in your purchasing decision. If the artwork you deal with is primarily line art, then a modestly priced scanner will produce very pleasing results. If you occasionally need to scan a halftone photograph, the same scanner will produce workable results, but will only approximate the appearance of the original photo. This is because scanners designed to produce their best work with line art treat an image as absolute black and white. When halftone photographs are scanned, the various levels of gray in the photo must be converted to either black or white. There is nothing in between.

Most scanner software can approximate a gray level by a process referred to as "dithering." The dithering process arranges the dots in an area of the image that is some level of gray in the original in a pattern that will give the appearance of gray in the output of the scanner. This will work fine if you only occasionally scan halftone photos, but aside from its obvious limitations on gray scale reproduction, the resulting image cannot be scaled very easily without picking up a herringbone pattern. This is due to the compression of the available data into a smaller area. Hence, the pattern of dots and spaces used to approximate a specific gray level will compress down to an entirely different pattern and thus destroy what the scanning software used for the gray level. Also, halftone photographs that are dithered will print with the same results regardless of the output device. So if you produce your documents on a high-resolution typesetter, you will achieve no better results in the halftone photograph than if you printed your document on a 300 DPI laser printer.

A scanner's software will also determine whether you will require a separate paint program. The image editing capabilities of scanner software encompass a wide range of functions from simple cleanup of the image to tools as sophisticated as most paint programs. Most scanner software packages also allow direct scaling of the image at the time of the scanning process and a reduction in the scanned resolution to either 150 DPI or 75 DPI. This latter capability is provided to speed the scanning process for rough drafts, preview copies, and the like where quality is of a lower priority than speed.

On the other hand, if you deal almost exclusively in halftone artwork, you will require a more expensive scanner package. These scanner packages include both hardware capable of scanning halftone photographs with multiple levels of gray and the software necessary to take advantage of this additional information. Gray scale scanners will produce a file that has the information necessary to produce gray scaled images at 16 to 256 gray levels, depending on the price of the package.

However, remember that as the amount of information contained in your image file increases, so does the amount of memory you will require for storage. A full-page, 300 DPI image scanned at 16 gray levels will require about 4 megabytes of storage space. The results obtained from such an image when printed to a high-resolution typesetter may make this worthwhile, however. Gray scaled images printed on a typesetter will rival the quality of the original halftone to the point of being impossible to tell them apart with very close examination. And gray scaled images may be scaled without any loss of photographic information. That full-page halftone may be reduced to a quarter-page image, and the results will appear to have been achieved through a photographic reduction. Figure 4-4 illustrates the differences between a dithered halftone and a gray scaled halftone when printed on a Linotype 100® at 1270 DPI.

The decision on the type of scanner package that you require is clearly a choice that needs to be made based on your requirements and the computer resources available to you. Line art

Figure 4-4. A halftone photograph reproduced by dithering the gray levels on a laser printer (left) and printing the true gray scale image on a 1270 DPI typesetter (right).

and dithered images do not require herculean computer power or massive storage space, but will produce less pleasing results when reproducing halftone artwork. The gray scale scanning packages, on the other hand, will produce exceptional reproductions at the expense of computing power and storage requirements. The choice is yours.

Screen Capture Software

Have you ever needed an exact picture of what was being displayed on your computer screen? We all have at some time, and this is exactly the purpose of screen capture software. Screen capture software can be categorized into three groups: text, graphics, and text and graphics. These types of capture programs have some similarities that should be discussed before we jump into the specifics of each. By virtue of its purpose, capture software must be made memory resident to run in the background of your computer. That is, they are loaded into computer memory and left there, invisible to you and your computer, while you run other programs.

Because of the manner in which DOS interacts with your computer, conflicts between memory resident programs may cause serious problems. Therefore, before using any capture program, be sure that no other memory-resident programs have been loaded. One other problem may arise if you have defined alternate keyboard options from within WordPerfect. All capture programs will operate when some "hot key" combination is pressed (such as **Alt+P**). If you have defined the **Alt+P** combination to some function in WordPerfect, this will create a conflict. So consider this when performing keyboard remapping in WordPerfect. With these considerations in mind, let's proceed with a look at the different categories of capture software and how they are used.

Text capture software merely writes an ASCII file to disk that contains the characters that are displayed on the computer screen. These text files can be edited with any word processor that can accept ASCII files. Text capture programs are useful for capturing screens from character-based applications such as word processors, database programs, and spreadsheet programs. They are also usually small in size and easy to operate. The text screen files themselves are small as well because of the nature of the information being stored. In most cases, text screens measure 80 characters across and 25 rows down. So the maximum size of the resulting ASCII file is 2000 bytes. Text screens have no implications in a graphics application, so we won't say much more about text screen capture software except that ASCII text must be converted to a WordPerfect file before being imported into a frame.

Graphic screen capture software, on the other hand, is very important to anyone using graphics for document processing. This category of software ranges in complexity from simply capturing an image and writing it to a file to providing not only a capture of the screen but editing and conversion capabilities as well.

If you only require the simpler of the two, public domain software is your best bet. These public domain programs are often sold by computer user groups for almost nothing or you can go bulletin board hopping and pick up a couple of programs that will perform this task quite nicely. Not to be overlooked is WordPerfect's own Grab Program. This program will capture any standard Hercules, CGA, EGA, or VGA graphic screen and write it to a file in WordPerfect's own WPG format. These images can then be incorporated into your document as a standard Wordperfect graphic (WPG) file. Note, however, that a screen captured with the Grab Program and saved with the WPG file extension is not the same format as the WPG graphic files supplied with WordPerfect. This may lead to some confusion, as the WordPerfect-supplied WPG files are vector graphic files and a captured screen is a bit-mapped graphic file. To avoid mixing these two files types together, you may want to rename the captured screen files.

The third category takes you to the very peak of capture software: text and graphics capture applications. These are sophisticated, well-developed programs that not only capture text and graphics screens but provide a wide range of editing and conversion capabilities. The premier capture software in this group is HOTSHOT Graphics™ by SymSoft. At some point in your publishing career you will need to capture a text screen and then edit the image like any other bit-mapped graphic image. This may be as simple as sizing and scaling the image to more involved tasks such as cropping the image and annotating the results by shading specific areas for emphasis and adding your own text. Figure 4-5 shows a WordPerfect screen

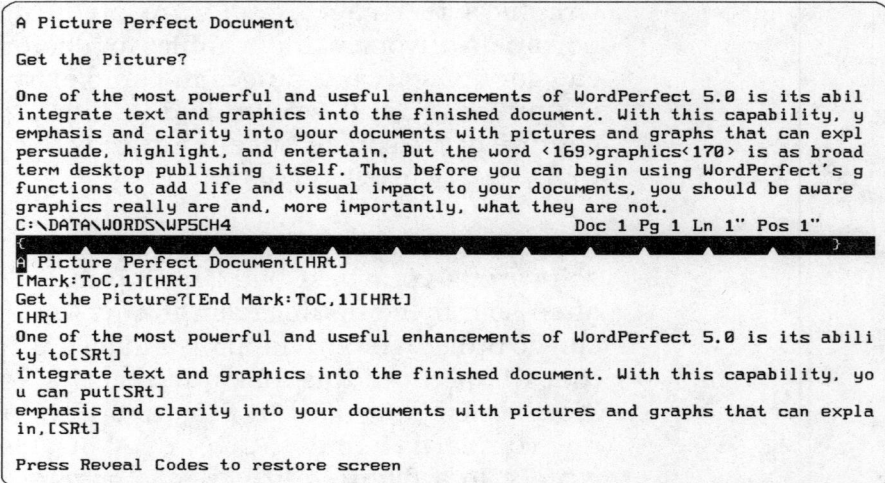

Figure 4-5. A WordPerfect screen converted to the PCX bit-mapped file format.

captured with HOTSHOT Graphics, converted to a PCX file, and loaded into Publisher's Paintbrush. HOTSHOT Graphics enables you to do this and much more. Aside from capturing any text or graphics screen on a multitude of monitor types and resolutions, the program offers you the ability to convert text and graphics screens directly to WordPerfect's .WPG format as well as the industry standard PCX, TIFF, IMG, and EPS formats. In case you were wondering, all of the text screens in this book were processed with HOTSHOT Graphics.

Another important use of the graphics and text/graphics software deals with its ability to capture displays that might otherwise be unavailable for use in your WordPerfect document. Recall our discussion of bridge software that enables you to view images from other machine types. Until the capture software is introduced into the picture, these images are just nice to look at on your computer. But capture software enables you to create files that are compatible with your software and thus incorporate them into your document. A typical scenario might find

Figure 4-6. An Amiga ray traced image converted from GIF format to the PCX file format for use with WordPerfect.

you downloading an attractive image from Compuserve that is in the GIF format. The type of machine that originally generated the image is of no concern to you because you have GIF file viewer software. You would like to incorporate the image into a document that you are preparing with WordPerfect, but Word-Perfect does not support the GIF file format. So you need some capture software to capture the image as it is displayed and write it to a disk file in one of the formats supported by Word-Perfect, including WordPerfect's own Grab program. Once this has been accomplished, it can be manipulated just as if the image had been created on your computer. Figure 4-6 is an image that has been captured and converted for use in Word-Perfect using these techniques. The image was originally created on an Amiga® computer.

Back to the Boards

One of the best places to begin searching for those graphic gems is the Tsunami Bulletin Board (415-726-2726) in northern California. The SYSOP of this bulletin board is Art Canfil. The organization of this bulletin board is a bit different than most, and an excellent one for a graphics-only system. The images are categorized by resolution and the number of colors in the images. This approach to cataloging the graphics files will quickly enable you to pick the images best suited for display on your computer and, consequently, within WordPerfect. The resolutions and colors of the available images range from two colors with 320X200 resolution to a whopping 256 colors with a resolution of 1024X768! This is a free user board but certainly worthy of your financial support, because you will be using this one a lot. As with the bulletin boards mentioned in Chapter 3, this bulletin board will probably be your starting point on the path to graphics fulfillment. Some of the images that you download and view may contain advertisements for other graphics-oriented bulletin boards.

Another very good source of graphic clip art is the Event Horizons bulletin board system in Portland, Oregon (503-777-1578). This system is a subscription service that requires an advance payment to cover the cost of $3.00 per hour of connect time. A typical 256 color file with a resolution of 320X200 screen pixels will be about 50K bytes. At 1200 baud, the file transfer time will be about 7 minutes. If you find this hourly rate to be steep or have a slow boat modem (meaning its like taking a slow boat to China trying to get a file from the bulletin board to your computer), just download their catalog at no charge and do your shopping by mail.

However, be forewarned about graphics-oriented bulletin boards in general, the current trend for many of these systems is to specialize in digitized explicit nudity. Who would have ever thought that a bunch of computer wimps with taped-together glasses and pocket protectors full of pens and pencils would be secretly carrying around porno on their floppy disks! But seriously, even some of these erotic files of bits and bytes demonstrate some of the remarkable capabilities being achieved in digitized computer imagery.

Vector Graphics

Most vector graphics are comprised of lines, circles, and shapes that are represented as a series of points on a two-dimensional surface. The exception to this is three-dimensional graphics where a third set of points is included to define the depth of the object. When trying to conceptualize this, remember your old analytical geometry classes where you were taught that a vector defines a unique point in space. For the purposes of our discussion of vector graphics, we will limit our examples to the two-dimensional variety. This limitation is also applicable because most vector graphics available to the desktop publisher are two-dimensional in nature. Figure 4-7 illustrates a simple

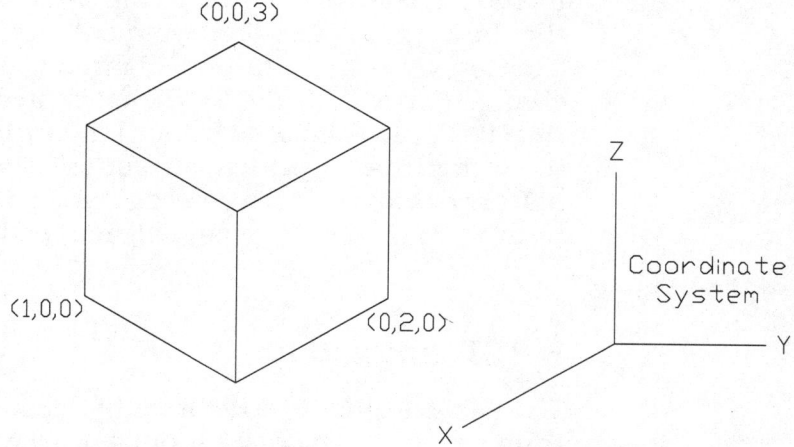

Figure 4-7. A vector drawing of a simple box with the coordinates of each vector shown.

box drawn in vector form with the corresponding coordinates for each vector point.

Because vectors are independent of any resolution restrictions, the quality of the output of vector graphics is dependent on the resolution capabilities of the printer. For this reason, vector graphics provide the best possible graphic output when printed with high-resolution typesetters. Although more limited in their artistic capabilities, vector graphic software applications can't be beat for line art such as technical drawings, business graphics, and block diagrams. Be aware that as technology changes and software that creates vector based drawings increases in functionality, you will find many more graphics tasks suitable for vector based drawings.

Bringing in the Vector Files

The output formats available from the graphics application will determine how these drawings are incorporated into WordPerfect documents. Most drawing software packages will include at least one standard file exchange format for output of the drawing to a file. The two most common formats are HPGL (Hewlett-Packard Graphics Language) and DXF (Data Exchange Format). The DXF file is created as any other file, but the HPGL file is created by actually "printing" the drawing to a file rather than a printer or plotter. If neither of these file formats are available with your drawing program, you may be able to capture the drawing as a bit-mapped image.

HPGL Format

The HPGL format is supported by most drawing programs and thus has, again by default of user acceptance, become the industry standard for the exchange of vector drawing files between different systems and software applications. The process of creating an HPGL is a very easy concept to understand. Drawing programs are designed to output their files to pen plotters. Unlike laser printers and typesetters, pen plotters require very simple commands to produce very complex line drawings.

These commands include moving the pen to a specific position, putting the pen in the down position, and moving the pen to another specific location, which draws a line between the two points. The pen is then raised to the up position and the process is repeated until the drawing is completed.

Furthermore, the pen's motion is not restricted to left and right movement, so diagonal lines are drawn as one unit rather than a series of dots placed in the appropriate place as the paper is moved downward, as in dot matrix printers. Figure 4-8 shows this difference in printing methods.

So how does all of this apply to you, the desktop publisher? The HPGL files created by these drawing programs for use in WordPerfect actually write an ASCII file that contains these plotter commands in a readable format. If you examine an HPGL file, you will see the actual pen up, pen down, and go to point X,X commands used by WordPerfect to recreate your vector drawing.

DXF Format

The DXF file format offers a second path for file exchange between different systems and applications. Differing in file structure from the HPGL file, the DXF file is an encoded representation of the mathematical relationship of the objects in the drawing. If you want to use a DXF drawing in WordPerfect, you will need to use WordPerfect's Graphic Conversion Program (GRAPHCNV.EXE). The Graphic Conversion Program converts DXF files to WordPerfect's own WPG format.

Capturing Vector Graphics

If your drawing software does not support output of either HPGL or DXF files, your last resort may be the screen capture software previously discussed. Even though the drawing that is being prepared is vector based, the image displayed on your monitor is just that, a bit-mapped image.

Be forewarned, however, that screen capture software may not operate properly with your software because of the way in which the drawing program interacts with your hardware and your operating system. If the screen capture software does work, the image captured will no longer be a vector drawing, but rather a bit-mapped image with its resolution limited by the resolution of your monitor.

Colorful Graphics

Most paint and drawing programs provide for selection of colors used in the graphic to differentiate different layers in a multiple layer drawing, identifying different objects within the graphic, or to produce a realistic image. Color is an extremely useful tool in the hands of the draftsperson or artist, but some considerations are in order when the graphics being produced with multiple colors are intended for use within a WordPerfect document. WordPerfect will display a beautiful rendition of your graphic in full color using the View Document feature.

However, WordPerfect cannot print graphics in color, either bit-mapped images or vector drawings, even on printers that support color printing. Color graphics are converted to dithered gray scaled images. Therefore, it is advisable to avoid using color as a means of conveying information in your graphic.

For instance, if you create a graphic image from a 1-2-3 spreadsheet, do not use different colors to indicate different data ranges. Instead, produce a black and white image and use different hatch and fill patterns to distinguish the different data ranges. The results will communicate the information in a much more pleasing, accurate, and professional in appearance.

If you insist on using colors in your graphics, be aware that WordPerfect will convert the colors into various shades of gray and then apply a dithering technique to the graphic in an attempt to produce a satisfactory black and white graphic on your laser printer. This is a worthy undertaking on WordPerfect's part, but the results are all too often less than acceptable for professional documents. This limitation is a case in point for desktop publishing in general—desktop publishing applications are not always the most efficient and easiest method of completing the job. Keep an open mind and rely on the old production methods when they are best suited for the task. In this instance, letting the printer (the human one) put the color image in the document manually is the best solution to the problem.

Styles Revisited

Now that we have a good handle on what types of graphics files are compatible with WordPerfect, let's put this information to work to produce our sample newsletter. We will incorporate both bit-mapped and vector graphics in the newsletter. We will also be editing these graphics using WordPerfect's own set of graphics manipulation tools. Finally, we will use WordPerfect's own set of line drawing functions to enhance the appearance of our newsletter.

The first thing we need to do is create the WordPerfect style for the banner of our newsletter. First, look at Figure 4-8 to see how the complete banner will look. As you can see, we are using one of the 30 vector drawings supplied with WordPerfect in the

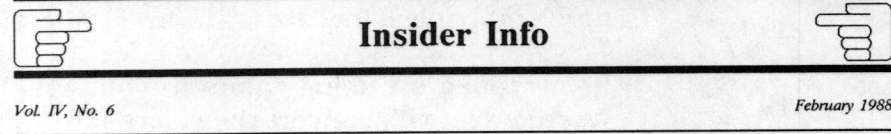

Figure 4-8. The banner as it should appear when the completed newsletter is printed.

WPG file format. Also, we use WordPerfect's horizontal line function to offset the publication number and date. We can create a style that includes everything in the banner except the graphics. To automate the incorporation of the graphics in the banner, we will create a macro that makes the frames for the two pointing hands, loads the drawings, reverses one of the hands, and scales the drawings to the proper size. That's quite a bit of work, so let's get started.

The Banner Style

To define our banner style, we will repeat the steps that we took in Chapter 3 to create the text styles. However, because Word-Perfect 5.0 is a document processor (character based) rather than a page composition application (graphic based), some experimentation will be required to place all of the elements in the correct positions. It is advisable to define the banner first in a blank WordPerfect document, without trying to create it as a style. By placing each element in the desired position and then using the View Document function to observe the results, we can get all the elements positioned correctly before copying the settings into the style definition.

Entering the Banner Text

In order to position elements in the banner correctly, we must first turn on the page format style we defined for the newsletter in Chapter 3.

Press	**Alt+F8** (Style)
Highlight	Newsletter
Press	**Return** (turn the style on)

The first element of the banner to be defined is the name of the company. This text will be set in Dutch 14-point bold italic flush right with the right margin on two lines. In Chapter 3 we used the Printer Program to examine the printer resource file to determine what automatic font changes had been assigned to the Dutch 12-point font. If you did not note these AFCs, go back to Chapter 3 and review Figure 3-18. The Dutch 14-point bold italic font is used when Large is selected, so we can set the new font with the Font Size function.

Press	**Ctrl+F8** (Font)
Press	**1** (Size)
Press	**5** (Large)

Now type the company name as follows:

Press	**Alt+F6** (Flush Right)
Type	Barmecide Mutual
Press	**Return**
Press	**Alt+F6** (Flush Right)
Type	Funding Corporation
Press	**Ctrl+F8**
Press	**3** (Normal)

This completes the company name portion of the banner and sets the font back to the normal Dutch 12-point font. The next element to be added is the horizontal line above the newsletter title. WordPerfect provides two types of line functions: line draw and graphic lines. Line draw is useful for creating simple diagrams, but the graphic line function allows you to set the width and gray level of the line The graphic line is also a printer command rather than characters, so these lines may be used without affecting any text around it. For this reason, we will use the graphic line function.

Press	**Alt+F9** (Graphics)
Press	**5** (Line)
Press	**1** (Horizontal Line)

The screen shown in Figure 4-9 shows the options available for creating horizontal lines. Option 1 is used to set the horizontal line position. In our banner we want the line to run from the left margin to the right margin, so the default is used. If, however, we wanted to start the line at some other point, we would use option 1 to set its position. Once the position was

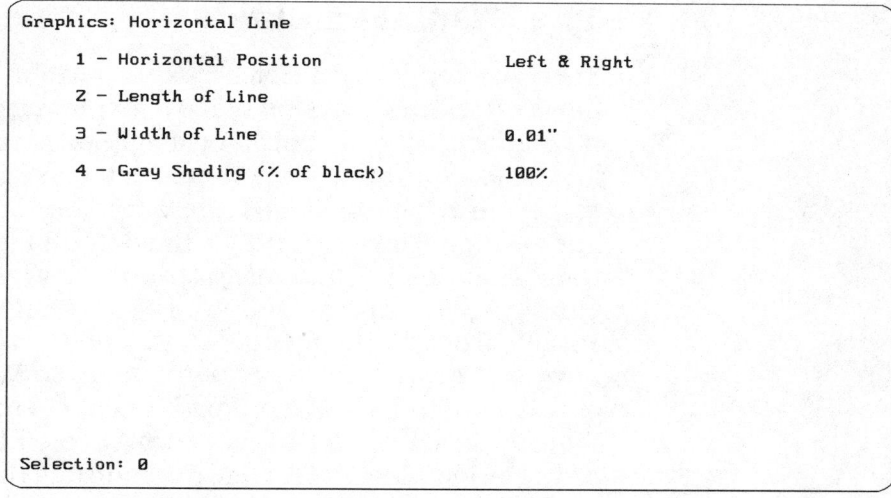

Figure 4-9. The Horizontal Line *options menu.*

set, we could also use the length option (2) to adjust the line's length to our requirement. For our newsletter banner, we will use neither of these options, but we will set our line width to 0.05 inch.

    Press   3

    Type   0.05

Finally, we also have the option of selecting some percentage of black with which the line will be drawn, from 0 percent (no black and thus white) to 100 percent (solid black). Percentages between 0 and 100 will produce a shade of gray; the smaller the percentage, the lighter the shade of gray. Our line will be solid black (100 percent), so now change will be required to the default value. The first horizontal line has now been defined so press **F7** (Exit) to complete the line definition.

The Misplaced Line

Even though we will not be using vertical lines in our sample newsletter, this is a good place to explain a characteristic of vertical lines that you should be aware of. If you select the vertical line function, you will see the screen shown in Figure 4-10. This screen provides basically the same options as the horizontal lines option. However, notice the default for the horizontal position. This default, Left Margin, would lead you to believe that if you had a 1-inch left margin, the vertical line would be drawn 1 inch from the left edge of the page. This is not the case, however. Although this is not a "bug" in WordPerfect, it is one of those instances when WordPerfect seems to outsmart itself. WordPerfect knows that your text is also being printed 1 inch from the left side of the page and adjusts the position of the line to the left about 0.1 inch so as not to overprint the text. The result is that if the default Left Margin is used to draw the line, the line will actually be drawn approximately 0.9 inches from the left edge of the paper. This will be a problem if you are trying

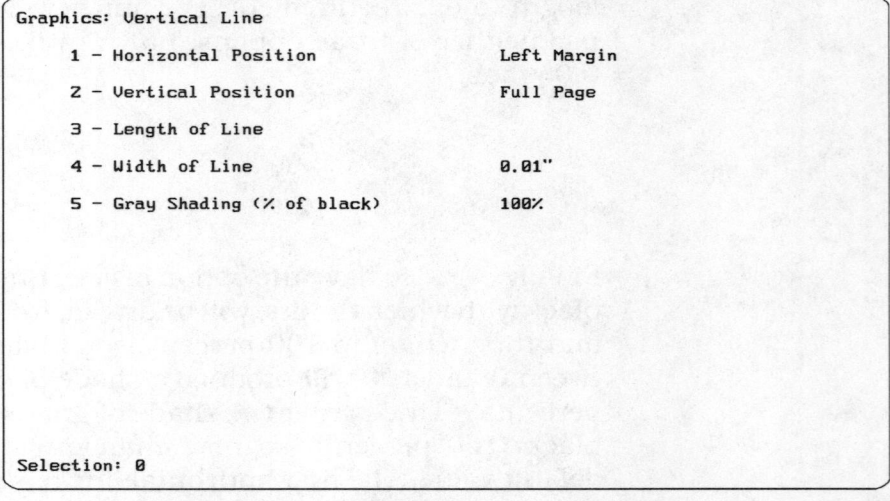

Figure 4-10. The Vertical Line *options menu.*

to create a table header, for instance. The horizontal lines will not meet the vertical lines at the corners.

To get the line to print at 1 inch from the left side of the page (the "real" left margin), you must manually enter 1 inch with the Horizontal Position option. This requires little effort because the default position displayed when you select the Horizontal Position option (**1**) is the current position of the cursor in your document. So if the cursor is on the left margin, all you need do is press **Return** to accept the measurement.

Completing the Banner Text

After that short digression, we now return to our banner style creation. We will begin by adding some space between the first horizontal line and newsletter title and then we will set the base font to Dutch 18-point bold.

Press	**Return** (twice)
Press	**Ctrl+F8** (Font)
Press	**1** (Size)

The Dutch 18-point bold font is assigned to the Extra Large size. Therefore, to select the Dutch 18-point bold font, we need only to select Extra Large as the font size. WordPerfect will use the Dutch 18-point bold font until we switch back to normal text.

Press	**7** (Ext Large)
Press	**Shift+F6** (Center)
Type	Insider Info
Press	**Return**

To return to the normal font, you can either press the right arrow key on the cursor keypad once to move the cursor beyond the Extra Large font code, or reselect the normal font with the Font function. For this example, we will do the latter.

Press	**Ctrl+F8**
Press	**3** (Normal)
Press	**Return** (*twice*)

Pressing **Return** twice puts some space between the newsletter title and the horizontal line we are going to add next.

The second horizontal line is the same as the first except we will accept the default of 0.01 inches as the width. So repeat the steps for creating a horizontal line described above, except do not change the default line width, and press **Return** twice.

The publication number and date will be entered next, so we need to set the base font to Dutch 8-point italic font. Our examination of the printer resource file tells us that this font has been assigned to the Fine size for the automatic font change.

Press	**Ctrl+F8** (Font)
Press	**1** (Size)
Press	**3** (Fine)
Type	Vol. IV, No. 6 (*the publication number*)
Press	**Alt+F6** (Flush Right)
Type	November 1988 (*the publication date*)
Press	**Ctrl+F8**

Press	**3** (Normal)
Press	**Return**

Now complete the banner by inserting the final horizontal line with a width of 0.01 inches (the default) as previously described.

This finishes the text portions of the banner, but we still need the two pointing hands. We will have to set those graphics as a macro, which we will do next. Before we proceed to the creation of that macro, however, verify that all of the elements of the banner created thus far are in their correct position by using the View Document function.

Press	**Shift+F7** (Print)
Press	**6** (View Document)

Once you are satisfied with the appearance of the banner, save it in a file named BANNER. The banner text will remain on the screen.

Press	**F10** (Save)
Type	BANNER
Press	**Return**

The banner remains on the screen while we size and place the pointing hands.

Pointing a Finger

Again, experimentation is the key to creating the pointing hands graphics. Use the View Document function (**Shift+F7, 6**) liberally during this process to help position the graphics. To perform this experimentation, we will have to create the graphics by themselves before creating the macro that automates the creation process. Before creating the graphics, we need to turn off the borders for figures that WordPerfect uses by default.

Press	**Alt+F9** (Graphics)
Press	**1** (Figure)
Press	**4** (Options)
Press	**1** (Border Style)
Press	**1** (None) (*four times for each side of the figure*)
Press	**F7** (Exit)

We will turn these borders back on when we have completed our pointing hands. Next, we will actually insert the first pointing hand graphic in the banner.

Press	**Alt+F9** (Graphics)
Press	**1** (Figure)
Press	**1** (Create)

The Figure Definition menu is displayed. We will create the left pointing hand first.

Press	**1** (Filename)
Type	HAND.WPG

Figures may be attached to a paragraph or treated as an indiviual character. For this graphic, however, we will specifiy the graphic as the page type because the figure must be positioned at an absolute point on the page. Therefore, we will set the graphic to be anchored as a page graphic at a specific location.

Press	**3** (Type)
Press	**2** (Page)

If we allow the text portion of the banner to flow around the text in the banner we will never achieve the results we want, so select option **7** and press N to set Wrap Text Around Box to **No**.

We next have to position and size the drawing. Because this is a vector drawing, we can size this graphic without being concerned with how our actions will affect the resolution of the printed image. So we can experiment all we want with the graphic to obtain the exact position and size we require.

To quicken this experimentation, it has been determined that the vertical position should be set to 1.05 inches and the horizontal position should be set to 1.5 inches.

Press	**4** (Vertical Position)
Press	**5** (Set Position)
Type	1.05
Press	**5** (Horizontal Position)
Press	**1** (Margins)
Press	**1** (Left)

When any graphic is loaded into a frame, WordPerfect sizes the image in height based on a default width of 3.25 inches. We have the option of resizing the image based on a specific width (height calculated by WordPerfect), height (width calculated by

WordPerfect), or width and height (WordPerfect keeps its nose out of our business). For our graphic, we need to set the height to fit between the horizontal lines (we are not concerned about the width).

Press	**6**	(Size)
Press	**2**	(Height (auto width))
Type	0.4	

WordPerfect automatically calculates the new width to be 0.52 inches. When the graphic definition is complete, your Figure Definition menu should look like Figure 4-11. Press Return to complete the figure definition.

```
Definition: Figure
        1 - Filename                    HAND.WPG (Graphic)
        2 - Caption
        3 - Type                        Page
        4 - Vertical Position           1.05"
        5 - Horizontal Position         1.5"
        6 - Size                        0.52" (wide) x 0.4" high
        7 - Wrap Text Around Box        No
        8 - Edit



Selection: 0
```

Figure 4-11. The completed Figure Definition *menu for the first pointing hand graphic.*

Advance—WordPerfect's "Mr. Fixit"

There is a shortcut to positioning a graphic without resorting to the tedious experimentation process of changing the absolute position, checking the position, and then changing the position again. The Advance command is one of those terrific features of WordPerfect that is a treasure waiting to be unearthed. Just about any formatting problem you may encounter while composing a document can be solved with the proper Advance command. There are six ways in which the Advance feature may be issued: left, right, up, down, line, and position.

The Advance command will move the subsequent text or frame in the direction selected by the amount specified. Which option is used will depend on your particular circumstance. If the exact position of where the element is to be moved is known, the position option is favored. If you need to move some distance that is independent of other considerations, the direction options should be used.

Aligning Text
Suppose you are composing your document with proportional fonts and you need the text on several lines to line up vertically. You will encounter one of two problems: the text, when lined up on screen, will not print with the proper alignment, and text that prints properly will not line up on the screen. Using tabs may be of some help, but only if the tab settings do not interfere with the rest of the document's format. And if the text doesn't line up on screen, it may be of little concern to you, what of others that may work with the same document?

Consider the example in Figure 4-12. This document is being composed in the Dutch 12-point font. Notice that the on-screen layout is correct, but the cursor position for the "L" in line one is at 1.86 inches and the cursor position for the "W" in the second line is at 1.70 inches. This document will not print correctly. Figure 4-13 shows the reverse; the printed copy will be

```
Maybe this Line of the sample text is a table heading.

        We need this line of text aligned with the previous one.




















                                            Doc 1 Pg 1 Ln 1" Pos 1.86"
```

Figure 4-12. WordPerfect's placement of proportional text in the document editing screen requires special attention.

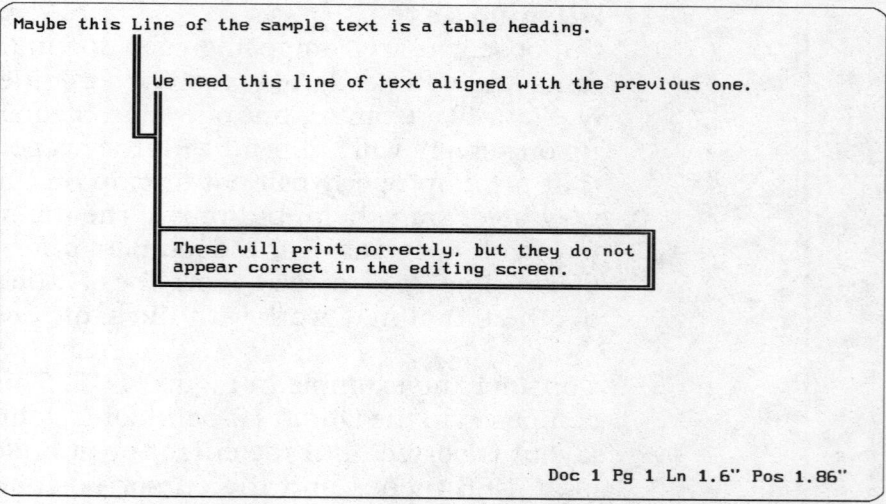

Figure 4-13. Proportional text will often print differently than it appears in the document editing screen

correct, but the on-screen layout does not reflect how the document will print. The answer to this problem lies in the Advance command. In this example, we will use the Advance command with the results shown in Figure 4-14. The value of the advance command was determined by noting the cursor position in the first line and inserting an Advance command with that value at the beginning of the text in the second line as shown below:

Press	**Shift+F8** (Format)
Press	**4** (Other)
Press	**1** (Advance)
Press	**6** (Position)
Type	1.86
Press	**Return** (*twice*)

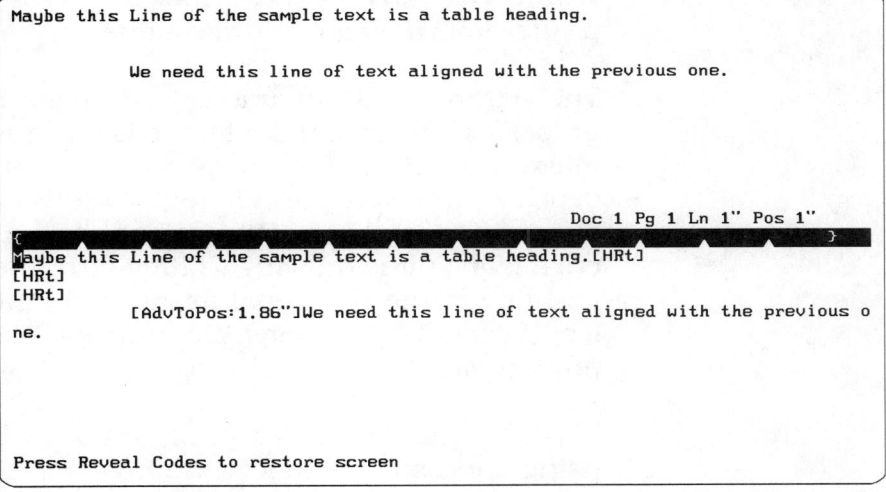

Figure 4-14. The Advance command corrects proportional text errors.

The position option was used because the text was to start at a specific position without regard to any other element. We could have used the advance right option, but we would have had to calculate the distance to the right that we needed to move (the desired position minus the cursor position). Now the on-screen document and the printed document are both correct. And since the advance command is not visible unless the Reveal Codes command is evoked, the document is not confusing to others that might also need to work with it.

Line Drawing with Proportional Fonts

WordPerfect tells you that its line draw feature does not work properly if you use a proportional font for your text. Before we can tell you the reason for this limitation, some explanation of the difference between a line drawing and a graphic line is required. If you use WordPerfect's line draw function (**Ctrl+F3, 2**), the lines are visible in your document in the editing mode. You may deduce correctly, therefore, that these lines are composed of individual characters that are sent to the printer just as any other character. Lines created with the graphic line function (**Alt+F9, 5**), on the other hand, are not visible in the editing mode. WordPerfect creates these lines by sending a command to the printer instructing it to draw a line.

The reason that the character form of line drawing will not work properly with proportional fonts is that the characters used to make the lines are monospaced. Thus the line draw feature depends on a constant character width for correct placement of intersecting lines. Proportional text placed inside a box created as a line drawing will result in the right side and bottom line of the box being misaligned. This is due to the line length and height being changed by WordPerfect when the proportional text was selected.

This limitation on line drawing can be overcome, of course, by using the graphic line feature. However, it is a very time-consuming process to place the lines and they will not be visible in the editing mode. Once again, however, the Advance command can overcome this problem quite easily.

Let's use the Dutch 12-point font again and draw a box around a step number. The editing screen is shown in Figure 4-15 and the View Document screen of the box in Figure 4-16 accurately shows how the box will be printed. This is not exactly what we had in mind. Therefore, we will use the proportional fonts only for the text and the built-in Courier monospaced font for the box. Notice that the top right corner of the box is at the 2.6-inch position. Go down to the right horizontal line of the box and set an Advance to Position command with a value of 2.6 inches to straighten out the box. Also advance the bottom line up by 0.1 inch. The results are shown in Figures 4-17 and 4-18.

The Advance command will work on just about any positioning problem you have, be it text or graphics. For our pointing hand, for instance, we could have set its position at the top of the page and used the Advance Down command to move it into the correct position. With a little practice and experimentation, you can get an element of your document to do just about anything you want with the proper Advance command.

Creating the Other Hand

To create the right pointing hand, we will use the same steps as we did to create the left pointing hand and the Edit option. Repeat the process we followed to create the first pointing hand, but use the right margin for the horizontal position. Now we will turn the hand around so that it is pointing to the left.

Press   **8** (Edit)

The editing screen shown in Figure 4-19 is displayed. This is a vector drawing that enables us to use the Rotate option to change the position of the graphic. However, we are not interested in

136 *Desktop Publishing with WordPerfect 5.0*

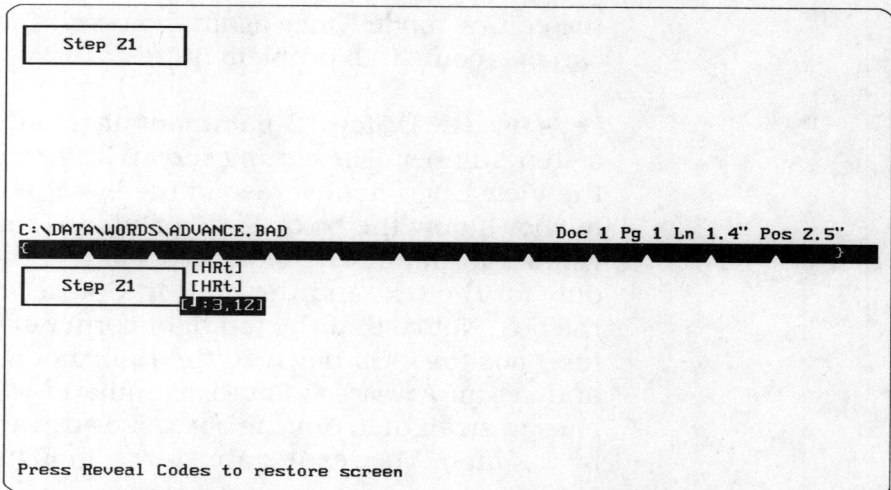

Figure 4-15. The text editing screen showing the codes for the step number box.

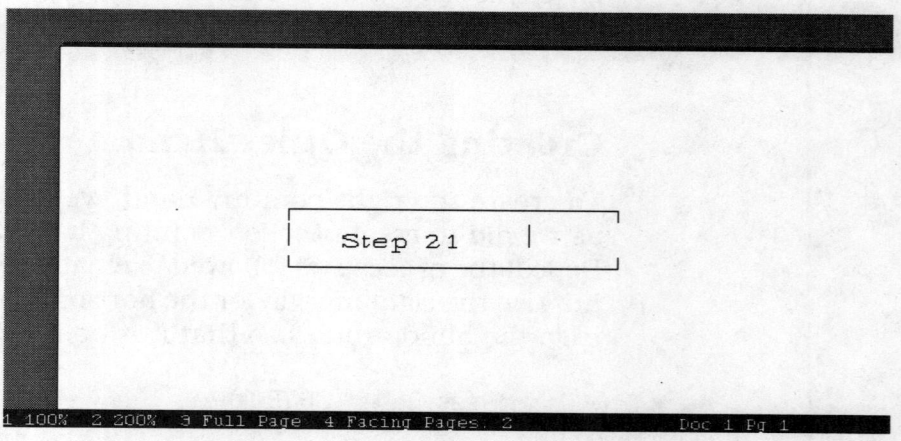

Figure 4-16. The View Document screen showing how the codes in Figure 4-15 will be printed.

A Picture Perfect Document   137

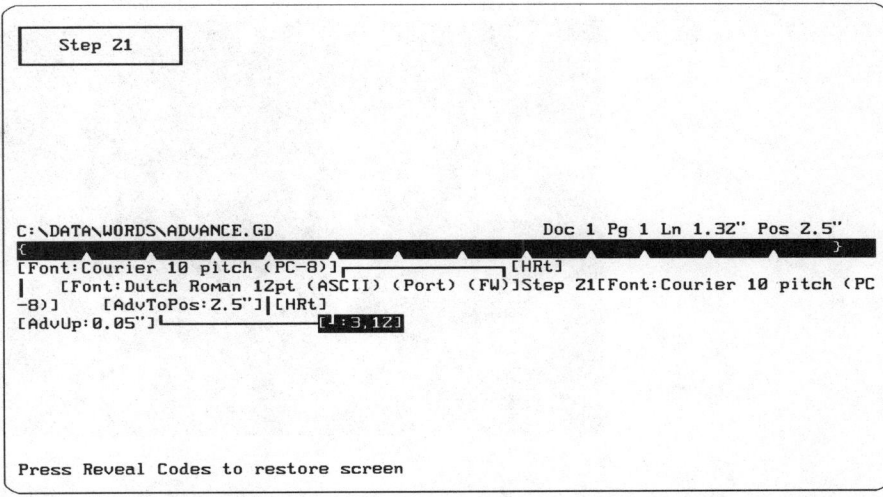

Figure 4-17. *The text editing screen showing the codes for the step number box corrected with the Advance command.*

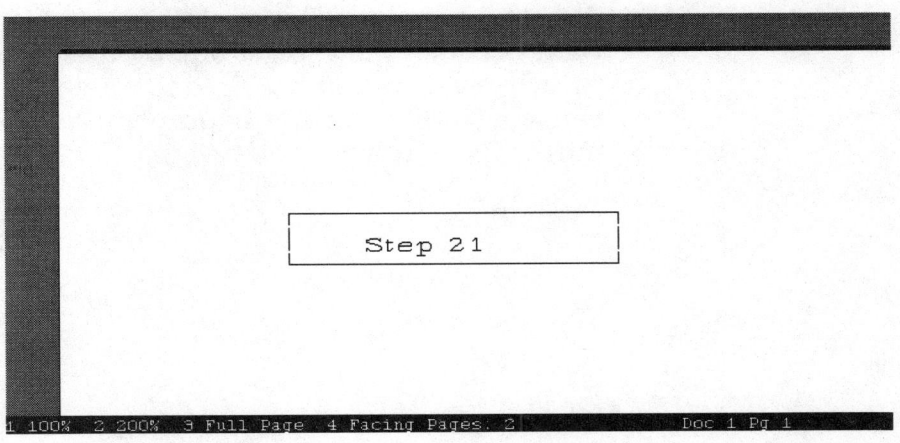

Figure 4-18. *The View Document screen showing how the codes in Figure 4-17 will be printed.*

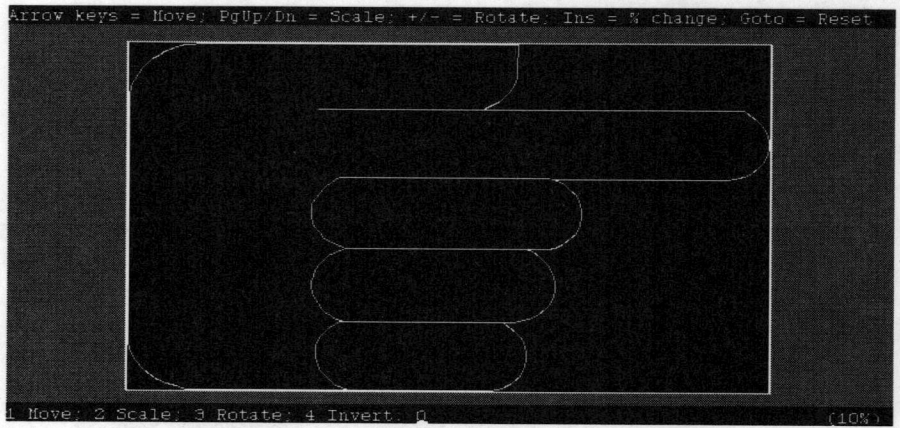

Figure 4-19. WordPerfect's graphic editing screen with the HAND.WPG drawing loaded.

changing the position of the hand, we want to turn it around. Any time you ask WordPerfect to rotate a vector drawing you are given the option of mirroring the drawing. The mirrored drawing is reversed horizontally so that left becomes right and right becomes left. To get our right pointing hand pointing in the correct direction, we need to rotate the hand 0 degrees (because we still want the hand pointing horizontally) and then mirror the graphic.

Press	**3** (Rotate)
Type	0
Type	Y

Your graphic should now look like the one in Figure 4-20. If it doesn't, you did something wrong, so press **F7** (Exit), reload the HAND.WPG drawing, and repeat the editing process. If the pointing hand looks correct, press **F7** (Exit) and **Return** to exit the

A Picture Perfect Document 139

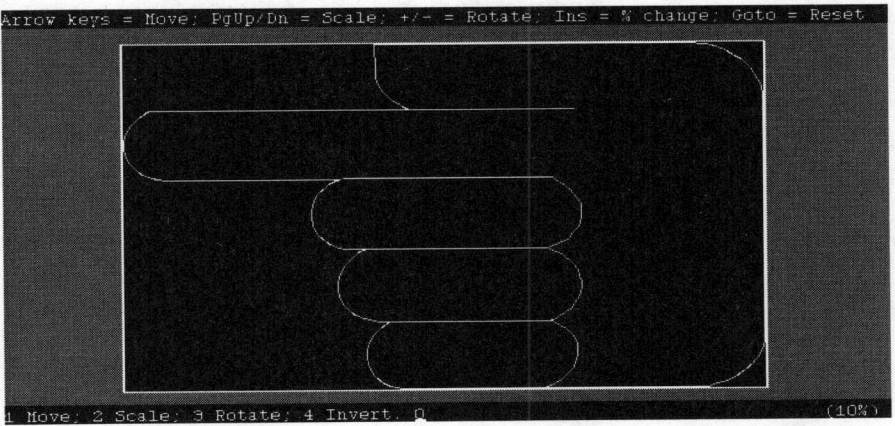

Figure 4-20. The mirrored image of the HAND.WPG drawing.

figure creation process. This completes the placement of the pointing hands graphics in the banner, but we need to reset the figure border options so that they are correct for the rest of the newsletter.

Press	**Alt+F9** (Graphics)
Press	**1** (Figure)
Press	**4** (Options)
Press	**1** (Border Style)
Press	**1** (None) (*four times for each side of the figure*)
Press	**F7** (Exit)

Once we have defined all of the particulars for the two graphics used in the banner and used the View Document feature to satisfy ourselves that everything is positioned correctly, we can begin automating the process for creating other newsletters. We start by creating the style for the text portion of the banner that will be saved as part of our newsletters style library. First, we will load our existing newsletter style library by recalling the NWSLTR.STY file we created in Chapter 3.

Press	**Alt+F8** (Style)
Press	**7** (Retrieve)
Type	NWSLTR.STY

The style library defined in Chapter 3 is displayed. We will use the Create option to add a new style to this library.

Press	**3** (Create)
Press	**1** (Name)
Type	Banner
Press	**3** (Description)
Type	Newsletter Banner

This style will be an open style since nothing in the style effects the appearance of the entire newsletter.

Press	**2** (Type)
Press	**2** (Open)

We are now ready to enter the codes that will create the banner at the top of the newsletter.

Press	**4** (Codes)

```
                                              Barmecide Mutual
                                              Funding Corporation

                              Insider Info

     Vol. IV, No. 6                                February 1988


Press Exit when done                        Doc 1 Pg 1 Ln 1" Pos 1"
{                                                                  }
[L/R Mar:1.5",1"][T/B Mar:0.5",0.75"][Pg Numbering:Bottom Alternating][Col Def:3
,1.5",3.3",3.6",5.4",5.7",7.5"][LARGE][Flsh Rt]Barmecide Mutual[C/A/Flrt][HRt]
[Flsh Rt]Funding Corporation[C/A/Flrt][HRt]
[large][HLine:Left & Right,6",0.05",100%][HRt]
[HRt]
[EXT LARGE][Cntr]Insider Info[C/A/Flrt][HRt]
[ext large][HLine:Left & Right,6",0.05",100%][HRt]
[HRt]
[FINE]Vol. IV, No. 6[Flsh Rt]February 1988[fine][C/A/Flrt][HRt]
[HLine:Left & Right,6",0.01",100%][Fig Opt]
```

Figure 4-21. The text and graphic codes for the banner defined as a style in the style codes screen.

Since we saved all of the codes for creating the text portion of the banner in a file called BANNER, we will just import this file into the codes screen.

| Press | **Shift+F10** (Retrieve) |
| Type | BANNER |

The file is brought into the codes screen and displayed as shown in Figure 4-21. Now save the new banner style.

Press	**F7** (Exit)
Press	**Return**
Press	**6** (Save)
Type	NEWSLTR.STY

Type   Y (*we are updating the old style library*)

Press   **F7** (Exit)

How about Those Macros!

We now create a macro to automate the process of placing the pointing hands into the banner.

Press   **Ctrl+F10** (Macro Def)

Type   PHANDS (*do not type a file name extension*)

Type   Banner Graphics

Now repeat the keystrokes required to produce the two graphics. When you have completed the macro definition, save the macro the PHANDS.WPM.

Press   **Ctrl+F10** (Macro Def)

The WPM extension is automatically appended to the file name to indicate that the file is a WordPerfect macro. Note that you now have four graphics in your banner. This provides a good check of the macro's accuracy. Use the View Document function with 200 percent magnification to view the pointing hands graphics. If you can tell that one graphic overlays the other one (except for line thickness), you have made an error in entering the information in the Figure Definition menu within the macro.

5 | Satisfaction through Composition

The Foundation Is Laid

We have done a number of things in the previous chapters to prepare both WordPerfect and the printer to produce our newsletter. The page layouts for the sample newsletter have been designed (they are shown again in this chapter for convenience). The files have been converted to a WordPerfect 5.0 supported format, and a new keyboard definition has been created to include some special functions.

Several graphics files have been created that can be read and manipulated by WordPerfect's graphics functions. The fonts to be used in the newsletter have been created and the printer resource file has been updated to include all of the information necessary to access these fonts. Furthermore, styles have been created for the newsletter page format and banner.

Everything has been done except actually putting all of these pieces together into a newsletter ready to be printed. The actual composition process is where we begin to see the fruits of our labor. It is also where we have the greatest chance for making an error in layout and, conversely the greatest opportunity for success.

Setting Up for Composition

Before we actually begin to compose all the elements of the newsletter, we should take advantage of some of the shortcuts we set up in the previous chapters. First, we should reconfigure the keyboard by using our own keyboard definition.

Press	**Shift+F1** (Setup)
Press	**6** (Keyboard Layout)

A list of the available keyboard definitions is displayed, including the one defined in Chapter 3, MYBOARD. We will select this keyboard definition as the active one.

Highlight	MYBOARD
Press	**Return**
Press	**F7** (Exit)

We will not use any of the key definitions in this keyboard definition for composition of the newsletter, but it is a good habit to load it each time you begin WordPerfect.

Entering the Newsletter Basics

The two basic parts of any newsletter that you will create is the page format and the banner. With the exception of the publication number and date, these elements will be constant for each newsletter. This consistency provides a sense of familiarity to the reader that is a key part of any document being accepted by the reader. How would you feel about your favorite magazine if every time it was published it had a totally different look and format? It wouldn't be very long before, not only was it not your favorite magazine, you probably wouldn't even purchase it. And so it goes with any document you produce—familiarity of appearance and format is the key to initial acceptance of your work by your audience.

Calling All Styles

We have created a style for each of these elements to assure such consistency. So let's put these elements in place. Starting from a blank document, retrieve the set of styles that were created earlier for the newsletter.

      Press   **Alt+F8** (Style)

      Press   **7** (Retrieve)

      Type   NEWSLTR.STY

Figure 5-1 displays all the styles we have created for the newsletter. Because the page format is the lowest level of style

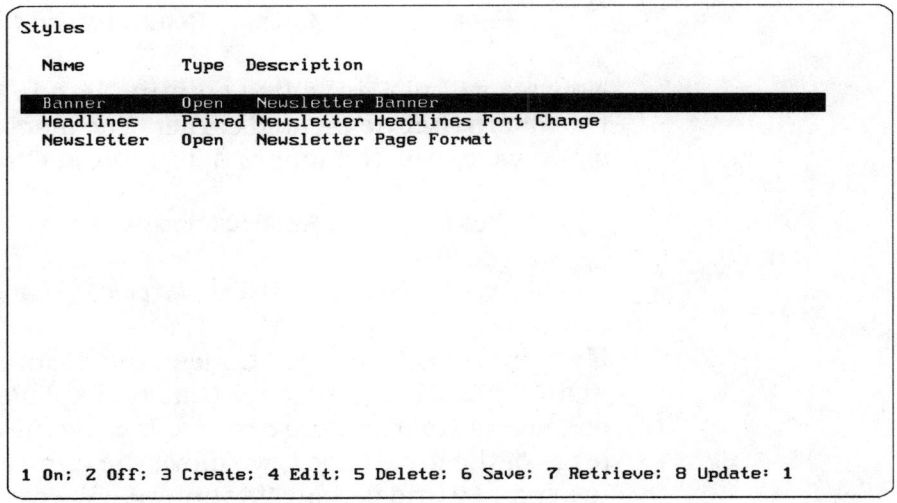

Figure 5-1. The styles available for use in our newsletter.

we created (everything else on the page is dependent on the page format), we want to turn on this style first.

Highlight	Newsletter
Press	**1** (On) or **Return** (*option 1 is the default selection*)

The Newsletter style is placed at the beginning of the document. This is an open style that can be turned on and forgotten. As you will recall, the Newsletter style contains the margin settings and the definition for the three-column format.

Now that the basic format of the page has been set, we can place the first element of the newsletter, the banner, on the page. Since we have defined a banner style that will place all of the various elements of the banner (except the graphics) in the proper positions, we will turn on the banner style by repeating the steps above.

Highlight	Banner
Press	**1** (On) or **Return** (*option 1 is the default selection*)

Now we will place the two pointing hands in the banner using the macro that we created earlier. The macro was stored on disk when we exited the macro definition in Chapter 4.

Press	**Alt+F10** (Macro)
Type	PHANDS (*the pointing hands macro*)

If we press **Alt+F3** (Reveal Codes), the document should look like Figure 5-2. Notice that all that is displayed are the two style codes and the two figure codes. If we want to examine the contents of the style codes, we move the cursor over the style code to expand it and display its contents. We could view the specifics of the two figure codes using the Edit Figure function.

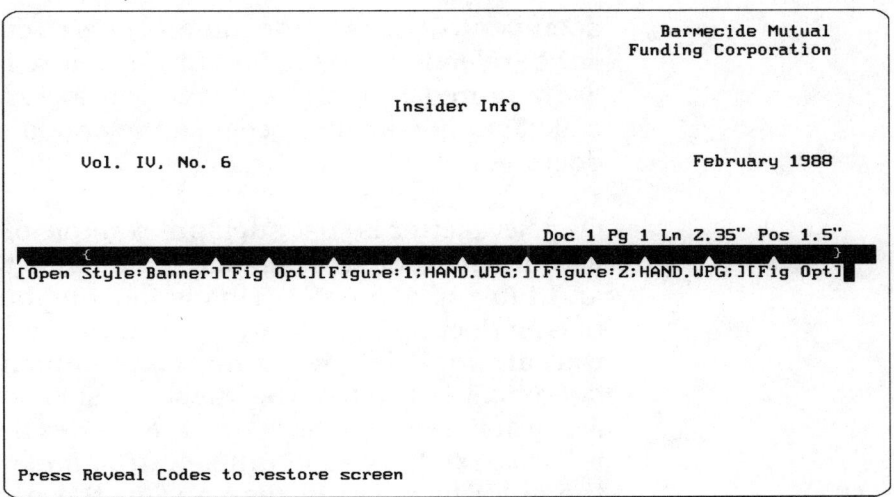

Figure 5-2. The page format, banner, and graphics codes for the newsletter.

Press	**Alt+F9** (Graphics)
Press	**1** (Figure)
Press	**2** (Edit)
Type	**1** or **2** (*the figure number to be examined*)

You can verify the appearance of the newsletter so far by using the View Document feature. Now press **Return** once to put some space between the banner and the other elements on page 1 of the newsletter.

Using Master Documents

WordPerfect offers a feature that eases the management of any document that is comprised of more than one file—the master document. A master document is a document that contains either references to the files (or the entire files themselves) that are required to make up a single document. These files are called subdocuments because they are a subset of the master document.

Our newsletter is just such an example of a master document (the newsletter itself) and subdocuments (the individual stories and table of contents). This is ideal if you want to set up the master document once and save it, then edit the subdocuments that are included in the master document. When the master document is printed, the latest revisions of the subdocuments are automatically inserted in the master document. Disk space is also saved because unlike our sample newsletter, wherein the story files are on disk and in the newsletter, the master document does not contain the actual contents of the subdocument files until it is expanded.

As you can imagine, the master document feature is very easy to use and results in a much more manageable approach to building a single document from several source files. However, because of the illustrative purpose of the sample newsletter, we will not be using the master document feature. This feature actually streamlines the process of compiling the newsletter too much to be used here.

Composing the First Page

The newsletter will be in three-column format. We have already defined the columns in our page format style, but before we begin we need to turn the columns on.

Press	**Alt+F7** (Math/Columns)
Press	3 (Column On/Off)

We also need to set some graphics options so that the frames align properly with the text. For this newsletter, we will just use the User-defined Box for all of our frames. The only reason WordPerfect gives us the other options is so we can differentiate between different frame types for setting options, inserting captions, building tables of contents, and so forth for each type. Since we won't be generating a table of contents for figures or tables, we will stick with the user-defined type of frame.

WordPerfect provides a default setting of 0.16 inch outside margin for all frames. To get our frames the same width as the text around the frames, we will reset these margins to 0 inches.

Press	**Alt+F9** (Graphics)
Press	**4** (User-defined Box)
Press	**4** (Options)
Press	**2** (Outside Border Space)

Set each of the four measurements to 0 inches. This will align the edges of the frames with the text around the frames and keep everything nice and neat.

Creating the Table of Contents Frame

We are ready to put in the frame for the table of contents. The page layout for page 1 is shown again in Figure 5-3. We don't have a clue as to what the table of contents will be yet, but the need to reserve space for it exists just the same. Later, when we complete the newsletter, we will make a file containing the table of contents and then edit this frame to include the text.

Press	**Alt+F9** (Graphics)

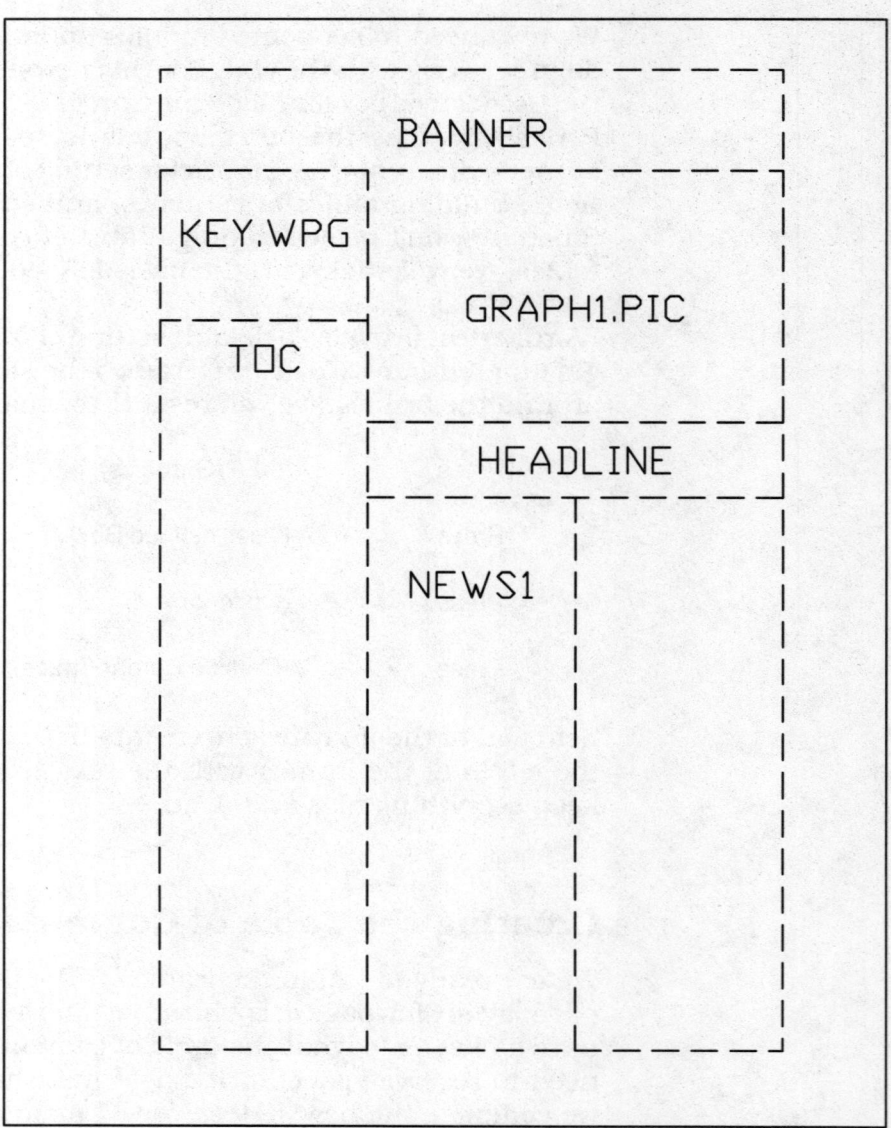

Figure 5-3. The page layout for page 1 of the newsletter identifying the position of the table of contents frame.

Press	**4** (User-defined Box)
Press	**1** (Create)

This frame will be of the page type because we want WordPerfect to automatically calculate the correct position and size of the frame. We want the frame to be placed directly below the banner in the left column (column 1), so its position needs to be set accordingly.

Press	**3** (Type)
Press	**2** (Page)
Press	**4** (Vertical Position)
Press	**5** (Set Position)

WordPerfect uses the current cursor position for the default value of the vertical position. If we have not moved the cursor from immediately below the banner, this value will be correct.

Press	**Return** (*accept default value*)
Press	**5** (Horizontal Position)
Press	**2** (Columns)

The Columns option indicates that we intend to have the frame span either one or two columns, but not all three. We will then tell WordPerfect which columns will be spanned and the position of the frame.

Press	**Return** (*column 1 is the default value*)
Press	**4** (Both Left & Right)

We have now told WordPerfect to place the frame in column 1 and that it will span the column from the column's left margin to its right margin. We will let WordPerfect size the frame for us based on these specifications.

    Press   **6** (Size)

    Press   **4** (Both Width and Height)

Now enter 5 inches for the width and 10 inches for the height. These values are certainly larger than is allowable and should do the trick. WordPerfect will size the frame for us so as not to exceed the width of column 1 or the height from the current cursor position to the bottom of the page.

    Type   **5** (*inches for width*)

    Type   **10** (*inches for height*)

Sure enough, WordPerfect has recalculated the correct width and height for the table of contents frame as shown in Figure 5-4. You can use this method anytime you want to create a frame but are unsure of the exact dimensions the frame requires.

Putting in the First Graphic

The first graphic that we will place on the page will be the file GRAPH1.PIC. This graphic, as indicated by our page 1 layout, spans columns 2 and 3 immediately under the banner. Therefore, the width will be fixed according to the width of columns 2 and 3 and WordPerfect will calculate the correct height. This frame will be a page-type graphic because we want it stationary on the page at a fixed location, without regard to the elements on either side of it. We will begin by moving the cursor to column 2.

```
Definition: User-defined Box
    1 - Filename
    2 - Caption
    3 - Type                        Page
    4 - Vertical Position           2.1"
    5 - Horizontal Position         Column(s) 1, Left
    6 - Size                        1.8" wide x 8.9" high
    7 - Wrap Text Around Box        Yes
    8 - Edit




Selection: 0
```

Figure 5-4. The complete Table Format *screen for the table of contents frame.*

Press	**Return** (*move to column 2*)
Press	**Alt+F9** (Graphics)
Press	**4** (User-defined Box)
Press	**1** (Create)
Press	**1** (Filename)
Type	GRAPH1.PIC

This will load the file GRAPH1.PIC into the frame we are creating. The size of the frame will be calculated by WordPerfect to obtain the best possible fit while retaining the aspect ratio of the original graphic. We will now set the type, horizontal position and vertical position.

Press	**3** (Type)

Press   **2** (Page)

Press   **5** (Horizontal Position)

Press   **2** (Columns)

The graphic will span columns 2 and 3 from the left margin of column 2 to the right margin of column 3.

Type   2-3

Press   **4** (Both Left & Right)

Press   **Return**

WordPerfect automatically recalculates the size of the frame so that it spans columns 2 and 3 and maintains the proper aspect ration (height to width). After setting the vertical position to the current cursor position, the complete User-defined Box Definition screen should look like Figure 5-5.

```
Definition: User-defined Box
    1 - Filename                GRAPH1.PIC (Graphic)
    2 - Caption
    3 - Type                    Page
    4 - Vertical Position       2.11"
    5 - Horizontal Position     Column(s) 2-3, Left & Right
    6 - Size                    3.9" wide x 2.91" (high)
    7 - Wrap Text Around Box    Yes
    8 - Edit




Selection: 0
```

Figure 5-5. The completed definition for the GRAPH1.PIC frame.

Placing The First Story

The first story to appear in the newsletter is in a file called NEWS1.WP5. There are two things that we will do to this file in order to begin it on page 1. First, we have to remove the headline of the story. Since we want the headline to also span columns two and three, we will put the headline in another frame. Then we will insert the story into the frame, determine how much of the story will fit on page 1, and then break the file into two parts so that the story can be continued on page 3. Each part of the story will be saved to a separate file. Begin by switching to Document 2 and loading the file.

Press	**Shift+F3** (Switch)
Press	**Shift+F10** (Retrieve)
Type	NEWS1.WP5

Make a note of the headline of the story "Deposits Top 1 Billion $$$" and then delete the headline and hard return so that "Hartford, CT" is the first thing in the file. Then save the file under the same name, exit Document 2, and switch back to Document 1. We will reset the options for the user-defined box so that no lines are drawn around the box and then create the box for the headline of the story.

Press	**Alt+F9** (Graphic)
Press	**4** (User-defined Box)
Press	**4** (Options)
Press	**1** (Border Style)

Set the Border Style to None on all four sides of the box and press **F7** (Exit). Now create the frame for the headline of the story.

Press	**Alt+F9** (Graphics)
Press	**4** (User-defined Box)
Press	**1** (Create)

Notice that we are not going to specify a file name for this frame. We will use the Edit option instead to type the text directly into the frame. First, we will set the frame type as a page frame, then set the vertical position and horizontal position. We will also specify a height for the frame based on the amount of text we enter into it.

Press	**3** (Type)
Press	**2** (Page)

We will now set the vertical position for the frame. Notice that the default setting is Top. We cannot use the default setting because WordPerfect will attempt to put the frame at the top of this page. Since there is no room at the top of this page, WordPerfect will place the frame at the top of the next page. We can reset the placement of the headline frame by simply selecting the Vertical Position option. WordPerfect displays the current vertical location of the cursor and we need only press **Return** to accept the value.

Press	**4** (Vertical Position)
Press	**5** (Set Position)
Press	**Return** (*accept the cursor's current position*)

We now set the horizontal position in the same manner that we set the horizontal position from the graphics frame.

Press	**5** (Horizontal Position)

Press	**2** (Columns)
Type	2-3
Press	**Return**
Press	**4** (Both Right & Left)
Press	**6** (Size)
Press	**3** (Both Width and Height)

Accept WordPerfect's calculation of the width by pressing **Return** and set the height to 0.5 inches and press **Return**. All of the frame's parameters have now been set and we are ready to put the headline into the frame. The wonderful thing about typing text directly into a frame is that WordPerfect treats the contents of the frame as a minidocument. All of WordPerfect's text editing capabilities (with the exception of page format commands) are available within the text frame. We will even use our headline style in this frame.

Press	**8** (Edit)
Press	**Alt+F8** (Style)
Highlight	Headlines
Press	**Return**
Type	Deposits Top One Billion Dollars
Press	**F7** (Exit)

The complete Definition: User-defined Box screen for the headline of the story should look like Figure 5-6. We will now add the body text of the story, find where the break from page 1 needs to be

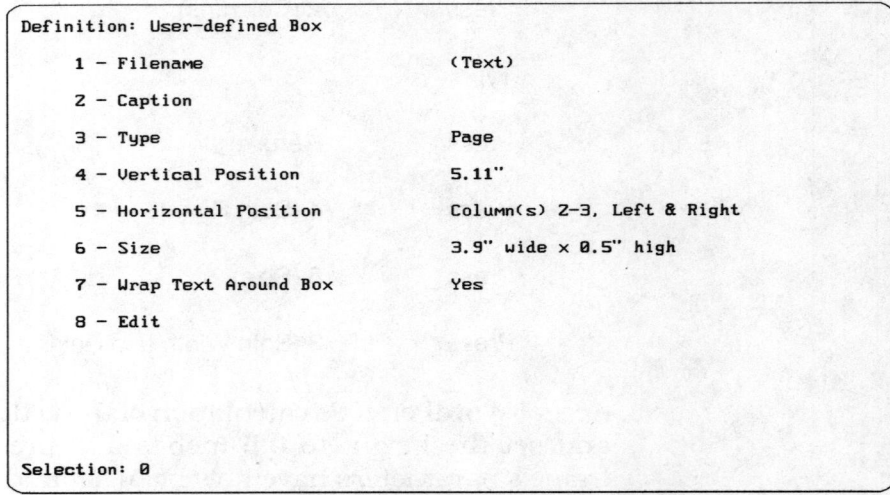

Figure 5-6. The complete box definition for the title frame.

needs to be made, break the file, and add an italicized "continue on page 3" line to the bottom of the page 1 file.

    Press   **Shift+F10** (Retrieve)

    Type   NEWS1.WP5

WordPerfect will ask if you want to retrieve to NEWS1.WP5 file into the current file. Type Y to load the file. Note that the last line of column 3 on page 1 ends with "finally get." We will break the file at the end of the last word in the previous line. The new last line will be the continued statement. Therefore, mark and delete this file from the newsletter, switch to Document 2, retrieve the NEWS1.WP5 file, mark the text to the end of the file beginning with "and hope," and save the block to a file called NEWS1-2.WP5. Then enter "continued on page 3" at the end of this file and save it as NEWS1.WP5.

You should now have two files for the first story: NEWS1.WP5 and NEWS1-2.WP5. Switch back to Document 1 and retrieve the NEWS1.WP5 file into the newsletter. Now we are going to align the statement "continued on page 3" flush with the right margin, block it with WordPerfect's Block function, and change the font to the Dutch 8-point italic font. Begin by positioning the cursor at the "c" in "continued."

Press	**Alt+F6** (Flush Right)
Press	**Alt+F4** (Block)
Highlight	continued of page 3
Press	**Ctrl+F8** (Font)
Press	**1** (Size)
Press	**3** (Fine)

Remember that we have an automatic font change that will select the Dutch 8-point italic font if we select Fine as the Font Size. Alternately, we could have chosen the Dutch 8-point italic font as the new Base Font and then reselected the Dutch 12-point Roman font after the continued statement. But why go to all that trouble, the power of WordPerfect is its ability to increase not only our capabilities for producing documents, but our productivity in doing it.

This completes the composition process for page 1 of the sample newsletter. If you have done everything correctly and in the proper sequence, page 1 of your newsletter will look like the printed page shown in Figure 5-7. If your page looks different when printed, check your codes with the Reveal Codes feature against the previous instructions. Use the View Document feature and make any corrections necessary to achieve the results shown before we continue.

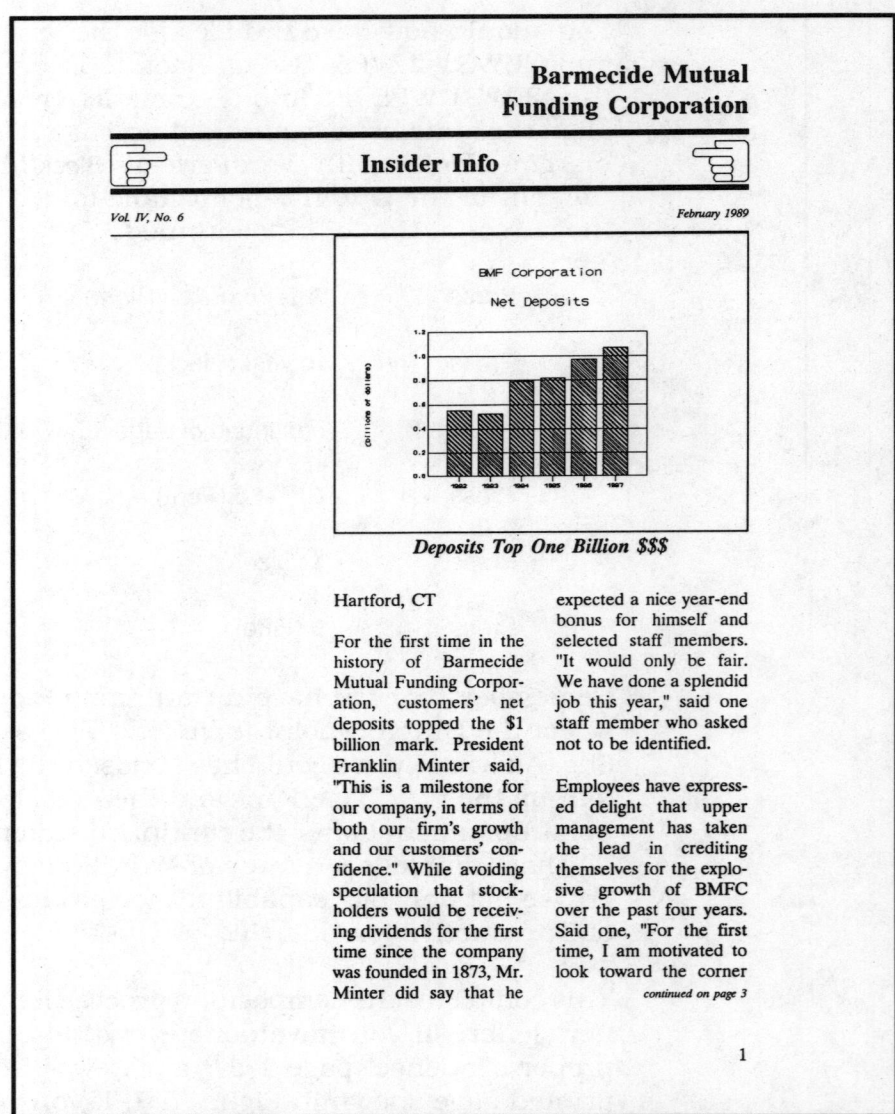

Figure 5-7. The complete page 1 of the newsletter.

Saving Our Work

It's always a good idea to save your work at points along the way as you are satisfied with the progress of the page composition process. This recommendation has a twofold purpose. First and foremost, as with any of the work you do with your computer, you should save the files periodically during the editing process in case a failure of your computer, the software, or a power outage causes you to lose your work. If you set up WordPerfect to perform automatic backups of your work, this is not much of a problem.

There is another and perhaps more logical (assuming you have WordPerfect doing automatic backups) reason for saving your work at a point at which you are satisfied with your progress. WordPerfect is a powerful program, and with power comes the inherent chance that you will try to do something fancy and foul up your document. You may or may not be able to determine what you did and the steps necessary to correct the problem.

If you are not able to undo what you and/or WordPerfect hath wrought and you saved your file the last time you were satisfied with its appearance, you can exit WordPerfect completely without saving anything and start over. In this way, you will never be inhibited to try something new with the almost endless varieties of page composition capabilities that WordPerfect has put in your hands.

Onward to Page 2

The page layout for page 2 of the newsletter is fairly straightforward in its design and implementation (see Figure 5-8). We have two stories on this page that come from the files NEWS2.WP5

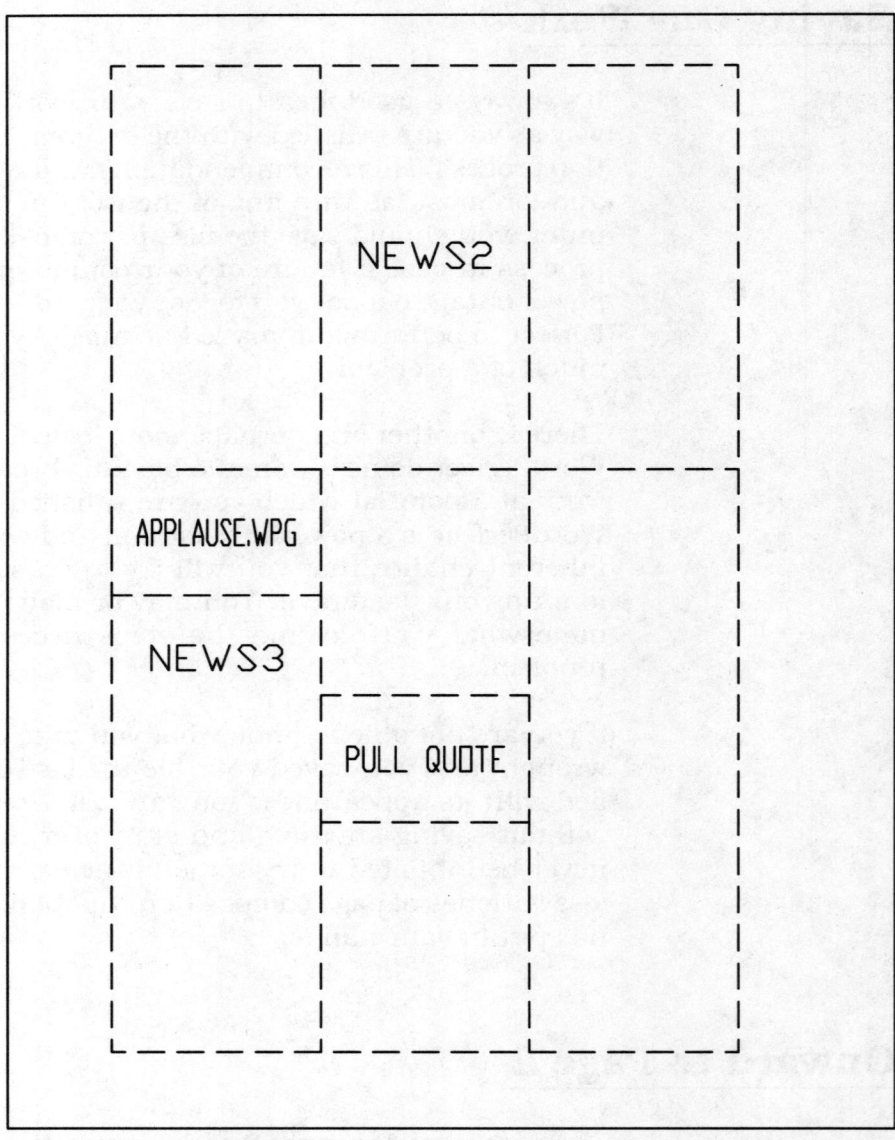

Figure 5-8. The page layout for page 2 of the newsletter.

and NEWS3.WP5. The NEWS2.WP5 story has a headline that spans the full width of the page and the headline for the NEWS3.WP5 story spans columns 2 and 3. NEWS3.WP5 has a WordPerfect WPG graphic at the beginning of the story and a pull quote centered in the center column. Because we have already laid the groundwork to automate much of this formatting, page 2 should prove to be smooth sailing.

Laying in NEWS2.WP5

To incorporate the NEWS2.WP5 and NEWS3.WP5 stories into page 2 of the newsletter, we will first set up the page format, then put NEWS2.WP5 onto the page, turn columns off, lay in a horizontal line, turn columns back on, and finally put in the graphic and the NEWS3.WP5 file. We will complete the page by adding the pull quote using a user-defined box. After evoking the newsletter page format style we will force this page to be page 2.

Press	**Alt+F8** (Style)
Highlight	Newsletter
Press	**1** (On) or **Return** (*option 1 is the default selection*)
Press	**Shift+F8** (Format)
Press	**2** (Page)
Press	**2** (Force Odd/Even Page)
Press	**2** (Even)

We need to set the headline for the NEWS2.WP5 file to span the entire width of the page. Therefore, we will not turn columns on before loading the file.

Press	**Shift+F10** (Retrieve)
Type	NEWS2.WP5

The file is displayed on the page in single-column format. We will block the headline and evoke the Headlines style to create the headline for this story. Position the cursor at the beginning of the headline.

Press	**Alt+F4** (Block)
Highlight	The headline text
Press	**Alt+F8** (Style)
Highlight	Headlines

The Headline style is evoked for the text currently marked. We now need to turn columns back on and adjust the column lengths so that NEWS2.WP5 fills the three columns evenly. The story presently fills approximately one full-length column, so splitting the story in three parts should yield good results. Columns are split by positioning the cursor at the point in the text where the text should begin in the next column and press **Ctrl+Return**. After the story has been split into three columns, some adjustments will probably be required to balance the columns of text with one another. After you have made the final adjustments, the story should look like Figure 5-9.

Separating the Stories

It is good practice to separate the different stories in your newsletter with rules to keep the reader from becoming confused as to where one story ends and the next begins. As with the banner, we will use WordPerfect's Line option of the Graphics function to draw a horizontal line from the left margin to the

```
-------------------------------------------------------------------------------
                   Company Mourns Employee's Passing

                              Mrs. Beatty could not be   cial records, thought to
Hackensack, NJ                contacted at press time,   be in Mr. Beatty's pos-
                              but the circumstances      session, was not found at
Mr. William Beatty, cor-      surrounding the death of   the scene.
porate financial auditor      Mr. Beatty have been
for 16 years, passed away     described by Hackensack    All of us at BMF Corpo-
Thursday, April 20, at his    police as "suspicious."    ration who worked with
home in New Jersey. He        Mr. Beatty was killed in   William mourn his pass-
is survived by his wife,      what appears to have       ing. Donations to his sur
Helen, and three child-       been a car-bomb explo-     vivors may be forwarded
ren, ages 7, 12, and 16.      sion. No personal effects  to Mr. Franklin Minter.
Funeral services are          were missing, prompting    Mr. Minter told Insider
scheduled for Tuesday,        police to eliminate rob-   Info "It is my upper-most
April 25. Services will       bery as a motive.          priority that the entire
commence at 2:00 pm at        However, a briefcase       Beatty family be taken
the Samuel Morris Mem-        containing certain finan-  care of."
orial Funeral Home.


C:\DATA\WORDS\NEWSLTR.PGZ                          Doc 1 Pg 2 Ln 0.5" Pos 1.5"
```

Figure 5-9. The NEWS2.WPG file split into three columns.

right margin to separate the NEWS2.WP5 file from the NEWS3.WP5 file. First we will turn columns off and then insert the line.

Press	**Alt+F7** (Math/Columns)
Press	**3** (Column On/Off)
Press	**Alt+F9** (Graphics)
Press	**5** (Line)
Press	**1** (Horizontal)

The current defaults for the horizontal line may be used, but we need to increase the width to 0.05 inches.

Press	**3** (Width of Line)

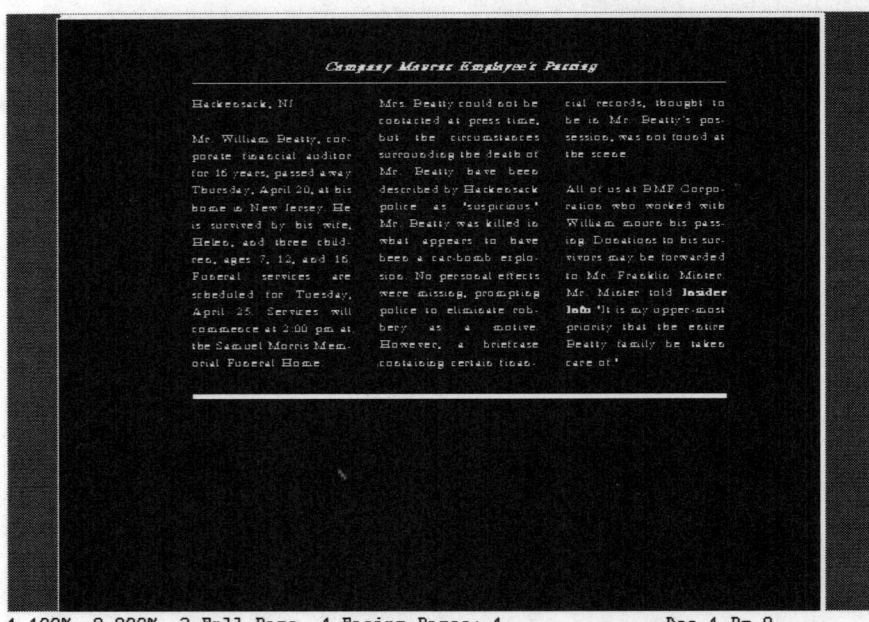

Figure 5-10. Page 2 of the newsletter using the View Document *feature.*

Type	0.05
Press	**Return** (*twice*)

Page 2 as seen using the View Document feature should look like figure 5-10.

We are now ready to load the NEWS3.WP5 file. We don't want to turn columns back on just yet because the headline for this story also spans all three columns.

Press	**Shift+F10** (Retrieve)
Type	NEWS3.WP5

Press	**Return**

Again we will apply the Headlines style to the headline of this story. Position the cursor at the beginning of the headline.

Press	**Alt+F4** (Block)
Highlight	The headline text
Press	**Alt+F8** (Style)
Highlight	Headlines

The Headlines style is again evoked for the text currently marked. We now need to turn columns back on. This time we are at the mercy of the length of the story itself as to whether the third column will be completely filled. We do have a couple of aces in the hole to help handle this problem, however. We have a graphic to be placed at the beginning of the story and a pull quote to insert in the middle. By adjusting the size of these two elements, we should be able to get fairly close to obtaining three balanced columns.

Press	**Alt+F7** (Math/Columns)
Press	**3** (Column On/Off)

The graphic frame will be created as a page-type frame. Therefore, we must put the graphic in before we insert the text in order to keep the graphic from being pushed to the next page.

Press	**Alt+F9** (Graphics)
Press	**4** (User-defined Box)
Press	**1** (Create)

We will set this frame up as a page-type frame to be placed on the left margin. Until we see how much adjustment needs to be made to get the columns balanced, we will set the width to be as wide as column 1 with automatic height calculations performed by WordPerfect.

    Press   **1** (Filename)

    Type   APPLAUSE.WPG

    Press   **Return**

    Press   **3** (Type)

    Press   **2** (Page)

    Press   **4** (Vertical Position)

WordPerfect's default setting for page-type frames is to set the vertical position to the top of the page. If we want to use the current cursor position as the vertical position, we can set the vertical position manually and WordPerfect will change its default to a measurement equal to the cursor's current position relative to the top of the page.

    Press   **5** (Set Position)

    Press   **Return** (*the current position of the cursor*)

    Press   **5** (Horizontal Position)

    Press   **2** (Columns)

    Press   **Return** (*accept the default of column 1*)

    Press   **4** (Both Left and Right)

That takes care of everything in this graphics frame. Now we can make adjustments to the text and see how the page looks. Remember, we still need to put in the pull quote, so don't panic if column 3 is short. Once the final adjustments are made, it looks like we are going to be pretty close to balanced columns once we get the pull quote put in. Let's go ahead and do that to see where the end of the text file ends in column 3. But before we do, we need to change the Border Style option for the user-defined box. We want a thick line above and below the pull quote to set it out from the body text.

Press	**Alt+F9** (Graphics)
Press	**4** (User-defined Box)
Press	**4** (Options)
Press	**1** (Border Style)

Set the top and bottom border styles to Thick **(6)** and exit the options menu by pressing **F7** (Exit). Next, move the cursor to about half way down the left margin of column 2 . (We could position the cursor at the top of column 2 and use the Center selection of the Vertical Position option, but that selection would center the frame on the page, not in our column, which is about two-thirds of a page long.)

Press	**Alt+F9** (Graphics)
Press	**4** (User-defined Box)
Press	**1** (Create)

We want the frame to remain fixed at a specific location on the page, so we will set the frame type to Page. We will also be adding the text for the pull quote directly in to the frame using the Frame Edit function. After reading the news story we decide the following line should be used for the pull quote, "The children were scared by the sudden noise and ran in all directions." This text can be created and saved to a file called PULQUOTE.WP5. When we get into the Edit function, we will retrieve this file just as we would any other file into WordPerfect.

Press	**3** (Type)
Press	**2** (Page)
Press	**4** (Vertical Position)
Press	**5** (Set Position)
Press	**Return** (*accept the current cursor position value*)
Press	**5** (Horizontal Position)
Press	**2** (Columns)

We will set this frame to be placed in column 2 with a width that will span all of that column.

Type	**2** (*to place the frame in column 2*)
Press	**4** (Both Left & Right)

Now we will add the text to the frame with the Edit function.

Press	**8** (Edit)
Press	**Ctrl+F8** (Font)

We will also select the Dutch 12-point italic font for the pull quote. The font for this text could have been saved with the file, but whoever wrote it probably didn't know what font we would be using for it.

Press	**4** (Base Font)
Highlight	Dutch Italic 12pt (ASCII) (Port) (FW)
Press	**Return**
Press	**Shift+F10** (Retrieve)
Type	PULQUOTE.WP5
Press	**F7** (Exit)
Press	**Return**

Now take a look at the page with the View Document function. Not too bad, but we will need to make some minor adjustments to the graphic and pull quote to get the NEWS3 story to balance in all three columns.

We might also use another trick of the publishing trade to fill the last part of column 3. If we have enough room, we can create a small frame at the end of column 3 and use the space for a "quote of the day" or some such other filler material.

It is not unlikely that a few minor adjustments will be required to the page elements to get everything just right. When you have completed any necessary minor adjustments on the elements on page 2, your page should look like Figure 5-11. Now save the job again and let's move on to page 3 of the newsletter.

Over the Hump with Page 3

Page 3 of the newsletter is put together using all the techniques that were used for pages 1 and 2. We will need to add two ruling lines to this page: a horizontal line between the NEWS1-2.WP5

Company Mourns Employee's Passing

Hackensack, NJ

Mr. William Beatty, corporate financial auditor for 16 years, passed away Thursday, April 20, at his home in New Jersey. He is survived by his wife, Helen, and three children, ages 7, 12, and 16. Funeral services are scheduled for Tuesday, April 25. Services will commence at 2:00 pm at the Samuel Morris Memorial Funeral Home.

Mrs. Beatty could not be contacted at press time, but the circumstances surrounding the death of Mr. Beatty have been described by Hackensack police as "suspicious." Mr. Beatty was killed in what appears to have been a car-bomb explosion. No personal effects were missing, prompting police to eliminate robbery as a motive. However, a briefcase containing certain financial records, thought to be in Mr. Beatty's possession, was not found at the scene.

All of us at BMF Corporation who worked with William mourn his passing. Donations to his survivors may be forwarded to Mr. Franklin Minter. Mr. Minter told **Insider Info** "It is my upper-most priority that the entire Beatty family be taken care of."

They Call This A Race?

The BMFC Runners Club held their annual "Spring Jump" run February 14 in Waterford. Distances of 2 and 5 kilometers were run starting at the Holy Street landfill. The races began with what sponsors hoped would become an annual event; a 10 meter tyke run for 1 to 3 year olds. However,

a small oversight by the organizers of the event may force the tyke run to be canceled in future years. According to witnesses, the toddlers were well-behaved as they took their positions on the starting line. When

The children were scared by the sudden noise and ran in all directions.

the starter's pistol was fired, however, the children were scared by the sudden noise and ran in all directions. After several hours of frantic searching for their lost loved-ones, the New Jersey Highway Patrol was

called in to assist parents in the search. About sundown the last lost child was located and waivers had been signed by all the parents concerned pledging not to file law suits against neither the sponsors nor BMF Corporation.

The senior division of this race was won by 63-year old Vince Norton. The results are being challenged, however, by 68-year old Ned Turner. Mr. Turner stated that he was leading Mr. Norton when he was pushed off the course by one of the scared children. The judges are considering his protest.

Figure 5-11. The completed page 2 of the newsletter.

text and the rest of the page, and a vertical line to separate the NEWS4.WP5 and NEWS5.WP5 stories.

After we set the page format, reset the page number to 3, and turn columns on, we will bring in the NEWS1-2.WP5 text that is to be placed at the top of the page. However, the NEWS1-2.WP5 file needs to have a "continued from page 1" added to it before it is ready to be incorporated into the newsletter. So go to a blank WordPerfect document, retrieve this file, add the text, save the file again, and switch back to the newsletter document. Now retrieve the file and change the text we added to the file to the Dutch 8-point italic font.

Press	**Alt+F8** (Style)
Highlight	Newsletter
Press	**1** (On) or **Return** (*option 1 is the default selection*)
Press	**Shift+F8** (Format)
Press	**2** (Page)
Press	**6** (New page Number)
Type	3
Press	**Return** (*three times*)
Press	**Alt+F7** (Math/Columns)
Press	**3** (Column On/Off)
Press	**Shift+F10** (Retrieve)
Type	NEWS1-2.WP5

```
┌──────────────────────────────────────────────────────────────────────┐
│  continued from page 1                                               │
│                                                                      │
│  and hope they finally get   employees to celebrate   attend. There is no cover │
│  what they have deserved     the occasion.            charge and the party will │
│  for so long." Other                                  begin promptly when       │
│  employees were too          Tentatively schedule for people begin to show up.  │
│  shocked by the good         Wednesday, March 13 at                             │
│  news to offer any           the Tusculoosa Bar &     Congratulations, BMF      │
│  response. However, a        Dance Hall, all non-     Corporation and Mr.       │
│  party has been organized    management employees     Minter, on a job well     │
│  by a large group of         are encouraged to        done!                     │
│                                                                      │
│                                                                      │
│                                                                      │
│                                                                      │
│  C:\DATA\WORDS\NEWSLTR.PG3                        Doc 1 Pg 3 Ln 2.63" Pos 1.5" │
└──────────────────────────────────────────────────────────────────────┘
```

Figure 5-12. The NEWS1-2.WP5 file set in three columns.

Block	*continued from page 1*
Press	**Ctrl+F8** (Font)
Press	**1** (Size)
Press	**3** (Fine)

You will recall that the printer resource file has an automatic font change that will select the Dutch 8-point italic font when the Fine font size is selected. Now we adjust the column lengths so that NEWS1-2.WP5 fills the three columns evenly. Remember that columns are split by positioning the cursor at the point in the text where the text should begin in the next column and press **Ctrl+Return**. We can split the columns so that your page look like the one in Figure 5-12 by adjusting the bottom margin to 7.7 inches at the start of the text and resetting the bottom margin to 0.75 inches at the end of the text. To begin, position the cursor at "and".

Press	**Shift+F8** (Format)
Press	**2** (Page)
Press	**5** (Margins - Top/Bottom)

Set the bottom margin to 7.7 inches. The text will now break into three columns as shown in Figure 5-13. As you can see, this setting will require us to add some filler to the end of the third column, so we choose one of WordPerfect's WPG graphic files. Position the cursor at the end of the story in column 3. The graphic frame will be created as a page type frame at the end of the text in column 3.

Press	**Alt+F9** (Graphics)
Press	**4** (User-defined Box)
Press	**1** (Create)

We can estimate the height of the frame, but some minor adjustments will have to be made to get it to vertically fill the remainder of column 3 exactly. As a starting point we will set the frame height to 0.5 inches and let WordPerfect calculate the width.

Press	**1** (File name)
Type	GOODNEWS.WPG
Press	**Return**
Press	**3** (Type)
Press	**2** (Page)
Press	**4** (Vertical Position)

176 *Desktop Publishing with WordPerfect 5.0*

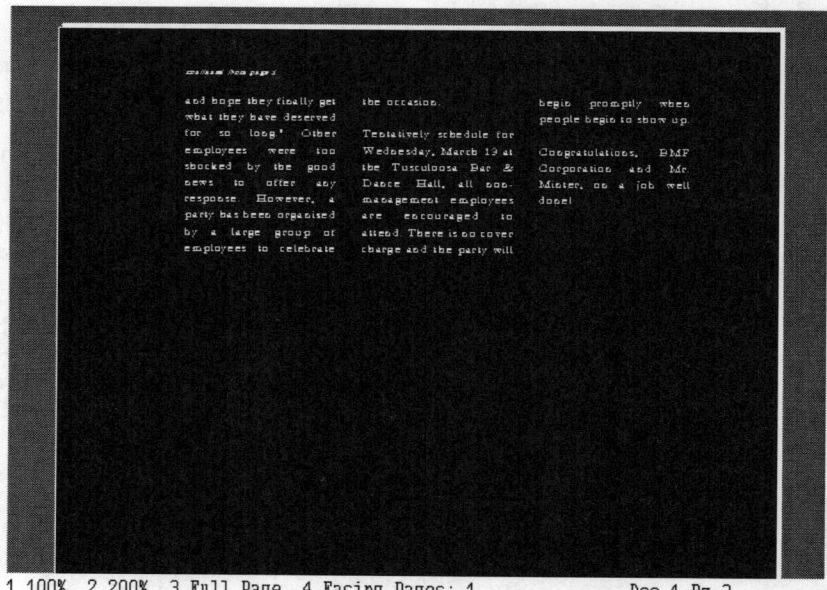

Figure 5-13. The completed NEWS1-2.WP5 story as seen with the View Document *feature.*

Press	**5** (Set Position)
Press	**Return** (*accept the current cursor position value*)
Press	**5** (Horizontal Position)
Press	**2** (Columns)

We will place the frame in column 3 and set the position to the right side of the column.

Type	**3** (*to place the frame in column 3*)
Press	**2** (Right)
Press	**6** (Size)

Press	**2** (Height (auto width))
Type	0.5
Press	**Return** (*twice*)

After checking the page with the View Document function, we see that an adjustment to the height of the graphic is required. Move the cursor to the last line of text in column 3.

Press	**Alt+F9** (Graphics)
Press	**4** (User-defined Box)
Press	**2** (Edit)

WordPerfect will default to the next user-defined box number in the document. This is true whether or not a frame currently exists for that number. For instance, if you place the cursor at the end of a document and try to edit what WordPerfect believes is the next frame an error message is generated because that frame does not exist. Consequently, if the cursor is positioned after the frame that needs to be edited, you would have to enter the correct frame number manually. Since we intentionally positioned the cursor immediately before the frame to be edited, WordPerfect's default number is the correct one.

Press	**Return** (*accept default frame number*)
Press	**6** (Size)

We can go ahead and use the Height (auto width) function and let WordPerfect use its own automatic calculation for the width.

Press	**2** (Height (auto width))
Type	0.6

Press	**Return**
Press	**F7** (Exit)

The graphic frame is now sized correctly to fill the remainder of column 3. We will now add the horizontal line to separate the story at the top of this page from the two stories that appear below it.

Press	**Return** (*twice*)
Press	**Alt+F9** (Graphics)
Press	**5** (Line)
Press	**1** (Horizontal)

The defaults for the horizontal line may be used, but we will increase the line's width to 0.05 inches.

Press	**3** (Width of Line)
Type	0.05
Press	**Return** (*twice*)

Now load the NEWS4.WP5 and NEWS5.WPG files as previously described and balance the columns. We need to add the horizontal line between the top story and the two bottom stories, so begin by positioning the cursor at the beginning of the NEWS5.WP5 text in column 2.

Press	**Alt+F9** (Graphics)
Press	**5** (Line)
Press	**1** (Horizontal Line)

continued from page 1

and hope they finally get what they have deserved for so long." Other employees were too shocked by the good news to offer any response. However, a party has been organized by a large group of employees to celebrate the occasion.

Tentatively scheduled for Wednesday, March 13 at the Tusculoosa Bar & Dance Hall, all non-management employees are encouraged to attend. There is no cover charge and the party will begin promptly when people begin to show up.

Congratulations, BMF Corporation and Mr. Minter, on a job well done!

Management Course Offered

A management course tailored to the unique requirements of BMF Corporation employees is being offered by Waterford Junior College. Topics covered during the eight-week course include social conduct for upwardly mobile managers, getting the most from under-achievers, and creative bookkeeping techniques. Anyone interested in learning about workings of the inner circles at corporations such as BMF Corporation is encouraged to attend.

Class size is limited to the first 120 applicants, so early registration for this course is essential. The class times, dates, and meeting place will be announced after the class size is determined.

For more information, call your employee assistance representative or write directly to Waterford Junior College at 1400 W. DuMont Street, Waterford, NJ 01234.

Ms. Everett Collects Garbage

Ms. Susan Everett works in the Internal Auditor Section by day, but in her own time, Susan collects garbage. A loyal employee of BMFC for 24 years, Susan says that her addiction to collecting garbage began some 40 years ago when she went to the local dump site with her husband, the late Thomas Everett. There, among the piles of genuine rubbish, Susan discovered the treasures that now sit in every part of her home.

"All of these things were junk to somebody, but I love them," Susan says with a gleam in her eyes. The mainstay of her vast collection is a huge assortment of glass bottles in every color and shape. "Bottles are maybe my favorite, they're so pretty." Other items to be found include furniture, kitchen appliances, and things that defy description.

Susan also likes to collect items that are big. As a matter of fact, Susan says "the bigger, the better." The family station wagon has long since been replaced by a 2-ton pickup truck.

We at BMF Corporation always take time to salute the unique individuals that are our corporation. And Ms. Everett certainly qualifies as one of those unique individuals. Good luck, Susan, and happy hunting!

Figure 5-14. The completed page 3 of the newsletter.

We can accept all of WordPerfect's defaults for this line because WordPerfect will automatically calculate its length as the width of column 2.

    Press   **F7** (Exit)

This completes the composition of page 3 and your page should look like Figure 5-14. If you need to make adjustments to achieve the correct appearance, don't hesitate to make them. Every job is an individual task that will require different adjustments to make the page balance out correctly.

Once again, when you are satisfied with the current state of the newsletter, save the newsletter before going on to page 4.

Finishing Up with Page 4

The elements in page 4 of the newsletter are no different than those that went into making the other three pages. Try this one yourself without being stepped through the process. Look at the page layout in Figure 5-15 and the completed page in Figure 5-16. Refer back to what we did to compose pages 1 through 3 and use WordPerfect's user's manual.

After you have completed the page, save the entire newsletter. Our next task is to generate a table of contents for the newsletter and put it into the appropriate frame.

Generating the Table of Contents

The last task to be done is the generation of the table of contents and placement of the table of contents text in the space reserved on page 1 of the newsletter. Each headline in the

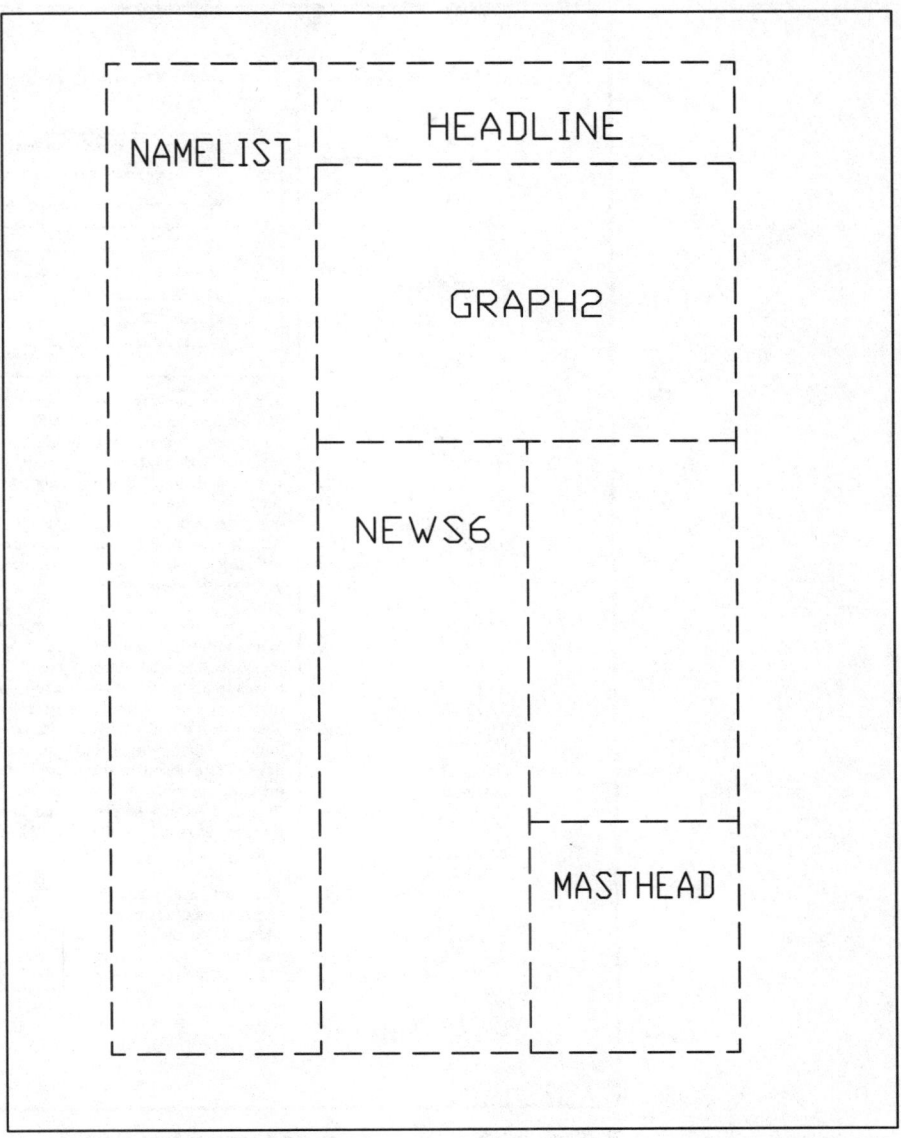

Figure 5-15. The page layout for page 4 of the sample newsletter.

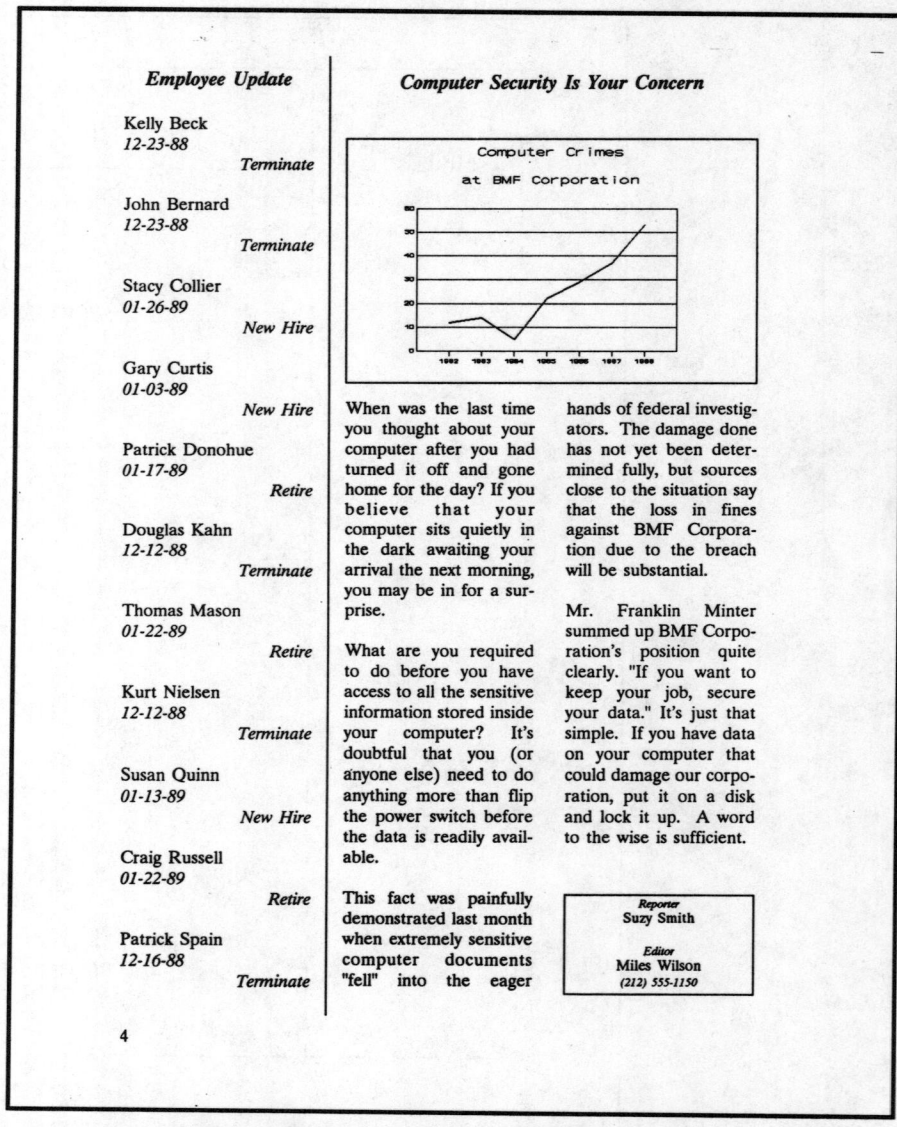

Figure 5-16. *The completed page 4 of the newsletter.*

newsletter requires marking so that WordPerfect can automatically compile the table of contents. This should be familiar territory because the process required to generate the table of contents is unchanged from WordPerfect 4.2. There is one new function that we will use here to simplify the creation process, however. Let's put the four pages of the newsletter into a single master document. By doing this, we can create the table of contents in one pass.

Press	**Alt+F5** (Mark Text)
Press	**2** (Subdoc)
Type	*your file name for page 1 of the newsletter*

Repeat this process for each of the four pages in the newsletter. Now expand the subdocuments so that you can mark the headlines.

Press	**Alt+F5** (Mark Text)
Press	**6** (Generate)
Press	**3** (Expand Master Document)

WordPerfect will expand the subdocuments, making the headline text of each story available for marking. Mark each headline for generation into the table of contents.

Press	**Alt+F4** (Block)
Highlight	the headline text
Press	**Alt+F5** (Mark Text)
Press	**1** (ToC)

Type	1 (*this is a first level entry*)

After you have marked each headline, go to very end of the master document and create a new page by pressing **Ctrl+Return**. We will generate the table of contents on this page. Then we will save the table of contents to a file, delete this page, and load the table of contents file into the frame we created on page 1 of the newsletter. Before we can do any of this, however, we must define the table.

Press	**Alt+F5** (Mark Text)
Press	**5** (Define)
Press	**1** (Define Table of Contents)
Press	**Return** (*accept the defaults*)

Now that we have marked each headline and defined the format, we are ready to generate the table of contents and save it to a file.

Press	**Alt+F5** (Mark Text)
Press	**6** (Generate)
Press	**5** (Generate Tables, Indexes, Autoreferences, etc.)
Type	Y (*we do not have any other tables generated*)

WordPerfect searches the entire master document looking for text that has been marked for inclusion in the table of contents. When WordPerfect completes this task, the table of contents is written to the point in the document where we defined the table. Now we need to block the table of contents and write the block to a file.

Press	**Alt+F4** (Block)
Highlight	*the table of contents text*
Press	**F10** (Save)
Type	TOC.WP5
Press	**Return**

We no longer need the table of contents or master document that we used to create it, so let's get rid of them.

Press	**Alt+F4** (Block)
Highlight	*the table of contents text*
Press	**Ctrl+F4** (Move)
Press	**1** (Block)
Press	**3** (Delete)
Press	**Backspace** (*deletes the hard page code*)

To load the table of contents file into the frame provided on page 1 of the newsletter, position the cursor immediately before the code that creates the table of contents frame in column 1 (use the Reveal Codes function to do this).

Press	**Alt+F9** (Graphics)
Press	**4** (User-defined Box)
Press	**2** (Edit)
Press	**Return** (*the default is the correct frame number*)

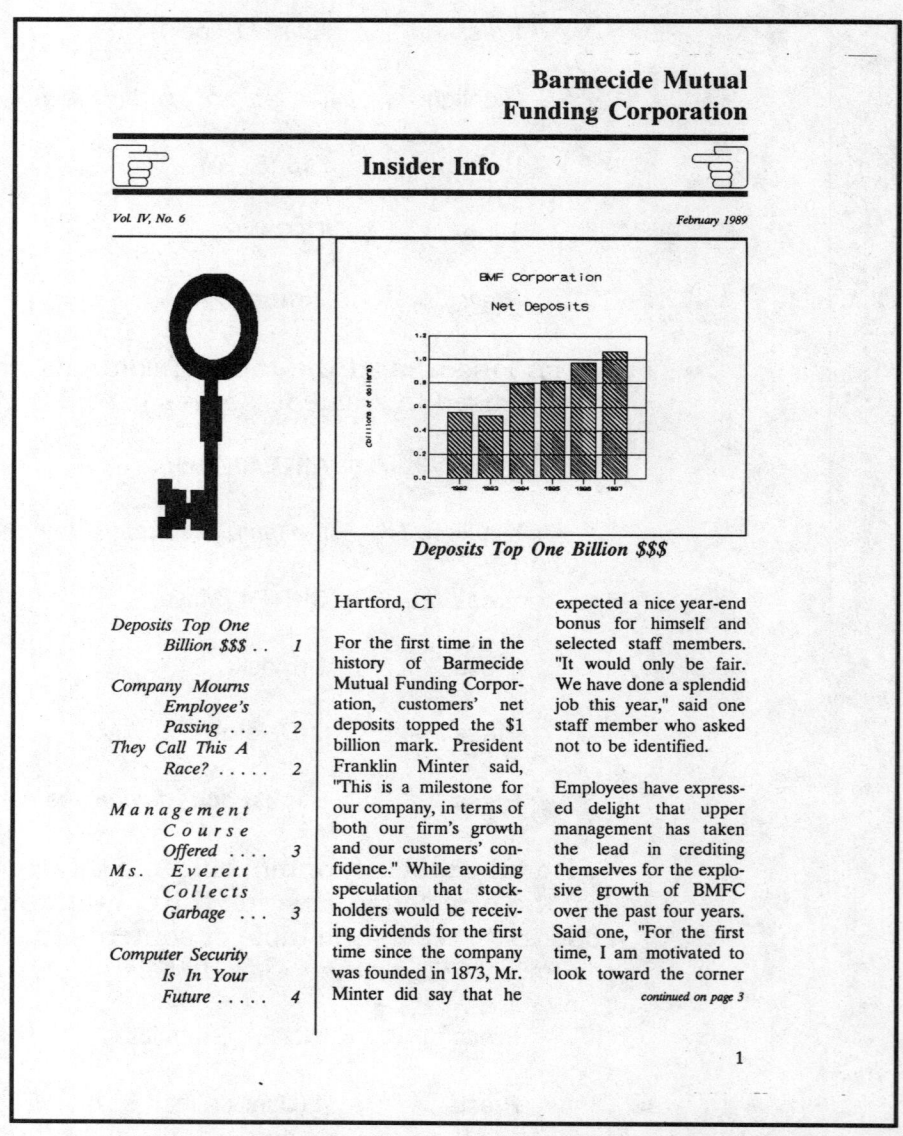

Figure 5-17. Page 1 of the newsletter with the table of contents in place.

We will use the Edit function to place the text of the table of contents in the frame.

Press	**8** (Edit)
Press	**Shift+F10** (Retrieve)
Type	TOC.WP5
Press	**Return**

The table of contents appears in the frame and may be spaced as necessary to occupy the entire frame. Additional text may also be added if required to fill the frame completely. Press **F7** (Exit) twice to return to the document editing screen. If page 1 of your newsletter looks like Figure 5-17, congratulations are in order. Save the page under the file name NEWSLTR.PG1. We now have a completed newsletter ready to go to print. However, what are our options for the final output of the document? Chapter 6 explores all the possibilities.

6 | Start the Presses!

Putting It On Paper

All that we have discussed has brought us to this point—putting those pearls of wisdom on paper so that others might share in our enlightenment. The quality of your output is totally dependent on the type of device that you select for printing, be it a dot matrix printer or a high resolution typesetter. The intent and the intended audience of your document will determine which output device is appropriate for your job. A bit of background, however, on each type of printer, the technology each uses, and the quality of the output you can expect from each may help you determine exactly what your printer requirements are. And you will be in a better position to understand how the printers for the systems described in Chapter 7 were chosen. So before we jump into printing our sample newsletter, let's look at all of the printer choices available.

Saving the Best for Last

For the most part, you probably won't require the typesetter on a daily basis. The steps required to put a document together are fairly constant. All of these tasks but the final typesetting accounts for approximately 90 percent of the time required to conceive, lay out, write, compose, check, correct, and print a document. Most of the printing tasks required for publishing a document, therefore, will fall to less expensive, faster, and smaller devices. Aside from the high expense, slowness, and size of typesetters, which should eliminate even laser typesetters from consideration as every day printers, photographic typesetters can by no stretch of the imagination be considered for use in an office environment. A photographic typesetter produces an output that must be developed just like any roll of film. This involves a reaction between paper and chemicals that has all the attendant ventilation and controlled environment restrictions that any developer process entails.

Raster Printers

You have probably grown tired of hearing the old raster (bit-mapped) versus vector discussion, but you also probably knew that when we got to talking about printers, you would have to endure it one more time. As it happens, the vast majority of printers available today have one thing in common with most monitors, fonts, and graphic images. They produce their output by arranging a series of dots on the paper to form text and pictures. The technologies differ widely on exactly how the ink got to the paper, but the principle remains the same.

Dot Matrix Printers
The workhorse of computer printing is the dot matrix printer. Dot matrix printers operate exactly as the name implies. The dot matrix printer uses a pattern of dots in a matrix to form characters and graphics. The dots are formed by a series of pins mounted in a "print head." The print head sets up electromagnetic fields around each pin. As the print command is received, the field is changed to either repel or attract each pin in the print head. Repelled pins are pushed outward against the

printer's ribbon while attracted pins are retracted into the print head. The fields are rapidly changed to the required polarity to create the necessary patterns as the print head moves across the paper. Any printing method that requires the physical impact of a part against a ribbon to transfer the ink to the paper is known as "impact printing." Dot matrix printers vary widely by price, determined by the number of features the printer has and the size of paper that can be used by the printer. Most dot matrix printers can usually print characters in several different sizes and densities. Density refers to the number of dots required to make a character and directly affects the speed of the printer. User-selectable density range from draft to near-letter-quality (NLQ). The higher the density of the printing, the slower the printing will be.

In addition to character sizes, the dot matrix printers can also print different character attributes from bold and italic to underlined and double width. These print attributes can be selected either from within the applications software or directly at the printer. Some dot matrix printers also provide the capability of printing in color by using a multicolor printer ribbon.

As stated earlier, dot matrix printers really gained their widespread acceptance by their ability to print high-resolution bit-mapped graphic images. Adding to this popularity was their relatively low price and, depending on the print mode selected, fast printing speeds. Printers that fall under this type include the ever-popular Epson series of dot matrix printers of which the LQ-2550™ is the newest 24-pin edition (Figure 6-1). Most of the other manufacturers that produce printers employing the dot matrix technology have adopted the Epson command set and made it the industry standard for dot matrix printers.

Ink Jet Printers

Another, newer technology has taken the dot matrix printer a step further. The ink jet printer still has a print head, but there

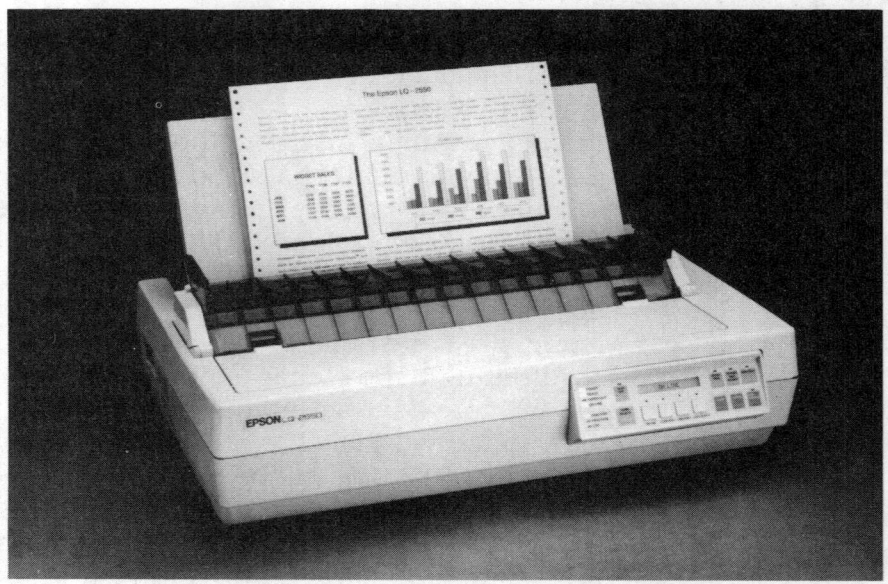

Figure 6-1. The Epson series of printers has defined the industry standard for dot matrix technology.

is no ribbon. Instead, the print head directs the ink in short bursts onto the paper to form the characters and graphics. Two ink jet technologies exist, the "bubble-jet" and the "drop-on-demand." The bubble-jet, so named because the Canon BubbleJet® ink jet printer first used the technology, employs small electric heaters to vaporize the ink under pressure. The vaporized, pressurized ink is then forced through the print head and onto the paper. The HP ThinkJet® printer also uses this printing method. Drop-on-demand printing, also called piezoelectric printing, uses an electrical-to-pressure transducer (a piezoelectric crystal) that is exposed to an increase in pressure when a print command is received. The crystal is distorted by an electromotive force, thus increasing the pressure on the ink surrounding the crystal and forcing it through the print head.

Ink-jet printers have become popular because of their ability to print in color and their ease of operation. Because there is no mechanical operation involved in transferring the ink to the paper, these printers are very quiet and have fewer mechanical parts to wear out or break. Black and white ink jet printers are also relatively inexpensive and a good choice for draft printing, while color ink jet printers are more expensive and are best suited to producing color transparencies for business and educational applications where multiple copies of the material are not required.

Thermal Printers
Thermal printers have a rather narrow range of applications that yield themselves to this type of printing technology. For the most part, thermal printers are restricted to use where ease of use and portability are the primary considerations. Portable computers that have built-in printers usually employ the thermal printer technology. Color printing is also available with some thermal printers, but the same limitations on the applications for any color printing applies to thermal technology as well.

Direct thermal printing is the simplest and oldest of the thermal printing techniques. The print head of the thermal printer is heated in such a manner as to cause a chemical change in a special thermal paper to form the text and graphics. This is the only type of printer that does not use some type of ink medium to form the characters on the page and thus requires fewer moving parts and less maintenance.

There is a disadvantage to this simplicity, however. Because of the chemical reaction required by the paper, special thermal paper is required and the print densities of thermal printers is usually lower than with other printing technologies. The thermal paper is not readily available at your local stationary store and must be special ordered. The dots produced by the thermal printing method are also not as well defined as other types of printers because a fine degree of control cannot be maintained over the chemical reaction process. Like paper scorched with a flame, the area where heat is directly applied becomes very dark, but the edges of the area exhibits some "bleeding," or a gradual lightening of the darkened area. And the special thermal paper has a very short life span when compared to other types of printing. Because the chemicals imbedded in the paper are sensitive to heat and light, they will yellow and fade over a few years to the point of being unreadable. For these reasons, direct thermal printers should be avoided for all but the roughest of rough draft printing where no archive of the document is required.

Thermal transfer printing is a much more popular method of thermal printing in PC applications. Thermal transfer printers return to the ink method of creating the desired text or image. The ink on a ribbon or transfer sheet is melted by the heated print head to adhere to the paper. These printers are lightweight and portable like their direct thermal printing counterparts, but they can use ordinary office paper for printing. However, because they employ an ink ribbon or transfer sheet, the maintenance of these printers begins to approach that of other technologies. Here again, color printing is possible if the ribbon or transfer sheet contains several colors of ink. In this case, the ink is deposited on the paper in several layers to produce the desired color. (Remember that WordPerfect supports only text color printing. Graphics will print in dithered black and white even on color printers.)

One other benefit of both types of printers is the reduction in noise created during printing. While noise may not be a consideration of yours when selecting a printer, bear in mind that your coworkers may well appreciate your consideration of the noise produced by your printer. Also, the the effects of computers and printers on the office environment are coming under increasing scrutiny from both government and insurance agencies for health and safety reasons. Your efforts to reduce the "noise pollution" created by your printer will benefit the entire workplace.

Laser Printers
As stated in Chapter 1, the development of the laser printer was instrumental in bringing the dream of true desktop publishing to fruition. Laser printers provide the best resolution and print quality of the output devices discussed thus far as well as providing this capability at very reasonable prices. There are two different types of laser printers from which to choose: those that print characters as a bit-mapped image (such as the Hewlett-Packard LaserJet series of printers) and printers that print characters based on mathematical expressions (vectors) of a character's appearance (the Apple LaserWriter exemplifies this type of printer). We will discuss the bit-mapped character type of printer here and reserve the vector-based laser printers for discussion later in this chapter.

The laser printer has all the features that desktop publishing demands. High resolution (300 by 300 dots per square inch), relative fast printing, quiet operation, and easy maintenance. These printers are at their best in printing multiple originals of a document, thereby eliminating much of the photocopying that must be done in any publishing environment. Once a page of text and graphics is contained in the printer's memory, the printing times for these copies decreases dramatically over the first original. A laser printer may take as much as 5 minutes to compose and print the original, but subsequent copies of that page are printed at a typical rate of eight pages per minute.

The time required to print that first original page is a function of the page description language (PDL) used by the printer. A printer control language (PCL) describes the appearance and controls the creation of the final page. There are currently three PDLs that are competing to become the standard for laser printers and photo-typesetters: Adobe's PostScript®, Xerox's Interpress®, and Imagen's Document Description Language®

(DDL). DDL is a document-oriented PDL, meaning that the entire docuemnt is treated as a whole contiguous unit.

On the other hand, PostScript and Interpress are page-oriented PDLs that view each page of the document as an individual entity. PostScript is rapidly surpassing the other two as the PDL of choice. Traditionally, the battle lines between Apple and Hewlett-Packard in the laser printer battlefield have been drawn around the implementation of PDLs. Apple's line of laser printers employs the PostScript PDL while the Hewlett-Packard line incorporates the DDL language. The battle appears to be coming to an end, however, because Hewlett-Packard has announced that it intends to provide PostScript support in its printers and approves the modification of current LaserJets with the PS Jet kit from The Laser Connection that provides the Adobe PostScript language.

The laser printer was born of the office photocopier. Both machines use a light source to transfer an image onto a photoconductive print drum. Rather than using reflective light to create a negative image from the original being copied, however, laser printers create a positive electrical image on the printer drum based on the information received from the computer. The toner is attracted to the positively charged organic-photoconductor belt in the laser printer as opposed to the copier in which the toner is attracted to the negative areas. As the laser printer's drum rotates, paper is pulled between the drum and an extremely fine wire called the "corona." The corona transfers the toner-created image from the drum to the paper, which is then fused permanently to the paper using either heat or pressure rollers.

The heart of all laser printers is the printer "engine." The most common print engine in use today is the Canon CX™ that originally was seen in the Canon Personal Copier series of office photocopiers. The Hewlett-Packard line of laser printers uses this engine, as do a large majority of the most popular laser printers. The engine of the Canon-based laser printer is a single cartridge that consists of the printing mechanism, belt, and toner.

Another, more recent print engine has been developed by Ricoh. Called the LP4120®, the Ricoh print engine does not contain the toner. With the Canon print engine, when you run out of toner, you must replace the entire print engine, including all of the optical components contained in it whether they needed to be changed or not. The Ricoh print engine, conversely, requires only the replacement of the toner without necessitating replacement of any other part of the system. The argument could be made, therefore, that the Ricoh-based printers are less expensive to maintain.

All laser printers can produce text at a resolution of 300 dots per inch. Each manufacturer chooses a combination of memory, processor, and a page description language or set of printer commands to best balance cost versus output quality. Depending on which way a particular manufacturer's scales tilt, the output of their printer will be dependent on the balance of these components and how well they handle the arrangement of dot patterns that are required to make the character or image.

Aside from the overall quality of the printed page, a laser printer's memory is a driving force on the printer's complete functionality. The printer memory is functionally equivalent to PC memory. Thus, the printer memory is divided into two types: random access memory (RAM) and read-only memory (ROM). The ROM in a printer contains the page description language and any built-in fonts that the printer provides. The printer's RAM is used for composing the page before it is printed and for holding any soft fonts that have been downloaded. A laser printer equipped with 512 kilobytes of RAM can only print one-fourth of a page of graphics at 300 dots per inch. As the image becomes larger, the resolution decreases so that a one-half page image is printed at 150 dots per inch and a full page image is printed at 75 dots per inch. Most laser printers are also capable of accepting downloaded soft fonts to increase the printer's flexibility. However, soft fonts decrease the amount of memory that is available for printing graphics.

Most laser printers may have their memory capacities expanded with add-on boards in much the same way that a PC's memory can be increased. With memory increases that bring a printer's total memory to 2 megabytes or more, full-page graphics and a wide variety of soft fonts may be used to create the finished document.

Bit-mapped laser printers can only print with bit-mapped fonts. Therefore, the quality of the printed page is also determined in large part by the quality of the bit-mapped font that you are printing with. The quality of these fonts varies from manufacturer to manufacturer, so it's best to see a sample printout of a particular font before investing in the package.

Typesetters

Typesetters that interface directly with computers are called photo-typesetters or laser typesetters. Photo-typesetters operate in much the same way as standard photographic developers. The image to be printed is transferred to photosensitive material usually by high-intensity light from a xenon flash lamp or a laser. The material used may be film, photographic paper, or offset plate. The resulting output of the image is of very high resolution (greater than 900 by 900 dots per inch in most cases) and produced at very high speeds of from 50 lines per minute to over 1000 lines per minute.

Photo-typesetters are very expensive devices that require a skilled operator and a wide range of supplies. Most of these machines also require special environmental and space considerations when they are being installed. Photo-typesetters are best suited for the production of final camera-ready copy. Their sheer cost, size, and complexity will probably eliminate them from any consideration of the day-to-day printing tasks you will require.

The Mathematics of Print—Vector Printers

Vector printers are identical to their bit-mapped counterparts in that the image is placed on the paper as patterns of dots. However, there is a very important difference in how the vector printer determines what those dot patterns should be. This difference amounts to how the printer is able to manipulate fonts. Some laser printers and typesetters can change the appearance of outline fonts directly within the device. They provide a page description language that allows outline fonts to be manipulated based on the font's mathematical representation of a character. Thus a character in an outline font can be sized, rotated, and otherwise changed internally by the printer.

As stated earlier in this chapter, the most popular page description language is PostScript from Adobe. When the Apple LaserWriter was introduced in 1985, the PostScript page description language was hailed as revolutionary. And it still is today. PostScript is being adopted by most laser printer manufacturers because of the performance/price advantages of this PDL and is, therefore, becoming the industry standard for this type of printer. And as with everything else in the computer business, several companies are busy developing clones of the PostScript PDL.

PostScript laser printers are usually better equipped to handle the tasks of desktop publishing than other types of printers. These printers come from the factory with enough RAM to print a full page of graphics at 300 dots per inch and ROM that contains 30 or more typefaces. Because PostScript uses outline typefaces stored in ROM, these typefaces can further be manipulated to obtain an almost endless number of fonts based on the ROM-resident typefaces. Soft fonts can also be downloaded to PostScript printers to further increase their capabilities.

PostScript also provides any easy path from the desktop laser printer to high resolution typesetters equipped with this page description language. For instance, you might compose a document in WordPerfect and print a proof copy of a non-PostScript laser printer. When you are ready to make camera-ready originals of the document, you would print the file again, but this time to a disk file using a PostScript printer definition. Both the Allied Linotype 100® (Figure 6-2) and Linotype 300® typesetters can then accept this file and provide true typeset masters without the need for translation programs or any changes being made to the file.

WordPerfect and Printers

WordPerfect provides printer drivers for literally hundreds of printers. In fact, some PC industry observers would tell you that WordPerfect became the market-dominating word processor based for the most part on its extensive printer capabilities. These drivers contain the command set used by each printer, be it a dot matrix, ink jet, laser, or just about any printer manufactured today. The selection process of which printer to use, then, is left to your requirements rather than what is supported.

What Do You Need?

The printer selection process may have already been made for you. You probably have some type of printer that you are currently using for printing documents. If you don't have a printer that takes full advantage of WordPerfect's powerful publishing capabilities, however, it probably won't be long before you yearn

Figure 6-2. The Allied Linotype 100 offers an Adobe PostScript interface for direct printing of WordPerfect documents.

for a printer that is up to the task. But before you leap, let's take a good look at the realities of printer selection. You will probably not make any points with the boss if you purchase a $30,000 Allied Linotype 100 typesetter for printing office correspondence, nor will you endear yourself if you go to a shareholders' meeting with the annual report printed on a $300 dot matrix printer.

The Right Printer for the Job

The production of most professional documents will involve three printing processes: the draft copy, the proof copy, and the final or camera-ready copy. Depending on the intent and the intended audience of your document, these processes may be combined or expanded to meet the requirements of that document. For instances, if you are preparing a flier advertising the company picnic, chances are the printing of both the proof copy and the final copy will be combined into one processes (the proof copy and the final copy are one in the same). On the other hand, if you are preparing that annual report, you may require several draft copies, a proof copy, a proof copy printed with camera-ready quality (a true WYSIWYG copy for highest management approval), and the final camera-ready copy.

If most of your work involves documents that are to be read by your peers or immediate supervisors, then dot matrix printers will probably suffice. For documents that are distributed throughout the company, a laser printer may be called for. And documents that will be placed in the hands of your customers should receive the top-rate treatment of a professional typesetter. Here again, the exact situation that you find yourself in will determine the exact type of printer you will require.

Most often, a mix of all of these printing technologies will be required. One interesting fact of the publication business is that as the quality of the print increases, the number of copies of the document that you will have to print decreases. To illustrate this, consider our example newsletter. If it were not for using the View Document function extensively during the composition process, we would have had to print the document several times to determine that we were laying out the elements of each page correctly. Depending on the resolution of your monitor and how close different elements are to each other on the page, you may still need to print these draft copies in addition to using the View Document function. This proof-and-correct method may require 10 printings of the same page.

After you have completed the page layout and are satisfied with the results printed by the draft printer, you will probably need to print a proof of the newsletter that closely approximates what the newsletter will look like when it comes back from the typesetter. This proof copy will go to your boss for approval. If you have done an absolutely perfect job, your boss may only find a few changes that need to be made. You make the requested changes, reprint the newsletter, and send it back to your boss for approval. If all goes well, you will get the approval and only two proof copies will have been required (this number is likely to be higher, however). You are now ready to send the newsletter to the typesetter for camera-ready copy. Hopefully, you will only need to do this once. This increasing

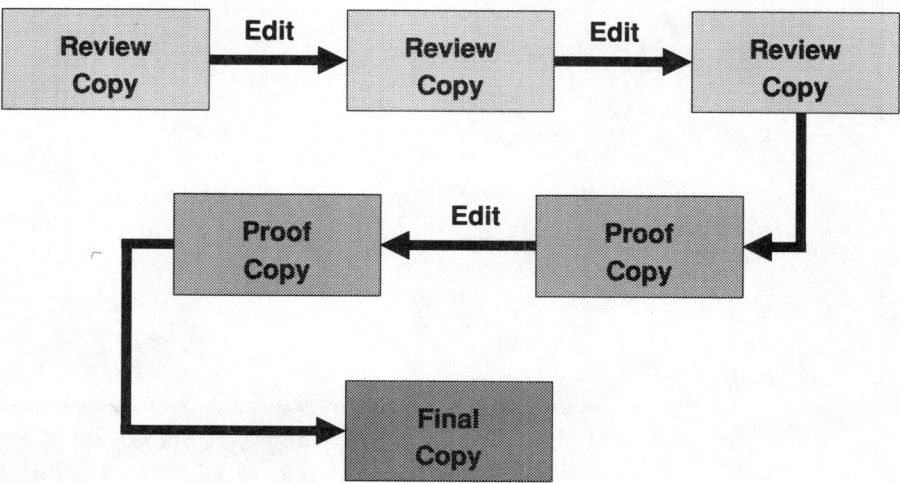

Figure 6-3. As the quality of the print increases, the number of copies required decreases.

quality/decreasing number of copies concept is illustrated in Figure 6-3.

In a large publication work group, each person may have an individual dot matrix printer for printing their own quick rough drafts. The group may also share a lesser number of laser printers for producing the proof copies. And finally, your company may choose to either purchase a typesetter or enlist the services of an outside print shop for production of camera-ready copy. This allocation of printer resources might look like Figure 6-4.

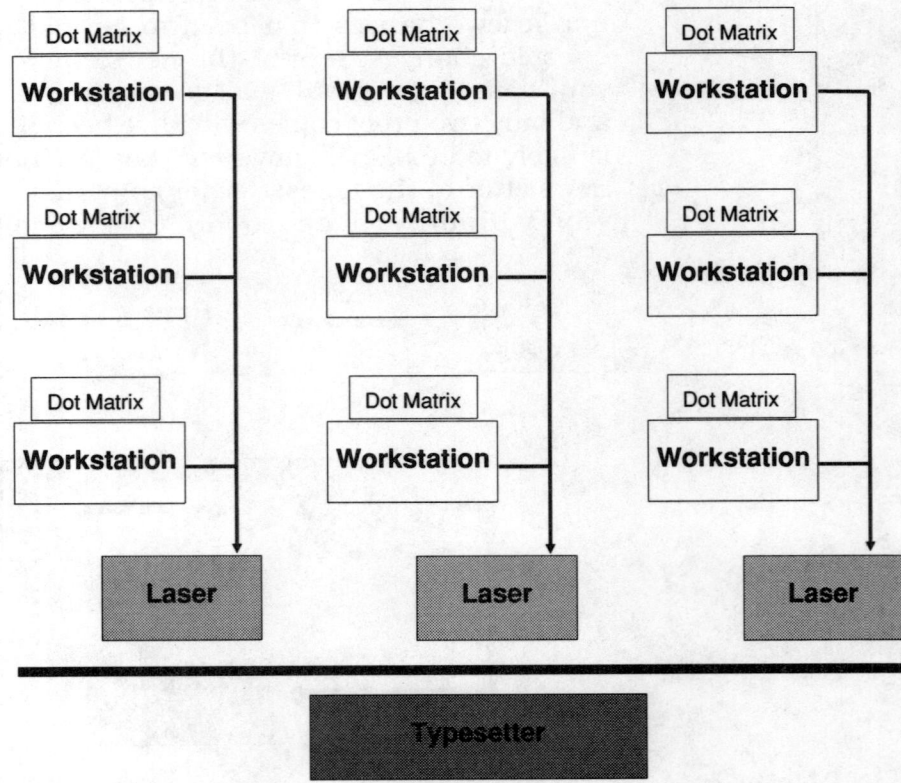

Figure 6-4. The distribution of printer types within a publication work group.

Cheating on Resolution

Perhaps you or your company does not have the funds to either buy a high resolution typesetter or hire an outside agency to provide the typeset copy. There is one other method that you may be able to use to create the appearance of high-resolution text and graphics. You can attain the appearance of an output resolution higher than that of your dot matrix or laser printer by using an office copier capable of producing reductions to reduce your masters to their final size.

Of course, this assumes that your final copy will have an overall measurement of something less than the standard 8 1/2-inch by 11-inch page or that you have the ability to print on pages larger than your final document size. This is not truly a high resolution output because the devices that provide camera-ready copy put more information (more dots) on the final page. The amount of information on the reduced page is not increased, the information is merely reduced to a smaller size. With some practice and experience for the types of text and graphics this technique works best on, you can produce a document that has an appearance close to that of true typeset output.

Printing the Newsletter

The time has come to print the newsletter that we have created. For this example, we will be using the Hewlett-Packard LaserJet Series II laser printer for the job, but the techniques are the same for whatever printer you choose to use. Notice, however, that the word "printer" was used. If you intend to use a typesetter (the machine and the human) for printing the document, you will have to use a typesetter that accepts PostScript files such as the Allied Linotype machines. We will cover this procedure later in the chapter.

First Things First

There is an old adage in the computer business that goes something like "If it doesn't work, make sure it's plugged in." At first glance, this would seem to be an obvious statement not worth repeating, but many man-hours of troubleshooting some mysterious computer problem have been expended only to find that a cable was not properly plugged in. So before you jump into printing the newsletter, let's double-check all of the hardware by answering the following questions.

Is the printer cable properly connected?

Is the printer plugged in?

Is the printer turned on?

When checking the printer's cable, remember to refer back to how you told WordPerfect that the printer is connected. It does little good to set up WordPerfect to use the COM1 serial port if, in reality, the printer is connected to the LPT1 parallel port. This is one of the most common errors made when connecting the printer to the computer.

Once you are satisfied that all is well, check the printer connection by typing a couple of lines in a blank WordPerfect document and then printing the document. If it prints correctly, we are ready to move on. If not, go back and recheck the prior items and make any changes necessary.

Initializing the Printer

The basic appearance attribute of any document is the font being used. Previously we created the six fonts that will be used in our newsletter and selected the Newsletter printer definition we created as the printer to use, so all we have to do now is download them to the printer and thus make them available for use.

| Press | **Shift+F7** (Print) |
| Press | **7** (Initialize Printer) |

Any soft fonts marked in the printer resource file as available when print job begins (indicated by an asterisk in the left margin of the fonts list) will be downloaded to the printer.

Note that if, at some latter time, we change the type of job we are working on and change to another printer that we created for that type of job, the fonts for our newsletter will be removed from the printer's memory and replaced with the new fonts when thew new printer is initialized. Otherwise, the newsletter fonts will remain in the printer's memory until the printer is turned off.

We can observe the progress of the font downloading by returning to the print option.

| Press | **Shift+F7** (Print) |
| Press | **4** (Control Printer) |

As each font is downloaded, it is displayed in the Status area of the Control Printer screen as shown in Figure 6-5. If the wrong path for the location of the font files has been set in WordPerfect, you will receive an error message. If this happens, cancel the print job and edit the printer definition to include the correct path name.

Each font in the font listed is downloaded in order to the printer. When downloading is complete, the Status area will display the No print jobs message. We are now ready to start the task of printing each page of the newsletter.

```
Print: Control Printer

Current Job

Job Number:  1                              Page Number:  None
Status:      Initializing                   Current Copy: None
Message:     Downloading AI0100AH.HPF
Paper:       None
Location:    None
Action:      None


Job List

Job  Document            Destination         Print Options
 1   (Initialize)        LPT 1



Additional Jobs Not Shown: 0


1 Cancel Job(s); 2 Rush Job; 3 Display Jobs; 4 Go (start printer); 5 Stop: 0
```

Figure 6-5. The Control Printer *screen during font downloading.*

Sending the Newsletter to the Printer

The only thing left to do is to send the newsletter to the printer. This is a straightforward process, but don't be impatient while the printer is composing the newsletter. It will probably take several minutes. The only decision to make on your part is whether you want to print the file from disk or recall the newsletter into WordPerfect and print it from there. Either method can be used so long as you did not set up WordPerfect to perform the Fast Save operation when you saved the newsletter. WordPerfect performs a fast save by saving the file directly to disk without formatting it. These files cannot be printed from disk and must be recalled into WordPerfect prior to printing. We will assume that the Fast Save option (WordPerfect's default) is OFF and thus, we will print the file from disk. If fast save had been on, you would need to recall each page into WordPerfect and either print from the screen or resave the page with the Fast Save option turned off.

Press	**Shift+F7** (Print)
Press	**3** (Document on Disk)
Type	NEWSLTR.PG1

WordPerfect will ask which pages of the newsletter to print, with All being used as the default. Because each page of the newsletter was saved to a separate file, you can simply press **Return** to accept the (All) default. Conversely, if you wanted to print pages 20 through the end of a document, you would enter 20. WordPerfect will accept just about any such form of entering page numbers.

| Press | **Return** (*accept the default*) |

After a few minutes, the first page of the newsletter begins to print. When printing is complete, the page should should look like Figure 5-7 in the previous chapter. You can continue with this process until all four pages of the newsletter have been printed.

Printing to a Typesetter

As mentioned earlier, WordPerfect will output files that are compatible with the Allied Linotype line of typesetters or any other typesetter that can read PostScript files. To prepare the newsletter for sending to a typesetter, select one of the PostScript printers as the current printer and print the file to disk.

| Press | **Shift+F7** (Print) |
| Press | **S** (Select) |

The printer definitions for all the supported PostScript printers are on the Printer2 disk in a file named WPRINT2.ALL. Insert this disk in the A: drive and then proceed.

    Press   **2** (Additional Printers)

    Press   **2** (Other Disk)

For this example, we will select the Apple Laserwriter Plus. If we were actually printing to a specific PostScript laser printer, we would want to select the printer that we had. However, because we are printing to disk, we can select any PostScript printer and the file will be printed correctly. WordPerfect asks where to find the additional printer definition files.

    Type   A:

    Highlight   Apple Laserwriter Plus

    Press   **Return** (*twice*)

The printer definition for the Apple Laserwriter Plus™ is read from the disk and a printer resource file named APLASPLU.PRS is created in the WP50 directory. When the font update process is complete, press **F7** (Exit). Now select the font that you will be using. This font must also be supported by the typesetter that will be printing the file.

You should check with your typesetter operator in order to agree on the font to be used and any other considerations required of the file. We must now tell WordPerfect that the file will be printed to disk. Be sure that the Select Printer: Edit menu is displayed.

    Press   **2** (Port)

    Press   **8** (Other)

Type	NEWSLTR1.TYP
Press	**Return**

Exit from the Select Printer: Edit menu and select the Apple Laserwriter printer as the current printer. Now print the first page of the newsletter as you would to any other printer. The file NEWSLTR1.TYP is created by WordPerfect and the page is printed to the file with all the PostScript commands embedded. This file may now be taken to the typesetter for production of camera-ready copy.

7 | The Complete System

Laying Out the Basics

When describing the complete desktop publishing system, there are things that can be discussed as absolute facts and others that will be dependent not only on your particular circumstances, but on the highly subjective nature of any art form. And desktop publishing is certainly an art form as much as any other art media. The absolute facts will usually confine themselves to the hardware selection process. For instance, if an application program requires 384 kilobytes of RAM to load and execute, there is nothing that can be done to escape the fact that your system will require at least that much RAM.

On the other hand, selecting the right paint program, computer-aided drafting (CAD) application, and even the document processor itself, is a very subjective process. The final decision of which package to purchase is often based on the relative "value" of one package over another. You may not require all of the power that the most expensive CAD program offers. And the most expensive CAD program on the market may not offer a function that you can not live without that a more modestly priced CAD program can readily accomplish. So before you open your checkbook, have a firm idea of your requirements.

With this in mind, let's look at three systems: a starter system, an intermediate system, and a power-user system. Each is designed around WordPerfect 5.0 and tuned to provide the most capabilities from that software within the limits of cost and desktop publishing expertise. The pieces that make up each system have been selected to best balance cost versus functionality, sometimes the only gauge of an application's value. Each component has also been selected with an eye toward practicality. It would be quite simple to recommend that you purchase a $30,000 typesetter for the best possible output from WordPerfect, but it wouldn't be very practical since a single piece of equipment in this price range is beyond the budgets of most users.

Buy or Upgrade?

When making any purchase decisions about hardware, you will be faced with the question of whether it is better to upgrade your existing hardware or purchase new equipment. This is especially true of the computer itself. Of course, if you don't own any hardware to begin with, your choice is a simple one—buy the hardware. If you already own some equipment, you should be able to cull enough from this chapter to make some sound upgrade decisions if you choose to do so. In either case, the result will be the same—higher performance and increased productivity.

Aces and Spaces

Aces and spaces is a term used in the card game of Bridge that describes a hand that contains the four highest-valued cards in the deck (the Aces) and no other cards of significant value. This analogy might be applied to trying to put together a desktop publishing system built upon a DOS-based personal computer. In some areas of functionality, the PC has clear-cut advantages for performing the functions of desktop publishing. It is easily expandable to accommodate the peripheral equipment required for the task. It is also quite powerful when performing the mathematical calculations that are encountered during a typical desktop publishing session.

However, and this is a big however, the PC was not designed to perform the types of tasks required by desktop publishing software. The system's memory is limited to 640 kilobytes of memory, hard disk storage space is limited to 32 megabytes in a single drive, the original IBM PC and PC/XT have a relative slow 4.77 megahertz clock speed, and the monitor/video adapter board combinations (henceforth called the display group) available ranged in resolution from 320 pixels by 200 lines to 640 pixels by 350 lines. These resolutions are most often referred to simply by their numbers such as 320X200 and 640X350 and none of them provide the display resolution necessary to perform desktop publishing effectively.

Ironically, these shortcomings should probably be credited, along with the PC's open architecture, with prompting the huge success of the PC. The limitations that these hardware and DOS barriers created opened a large and inviting doorway for thousands of third-party vendors selling hardware and software add-on products designed to expand the PC's capabilities. Some products were very good, even exceptional, feats of engineering ingenuity. Others were horrible and embarrassing failures. But taken as a whole, all of these products do just one thing—try to make the PC do a lot of things that it was never designed to do.

So where does that leave us? Actually, we are much better off now than one might believe. The newest generation of PCs breaks down many of the barriers that blocked the path between PCs and desktop publishing. New software, designed to make the most of this hardware's capabilities, is beginning to appear at cost that is within reach of the average user. And the new PCs have also retained their open architecture design, meaning that those same third-party vendors can now concentrate on providing products that truly make desktop publishing with a PC a viable, and in some cases preferred, alternative to the Apple Macintosh.

What all of this boils down to is—don't be surprised if you can't just buy a IBM PC or IBM PS/2 personal computer, WordPerfect 5.0, and a laser printer and start desktop publishing. The road to that delicate balance of hardware and software that will meet your needs now, yet be expandable as your requirements grow and change, will be a long one with lots of twists and turns and more than a few dead ends. Hopefully, this chapter will act as a combination road map, tour guide, and advisor as we seek that perfect system.

The Big Three

When we discuss any hardware recommendations, there are three categories in which more means better: speed, storage, and resolution. These are the first things that must be considered when putting together a competent desktop publishing system in any of the three categories we will discuss. Even the most meager system can be made to perform within the bounds of acceptability with the proper upgrades and expansions in the right places. Let's take a look at the big three and lay down some basic rules of thumb about each.

Speed

It's absolutely true, speed is addictive. Speed may refer to something as basic as the computing speed of the computer or as esoteric as the data transfer rate to and from the computer's memory. Whatever the topic, faster speeds mean you can get from point A to point B faster and thus be more productive. And once you have sat behind the wheel of a personal computer zipping along at a 20, 16, or even a 12 megahertz (Mhz) clock speed, you will never want to return to the leisurely pace of 4.77 Mhz computers. Aside from being an immediate boost to your productivity, they are a lot of fun. Because speed is the core of a computer's performance and encompasses every aspect of our system, we will cover it in more detail than either storage or resolution. The later two are also more restricted in what we can do with them, so their coverage will be briefer.

The clock speed of a personal computer is, in the most basic of concepts, the speed at which your computer can perform calculations. In WordPerfect, these calculations range from simply recalculating a line length when you change font sizes to composing and displaying a graphic representation of two entire pages when the View Document command is evoked. Needless to say, the faster the computer, the faster these operations can be performed. And, in the case of the View Document function, the faster you can see the parts of your document that are incorrect, the faster you can correct the errors and move on.

Of course, computers are never that straightforward, and so it is with speed. There are other factors that will determine the overall speed at which your computer can perform. A computer running at 12 Mhz, for instance, can perform a certain number of instructions in a given time period (12 Mhz equates to 12 million processor cycles per second, but it may take several cycles to perform an instruction). However, PCs based on the Intel 80x86 family of microprocessors have the capability of off-loading much of their mathematical computations onto a special chip, the math coprocessor, if there is one in the system.

Additionally, computers can only operate on data as fast as they are able to read data into memory for processing from a source and write data from memory to a source for storage. Therefore, the input/output (I/O) speed of a computer will also determine how fast a task can be performed. This data I/O encompasses everything from reading your data from a file on disk or accepting data from a scanner, to writing the data on the computer screen or back to the hard disk. The computer's I/O speed is the most critical area for perfomance and also the most overlooked.

Speed Reading
The first part of data I/O, reading the data from the disk, is affected not only by the speed of the computer, but by the hardware that is used to perform the task. A hard disk, for instance, will be rated by its access time measured in milliseconds. Even though differences in hard disk access times measured in milliseconds may sound insignificant, the sum of these milliseconds required to read hundreds of bits of data at different locations on the disk can be quite significant indeed. So the faster the access time of a given hard disk, the better performance you will see from your system.

The data on your hard disk also needs a pathway into your computer's RAM, and that pathway may prove to be another bottleneck in your system's performance. The hard disk controller board provides the necessary interface to your computer and determines how fast data is transferred from the disk to your computer. Thus hard disk controller boards can be rated by their data transfer rates. The balance between the disk controller's transfer rate and the disk's access time will determine what level of performance you get in reading data from your hard disk.

Obviously it would do little good to have the world's fastest controller board controlling the world's slowest hard disk. The controller board would be sitting idle for most of its time waiting for the disk to catch up. In most cases, the manufacturer of the hard disk will match the disk to a controller board that offers the best balance between the disk's access speed and the controller's data transfer speed. However, if you need to tweak the performance of your system, the hard disk/disk controller combination would be a good place to begin your exploration.

Speed Writing

The speed at which your computer writes data to various output devices also determines the level of performance that you will see from your computer. Writing data to your hard disk is affected by the same factors as reading the data, so the same observations can be made. But the computer also writes data to two other places: the screen and the printer.

Screen writing is controlled by the video adapter board that you have in your computer. The faster a video adapter board can write data to the screen, the faster your computer will appear to function. It is not uncommon to put two computers side by side, one running at 10 Mhz and the other running at 12 Mhz and observe that the slower machine appears to be running faster. This can be caused by a number of factors, some of which we have already discussed. However, more times than not, this phenomena is due to the faster computer having a slower video adapter board. Most video adapter boards will perform satisfactorily, but if you have a performance problem that you can't seem to locate, the video adapter board may be the culprit.

The speed at which your computer can send data to your printer is probably the single biggest performance bottleneck in the entire system. The printer is not directly connected to the computer's data bus, as are most other components in the system. Instead, the data must be sent from the computer to the printer through a cable connecting the two. The speed at which data can be transferred to the printer is directly related to the type of interface chosen—serial or parallel.

A serial interface is referred to as an RS-232-C or RS-422 interface. Serial interfaces send and receive data through a single

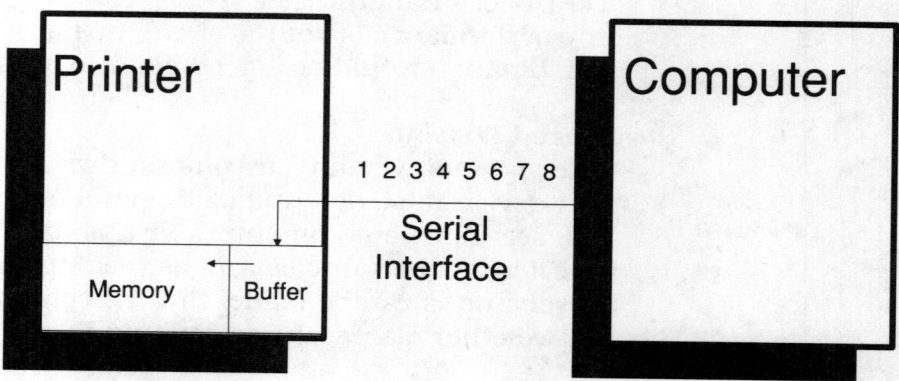

Figure 7-1. A serial interface may be required in some cases, however, it does not provide the fastest data transfers possible.

line, one bit of data behind the next, much like a long line of soldiers marching in single column. As each bit is received by the printer, the printer assigns it a place in memory, transfers the bit to the appropriate place, and then tells the computer it is ready for the next bit. In reality, this process is sped along by buffering the data. Buffering refers to the practice of placing a lot of data in a temporary "holding area" (the buffer) until the buffer is full. All the data in the buffer is then transferred to the proper place in the printer's memory and the computer requests another stream of data until the buffer is once again full. This process continues until all of the data has been sent. The serial interface data flow is illustrated in Figure 7-1.

The other type of interface used is the parallel interface, so-called because data is sent to the printer in parallel streams. The most common parallel interface, the Centronics, sends eight lines of data to the printer at one time as shown in Figure 7-2. It is apparent that the rate at which data is transferred to

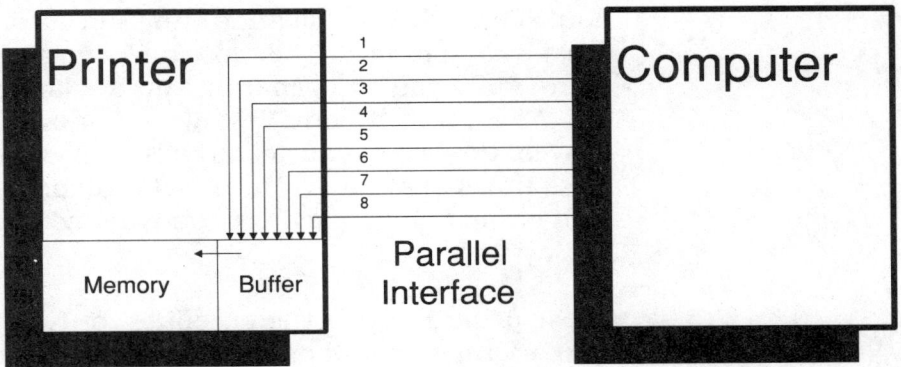

Figure 7-2. The parallel interface is preferred for fastest data transfers when the distance between devices will allow.

the printer is greatly increased when a parallel interface is used. There is a negative side to implementing a parallel interface, however. The distance between the computer and the printer must be kept to a relatively short distance (usually less than 10 feet). If you are the sole user of the printer and it is positioned next to the computer, this is not a problem. If, on the other hand, you are but one of a number of users connected to the printer through some sort of switch, you may be forced to use the serial interface port on your printer.

Storage

Storage is divided into two types: primary (RAM) and secondary (disk). The capabilities of both your computer and your printer will be determined by the amount of storage you have in each. The computer uses RAM storage for loading and running Word-Perfect and other applications. There must also be enough memory to load the data file you are working with. Your computer uses disk storage for your WordPerfect program files, soft font files, other application program files, and your data files (text and graphics). The more disk storage space you have, the more fonts you can generate and the larger your data files can be. As an added bonus to owners of large-capacity hard disk drives, the larger your computer's hard disk, the faster its access times and data transfer rate will be. You will thus provide two paths to increased productivity by moving to a larger hard disk.

Most printers, with the exception of typesetters, do not have disk storage, but all printers do have RAM storage. The printer uses RAM for holding downloaded soft fonts and for composing pages prior to printing. Consequently, a printer with more memory can use more data to compose the page.

For instance, a Hewlett-Packard LaserJet Series II printer can only print a one-half page graphic image at its full 300 DPI capability when equipped with the factory-supplied 512 kilobytes of RAM. So increasing the amount of RAM in your printer will enable you to both download more fonts to the printer and print graphics at higher resolutions. You may also see faster printing times because the printer can accept more data before its buffer becomes full and a request for more data is sent to the computer.

Resolution

The term "what-you-see-is-what-you-get" has been in vogue ever since the term desktop publishing was coined. A true WYSIWYG display group will show you, on screen, exactly what the printed page will look like. This is a lofty goal, and certainly one worth pursuing because a screen display that replicates the printed page exactly will save you printing time, wear on the printer, and printer supplies. However, this is a goal that, sadly, can never be realized using the display technology available today. A closer look at these technologies will reveal why.

A true WYSIWYG display group is dependent on two factors: the maximum resolution of the monitor and video adapter board combination, and the application software's ability to take advantage of this display group. Both of these factors will determine how close to the printed page we can get on-screen. There are monitors that offer extremely high resolutions that will display a page with an effective resolution of 100 DPI and WordPerfect 5.0 can display text and graphics on a monitor with this resolution. However, we can't quite get to absolute WYSIWYG from here.

First, the run-of-the-mill laser printer prints at 300 DPI, meaning that our screen shows only a third of the resolution we can expect when we print the page. And second, WordPerfect does not have "screen fonts" for each font that is available in the printer. A screen font is a font that corresponds in appearance to a font in the printer, but it is used to display text on the screen. Because WordPerfect does not use screen fonts, it must closely approximate the specific font's appearance with its own standard set of font appearance attributes.

As discussed in Chapter 1, this does not mean that we will be unable to preview the general appearance of the page before we print it, but it does mean that we can mark off true WYSIWYG display groups from our list of "must haves." WordPerfect can't do it, and neither can any other DOS-based document processor or page composition package.

However, the higher the resolution of our monitor and video adapter board combination (the display group), the closer we can get to doing it on the screen before we do it on the printer. Every page that we avoid printing by using WordPerfect's View Document feature with a high resolution display group increases our productivity.

A Mouse for All Systems

Mice are one of those little things in life that we swore we would never come close to, but now can't live without. It's true that WordPerfect does not support a mouse, but if you plan to do desktop publishing, you will surely have other applications that require one. Recommending the right mouse for you is like arguing about politics—it won't accomplish much. Like politics, there are two prevailing camps: the optical mouse lover and the loyal mechanical mouse fan. Everyone who uses a mouse has a personal preference for which type of mouse is best. Both have their good and bad points. Optical mice have no moving parts but require a special pad that will take desk space that always seems to be needed for something else. Mechanical mice can use any surface, but the moving parts get dirty and worn.

Whichever type of mouse you decide is best for you, you really can't make a bad purchasing decision. Major manufacturers include Microsoft, Mouse Systems, and Logitech. Prices are comparable among the two types (around $100), so pick the one that feels right for you. Then you, too, can have something to argue about passionately with a member of the opposite mouse camp.

Backing Up Those Words

There are two inescapable truths about computers. First, when anything goes wrong, it will go will go wrong at the least opportune time. And second, more work can be lost by a failed hard disk than by any other piece of your system. A lot of grief can thus be avoided by making regular backups of your hard disk onto tape. In case of a catastrophic hard disk failure (and there are seldom any other kind), your backup may be the only insurance that can save your whole business from going down the tubes. So every system, whether for desktop publishing or not, should have a tape backup system.

There are two types of tape backup systems from which to choose. One type makes a "mirror image" of your entire hard disk so that if you are forced to replace your disk, the process of getting your operation back up and running is as simple as copying your tape onto the new disk. This is fine if the whole disk fails and it will save you some time reinstalling your applications software (assuming it isn't copy protected), but what if a data file is accidentally trashed? The other type of backup system copies your hard disk on a file-by-file basis, allowing you to copy only those files that you need back onto the disk, thus saving you a lot of time over the first system.

Each of our systems will use a Tallgrass Technologies external tape backup system. These systems can be purchased in a variety of sizes, depending on the size of your hard disk. And they can be configured to make backups using either the mirror image or file-by-file backup techniques. An interface card that mounts inside for your computer is provided, as is software to manage the backup process.

The Economy System

The first system that we will put together is for those of us that have champagne tastes on a beer budget. By starting at the bottom rung of the ladder, we can increase the effectiveness of each system as we build toward that final "dream machine." This system will be remarkable productive considering the modest goals that we have, while providing all of the functions necessary to produce top-notch documents without sinking the budget boat in the process. More important, this system can be expanded to accommodate our growing requirements until it evolves into the super system described later.

Economy Hardware

The hardware that comprises our economy system is spartan, but it will provide the most capabilities for the dollar. Even this system will provide an excellent pathway for upward expansion, and everything in this system can be used as is or upgraded for use in one of the more complete systems. The idea is to obtain hardware that can grow with your needs without becoming surplus equipment. Regardless of how many times a computer has paid for itself, it's hard to part with a good computer just for the sake of upgrading your technology.

The Economy Computer

Of course, the computer is central to any system that we put together. Without it, we would have a lot of nice looking peripheral equipment and a lot of empty desk space. I won't be making many hardware vendor recommendations for this system because the system uses technology that has had time to mature and thus puts everyone in the market on fairly equal terms for performance. Because economy is the driving factor in this system, we have two choices on how the system is acquired. The first option is for the adventurous at heart. The second choice is a bit safer, but also a bit more expensive.

If you are comfortable with computers and like a challenge, there are some very inexpensive, plain vanilla PC compatibles out in the marketplace. If you are lucky, these computers will have names on them that you never heard of before. If you really like to gamble, the computer won't have any name at all. In either case, before you buy, ask some questions and poke around inside the machine.

Check the motherboard (the main board that everything else plugs into) for a familiar name like Western Digital. Most companies selling these "no name" computers buy the various parts from only three or four established vendors and put the parts together themselves.

Run the machine through its paces a few times. When the computer first boots, check the BIOS (Basic Input/Output System) copyright message. If there isn't one, stay away from the computer altogether. More than likely, though, you will see a copyright message from one of the major BIOS manufacturers such as Phoenix Technologies. These computers are generally worth exploring further. Run some of your software on it (maybe WordPerfect) and perhaps (if you already own a computer) put one of your expansion boards inside it. Look at the overall workmanship of the computer and ask about its warranty. When you feel that you have satisfied yourself that the computer contains parts by reputable manufacturers and is being sold by a reputable dealer, buy it.

Most computers on the low end of the scale run at the standard 4.77 Mhz and come equipped with 256 kilobytes of RAM and a single floppy disk drive. WordPerfect will perform well at this clock speed, but you will need to upgrade the memory to 640 kilobytes of RAM and add a hard disk. The 20 megabyte hard disk is the most plentiful on the market today. The larger 32 megabyte hard disk is becoming the new standard size for hard disks, and the prices for the 20 megabyte drive is falling accordingly. Most 20 megabyte hard disks have acceptable access times (60 to 80 milliseconds) and data transfer rates, so we will add one to our basic system. Thus far we have spent about $400 for the computer and $400 for the storage upgrades.

If you are not the least bit comfortable with computers, there are still some attractive selections at economical prices to be found in the PC clone market. Most of these computers are to be found through mail order firms, and it's difficult to determine from an advertisement in a magazine how reputable the company is. But try this test at a minimum before buying from anyone. Find an ad for the computer that you would like to buy and make a note of the firm's name. Then go to some back issues of that magazine (at least a year past, if possible) and see if the firm was advertising back then. Most company's that deal

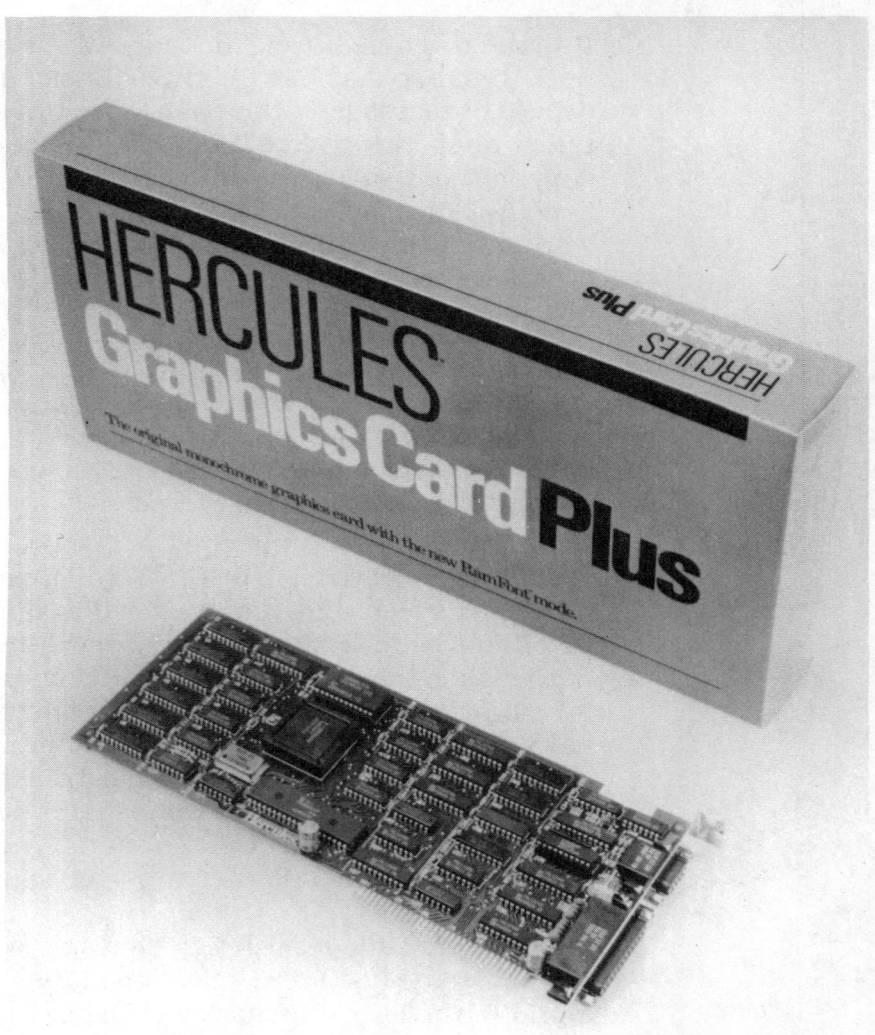

Figure 7-3. The Hercules Graphics Card Plus with RamFont mode is the absolute best in monochrome video adapters.

in poor quality merchandise are in the business for the quick buck and then disappear. The longevity of a company is no guarantee of getting a good product, nor does the youth of a firm indicate a questionable business motive. As in all such dealings, the old adage of "buyer beware" is best applied in heavy doses. And if all else fails, get a brand name PC compatible from your local computer dealer. It won't be as cheap as the other alternatives, but at least you will be able to sleep knowing that there is a dealer that will stand behind the product if you have problems later.

Economy Display Groups

If you have the option of buying the computer without a display group, do it. There are good deals to be found in display groups and you will surely do better on your own than taking the one offered with the machine. Any of the video adapter cards from the major manufacturers that complies with the Hercules video standard will provide excellent resolution (720X348) in a standard that has matured over the years and gained support from almost every application software package being sold today. For our economy system, we go straight to the source and pick up a Hercules Graphics Card Plus™ video adapter board (Figure 7-3). This little gem will give you as close to a WYSIWYG display of your document as you can get without spending thousands of dollars. This board comes with its own built-in memory called RamFont™ that contains 48 fonts that can display text in WordPerfect's editing screen that closely approximates the appearance of the typeface that you are using (Figure 7-4). This board will set you back about $170, and it is well worth the price.

To team up with the video adapter board, an inexpensive monochrome monitor will suit us just fine. As discussed in Chapter 4, color is nice to look at but has very limited uses in desktop publishing. With color monitors costing at least three times that of a monochrome monitor with exceptional quality, we can better spend the difference elsewhere. For our economy

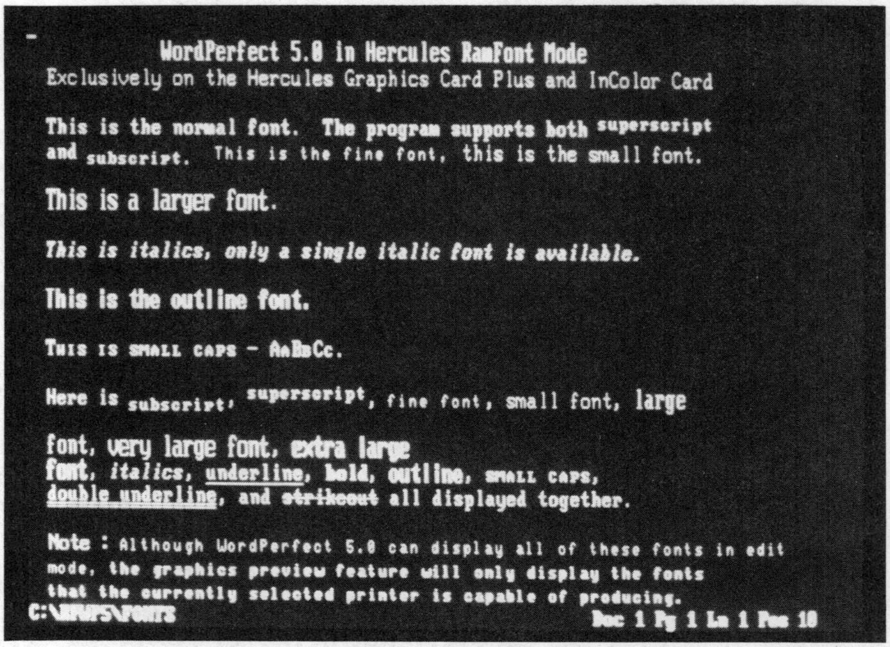

230 *Desktop Publishing with WordPerfect 5.0*

Figure 7-4. The display provided by the Hercules Graphics Card Plus with RamFont is the closest display to WYSIWYG in its price range.

system the Samsung MD-1278 monitor has been selected. The MD-1278 is a 12-inch monitor mounted on a tilt-and-swivel base that can be purchased in white, green, or amber configurations. Because of its attractive price and overall quality, this monitor is an excellent value at just under $100, but some shopping around can even save you a few more dollars.

Major Brand PC Compatibles
The other alternative is to buy a complete computer with display group, memory, and hard disk from one of the major players in the PC compatible market. These computers are best selections for those looking to get into desktop publishing with WordPerfect 5.0 and who do not care to go shopping for the components individually. A complete system consisting of the

computer, 640 kilobytes of RAM, 20 megabyte hard disk, Hercules-compatible video adapter board, and monochrome display will cost about $1500 as opposed to the approximately $1000 for the brand X system.

Economy Printers
When selecting a printer to use for your desktop publishing, the deciding factor will be more heavily weighted by your requirements than by your budget. This is an unfortunate situation, but a reality none the less. You can use the bottom line no-name computer with the minimum requirements for speed, storage, and display resolution, but if you required a laser printer with a resolution greater than 300 DPI, your system will still cost a tidy sum. For the economy system, we can assume that you will not be requiring anything greater than 300 DPI. If you do, there is no rule that says you can't use the computer recommendations here with printer recommendations made later for the more powerful systems.

Dot matrix printers, daisy wheel printers, and laser printers all have their own niche. Surprisingly, though, there are models in each of these printer categories that will cost roughly the same amount. For instance, the best Epson dot matrix printer is about the same price as a C. Itoh daisy wheel printer having moderate capabilities. And laser printers have begun to appear that can compete in this same price range, albeit with fewer capabilities than most laser printers. All three of these printer types are priced in the $1500 range.

But let's think economy. The output of a dot matrix printer may be sufficient for your needs even though they are limited in output to the fonts built into them. Most of these printers produce output in the 180 to 240 DPI range and cost about $700. There are also some daisy wheel printers in this price range, but they are unable to print graphics and thus should not be considered for desktop publishing. Before purchasing a dot matrix printer, make sure it is compatible with the Epson standard command set. The laser printer, on the other hand, should offer LaserJet emulation. If the printer you want to purchase does not support a standard, check with WordPerfect Corporation's Customer Support to see if a printer driver is available for that printer. If not, you should reconsider you decision, because building a printer definition for WordPerfect is not a task for the timid.

Economy Software

The software you select for use in desktop publishing is a matter of functions offered versus your requirements versus price. You will need a copy of WordPerfect 5.0 and DOS, of course. The only additional software that you may require is a paint program to create and edit graphic images for your documents. For the economy system, consider getting PC Paintbrush Plus from ZSoft. PC Paintbrush Plus offers a complete set of graphic editing tools and is very intuitive to operate. Both icon and pull-down menus are provided for fast and easy selection of each editing tool. For a mail order price of about $100, this program may well satisfy all of your graphics requirements. Its bit-mapped file format (PCX) has become one of the industry's dominate graphic standards and is directly supported by Word-Perfect, so no conversion will be necessary.

A System for the Masses

The next system we will build is called a "standard" system for desktop publishing because it offers the best output at a reasonable price for those serious about producing the kind of output that desktop publishing promises. The standard system offers higher performance and increased productivity by incorporating more of two of the **big three**—speed and storage. By increasing the processing speed of the computer and the amount of storage we have (RAM and hard disk), the productivity gains will increase accordingly. But to achieve the utmost in productivity from our system, we will need to augment the types of input that the system can accept. In our economy system, we limited our system's input to what we could enter at the keyboard—text into WordPerfect and graphics into PC Paintbrush Plus. In both cases, putting in the data was time-consuming.

For alternative, and more productive, methods of entering data, we will add a scanner and a modem. Both of these hardware items will enable us to generate text and graphics for our documents much faster and more efficiently than we did before. A color display group will also be incorporated into our system to take full advantage of some of the software we will be using. We will also step up a notch in our choice of printers, thereby producing output that lives up to the extra money we will spend for our system. The final configuration of our system will provide a powerful system that will do just about anything in desktop publishing that we can imagine, yet be flexible enough to grow and change as our needs and desktop publishing technology evolve.

The Standard Computer

The standard computer selected for desktop publishing should run at no less than 10 Mhz, have at least 1 megabyte of RAM, and a minimum of 40 megabytes of hard disk storage. Once again, if you are confident that you can be your own computer technician, there are "no-name" computers that meet these requirements with a price of around $1000. However, as previously discussed, be a wise shopper and look for the same kind of quality that the economy computer should offer. Otherwise, you can purchase excellent computers from such well-established manufacturers as IBM, Compaq, AST Research, and Dell Computers.

Dell Computers is a phenomena in the computer business. Originally a mail order firm (PC's Limited) located in Austin, Texas, Dell began selling its own brand of computers. At first, these computers were built in much the same way as other no-name brands, with components from three or four major manufacturers. But at some point, Dell decided they could make their own computers from scratch at competitive prices. The result is a line of PCs that is in the league with the major players. Dell computers are well-built, offer at least the same functionality as their competitors (and in some cases more), and are often less expensive than their competition. Dell computers also offers a warranty that is second to none—on-site repair for one year.

Therefore, the computer used in our standard system will be the Dell Model 200. This computer is a 12.5 Mhz machine that uses the Intel 80286 microprocessor. The system we will use also has a math coprocessor, 1 megabyte of RAM, and a 40 megabyte hard disk with an access time of 28 milliseconds. We will not get a display group from Dell Computers, opting instead for a display group from other sources. The total cost of this computer will be about $3200, a very reasonable price considering the amount of processing power we will have. It will also have five expansion slots (the hard disk controller board will use one of the six supplied) for additional boards and the system board can hold up to 4.6 megabytes of RAM, giving us plenty of room for expansion.

The Display Group

As we have previously discussed, there is not much requirement for color in desktop publishing until high-quality, reasonably priced color laser printers become available. However, there is some software worthy of our consideration that takes full advantage of the new high-resolution monitors and extended Video Graphics Array (VGA) video adapter boards.

These display groups will provide a display that is far superior to the earlier Enhanced Graphics Adapter (EGA) technology. The immediate benefit that we as desktop publishers can realize from these display groups is the ability to display more text on the screen at one time than has been previously available.

Until these new display groups began to appear, the maximum amount of text that could be displayed on screen was 2000 characters (25 rows of characters with 80 characters in each row). Most extended VGA video adapter boards can be configured to display 80 characters by 66 rows or 90 characters by 32 rows in addition to the standard 80 character by 25 row screen. Obviously, the more information you can view at one time, the easier it is to write and edit the information. Other benefits of these display groups include fast screen updating (most obvious when scrolling through a document) and the ability to use the new generation of graphics software beginning to appear.

Before making the following recommendation, there is one caveat to be observed. More than any other part of your desktop publishing system, the display group will be most heavily weighted by subjective opinion. What looks fantastic to you may not be acceptable to the next person. With so many subjective elements to be considered—resolution, colors, contrast, glare reduction, and so on—finding the right combination of monitor and video adapter board becomes a very personal project. So look at demonstrations of any combination you are considering before you buy anything.

With that said, the Genoa HiRes VGA™ video adapter board combined with the NEC Multisync Plus™ monitor was chosen for our display group. The Genoa HiRes VGA video adapter board is not only 100 percent compatible with the VGA standard, but offers emulation modes that will mimic every video standard developed for the PC: MDA/Hercules, Color Graphics Adapter (CGA), and EGA. This board also goes the VGA standard one better by offering extended modes of operation to provide the resolutions and text capabilities mentioned earlier. And the NEC Multisync Plus® monitor is not only an exceptional monitor in terms of its display characteristics, but it is probably supported by more hardware and software than any other monitor in the industry. This display group will cost about $1400, but you will probably be very pleased with the results.

Standard Peripherals

Peripheral items are those hardware elements that combine with the computer to increase its functionality. Included in this category of hardware would be such things as expanded memory boards, modems, scanners, and so forth. For our standard desktop publishing system, we will add a scanner for inputting text and graphics and a modem to enable us to communicate with bulletin boards, information services, and other people who might be helping us with our publishing (authors, editors, printing houses, etc.). The 1 megabyte of RAM that we got with the computer should be sufficient for our purposes, and because all that memory is located on the system board, we won't need a memory expansion board for this system. This will free all of our expansion slots for other hardware.

The Scanner
The scanner we select should provide full 300 DPI resolution for compatibility with our laser printer. It should also be capable of scanning in true gray-scale mode. There are no laser printers currently available that can print a gray-scaled image, but these files can be printed by typesetters to provide output that closely matches that of traditional screen printing. In addition, it should allow us to not only scan graphic images, but act as an optical character reader (OCR) as well. An OCR can be used to scan hard copy text from various sources directly in WordPerfect, thus saving the time and tedium of re-keyboarding the material.

Figure 7-5. The Hewlett-Packard ScanJet provides true gray-level image scanning for a bargain price.

The scanner for our system is the Hewlett-Packard ScanJet™ shown in Figure 7-5. This little marvel will do just about anything you want it to do, and then some. The ScanJet is a flatbed scanner that operates in much the same way as an office copier, scanning almost any object from photographs to pages in a book. Scanning graphic images in 16 levels of gray is a snap with the included Scanning Gallery™ software. The Scanning Gallery software allows you to preview the scanned image before it is saved and provides reductions to 13 percent or enlargements to 200 percent of the original image. The files created with the ScanJet are in the PCX format and are thus directly compatible with WordPerfect. The list price for all this power is a modest $1990 (about $1300 on the street). Combine the Scan-Jet with the $595 ReadRight™ software package also available from Hewlett-Packard, and you have a very proficient optical character reader system as well.

The Modem

The modem is our doorway to the outside world. The speed with which we get there and the hassles in doing so are what set modems apart from one another. Most modems have adopted the Hayes AT command set, but check to be sure that whichever modem you are about to purchase is compatible with this Hayes modem standard. Modems can be categorized by the maximum speed at which they can transmit and receive data. The faster a modem is, the less money you will spend on telephone calls and connect charges to information services. The two most common modem speeds available are 1200 bits per second (called the baud rate) and 2400 baud. Modems in both of these categories have the ability to fall back to the next lower speed. For instance, a 2400 baud modem can also communicate at 1200 baud and 300 baud while a 1200 baud modem can fall back to 300 baud.

Error detection and correction is also part and parcel of the better quality modems. Error detection and correction is provided to ensure that the data received is the same as the data sent. In addition to the actual data being sent, the sending modem also sends a special piece of information about the data to the receiving modem. The receiving modem looks at this information and compares it with the data received.

Sometimes a noisy telephone line will cause data to be changed along the way from one modem to the other. If the receiving modem detects errors in the data, it will attempt to correct them. If the errors are so prevalent that correction of the data is impossible, the receiving modem asks the sending modem to resend the data. This error detection/correction continues until all of the data has been received. Most communications software packages include some form of error detection and correction, but if it is built into the modem, the process is much faster. Therefore, the modem of choice should incorporate this feature.

The modem we have chosen for this system is the ATI Technologies 2400etc™. This modem is built on a half-length board for mounting inside the computer. It offers 2400 baud operation that is compatible with the Hayes AT command set. Further, it provides Class 5 MNP® error detection and correction, an excellent hardware based implementation that will provide faster file transfers when communicating with other modems equipped with MNP than software based methods. And its list price of $239 is hard to beat for modems with this feature.

ATI even throws in some communications software with this modem, but you are better off getting a copy of HyperACCESS™ from Hilgraeve. HyperACCESS will easily live up to your expectations in communications software including an intuitive user interface that keeps the learning curve to a minimum and a full-bodied programming language that will enable you to completely customize the program. And its data transfer times are among the best in the market. With a list price of $149, it's a steal that should be stolen for our system.

The Standard Printer

The Hewlett-Packard LaserJet Series II (Figure 7-6) could probably be recommend without so much as a single justification and not have anyone question the selection. However, for the sake of completeness, let's touch on a couple of key points to be considered when selecting the laser printer for this system. First, the printer should be reasonably priced. The LaserJet Series II certainly meets this criteria coming in at just $2500, it is an exceptional value for a laser printer of its

Figure 7-6. Hewlett-Packard's LaserJet Series II is the latest incarnation of the printer that defined the standard.

capabilities. The printer should also be widely supported by software and hardware manufacturers. In this category, the LaserJet Series II beats the rest hands down. With a market share of more than 70 percent of all laser printers sold, the printer command language (PCL) built into the LaserJet Series II is supported by over 700 software packages and the serial or parallel interface required is standard equipment in most computers today.

If there was one stone we could hurl in Hewlett-Packard's direction, it would be in the amount of RAM that is provided as standard with the printer. The 512 kilobytes of RAM that comes with the printer when purchased is not enough to print a full page of 300 DPI graphics nor does it give us much room for downloading soft fonts. We will need a memory upgrade for our LaserJet Series II, and not from Hewlett-Packard. Their memory upgrades are far too expensive for our tastes. So we turn to a company that makes memory expansion boards for the LaserJet Series II called JetWare Computer Peripherals. JetWare makes a product called the JetMemory™ board that will add 1 megabyte of memory to our printer for about the price as the same upgrade from Hewlett-Packard. However, unlike Hewlett-Packard's memory expansion kits, these JetMemory boards are expandable in 1 megabyte increments. For our system, we will get the 1 MB Starter board and a +1 MB Expansion board. Total cost is about $800, or the price of a single 1 megabyte upgrade from Hewlett-Packard.

The Standard Software

The software we select for our system should complement the investment we have made in hardware. It should interface with the hardware to take advantage of its strong point while minimizing those areas where we opted for price over capabilities. Generally, the software will fall into three categories: bit-mapped graphics programs, vector graphics programs, and font handling programs. Each of these programs has a very definite place in our desktop publishing system. We can produce very attractive and informative documents with only words, but the old saying is true—a picture is worth a thousand of them. We have the hardware we need to produce some very exciting pages, now let's go do it.

Bit-Mapped Graphics

Bit-mapped graphics are one of those necessary evils in desktop publishing. They take too much memory to store and are printer-dependent, meaning the printed quality is never quite what we would like. But we can come pretty close with a couple of software packages that will not only provide the very best in creating and editing bit-mapped images, but dazzle your boss (even if you are your own boss) and will be a lot of fun to work with too.

The first package is from ZSoft and is a significant extension to the PC Paintbrush Plus program. Publisher's Paintbrush adds the capability to edit images at the resolution of the printer rather than the resolution of the screen. And all of a full-page 300 DPI image can be edited in one screen at one of four different zoom levels. Version 1.5 goes even farther, providing support for several gray-scale scanners (such as our Hewlett-Packard ScanJet) and support for the 265-color modes of the VGA standard. But the amount of memory we have in our computer limits the size of the image we can edit. For instance, to edit one of our scanned 16-gray-level images, however, would require about 4 megabytes of RAM. Since we only have 1 megabyte, we must limit ourselves to either smaller gray-scale images or full page line drawings. This is not really a problem, since we will seldom be called on to incorporate a full page image in our documents. Most will be limited to one-fourth of a page or less. If you are frequently required to edit larger images, read on to the power user system.

The second application is unique in its approach to image creation and editing. Instead of being optimized to the printer's resolution, ColoRIX VGA Paint™ from RIX Softworks is optimized to take full advantage of the standard and extended resolutions of the VGA display group. As such, ColoRIX VGA Paint is the ultimate program for creating and editing color images in resolutions up to 1024X756 in 256 colors. Images in the maximum resolution of our display group (800X600) in 256 colors look like a color photograph projected on a television screen. These images can be cropped, airbrushed, colors can be smudged to produce smooth edges between two dissimilar colors, text can be added, and changed in just about any other way that a photo technician could do in a dark room. And for the desktop publisher, the images can be converted into a 16 gray-level PCX file for importing into WordPerfect. This program is a must see (and must have for a mere $195), so check your local computer dealer for a demonstration. You will be amazed at how far computerized imaging has come on the PC.

One other program that every desktop publisher should have is HOTSHOT Graphics from Symsoft. This package is specifically designed to capture images on the screen generated by software that WordPerfect does not support. HOTSHOT Graphics includes a screen grabber that once loaded, remains out of sight within your computer, ready to capture a picture of the screen to a file. If this software were only for graphics, it would be a very good program. But it will also capture text screens. Again, this capability alone would be nice, but nothing to shout about.

What makes HotShot Graphics™ worth shouting about is its ability to convert both graphics and text screens to one of several graphic formats, including PCX and WordPerfect's own WPG. As if that weren't enough, it includes a graphics editor that has many of the features found in Publisher's Paintbrush, and a complete set of text-oriented tools (annotation, reverse video, etc.) for manipulating captured text screens. HotShot Graphics is a gem of a program and one that greatly simplified creating the screen images used in this book.

Vector Graphics

Vector graphics are a desktop publisher's dream come true. These images are printer-independent and provide the best possible output available from the printer being used. They can also be rotated and scaled directly from within WordPerfect. Most spreadsheet programs provide output of business graphs to a file in the PIC format which is supported by WordPerfect. Drawing packages that produce files in the HPGL file format are also supported by WordPerfect.

For our system, we will use one of each type of package. For business graphics, we will get a copy of Borland's Quattro™ spreadsheet program. This program is completely compatible with Lotus 1-2-3 and other popular spreadsheet programs, yet it is smaller, faster, and cheaper. And for a list price of $249, you get not only graphic files in the PIC format, but the encapsulated PostScript (EPS) format as well. WordPerfect supports the EPS format, and the printed output from this format looks excellent, but we would need a PostScript printer to print them.

The drawing package we have selected is the DesignCAD 3-D™ package from American Small Business Computers. This software offers many of the advanced features you would expect to see only in much higher priced CAD packages, such as hidden line removal and shading of three-dimensional objects. But perhaps the best feature of DesignCAD 3-D™ is its file export formats. In addition to the standard HPGL format, this software also allows you to create encapsulated PostScript files for printing your drawings at the maximum resolution of your printer.

If you need to export your drawings to other CAD applications, you also have the option of creating IGES files that can be read by most mainframe drawing applications. This software can also import files from most other CAD systems, a real lifesaver if you work regularly with drawings created by outside sources. The price for DesignCAD 3-D is about $300, a real bargain when you look around at programs offering considerably less and costing much more.

Font Management
One of WordPerfect's most enhanced features is its font handling abilities. But, like all things that powerful and flexible, font management in WordPerfect can become a nightmare of coded font names, huge printer definition files, and complex installation processes. So where do we turn for help in managing this complex task? We turn immediately to Softcraft's Word

Processor Font Solution Pack™. Word Processor Font Solution Pack provides a complete system, through three separate programs, for making, installing, and modifying any Hewlett-Packard soft font. A fourth program included in this package is used to enhance graphics files that are in the PIC format.

The first of these programs, Softcraft Fontware™, takes any Bitstream outline typeface and generates fonts in any point size we choose. The process is simple and straightforward, producing fonts with names that conform to the Hewlett-Packard naming convention. The technology used to generate the fonts is licensed from Bitstream, so the fonts produced are every bit as good as those produced by the Bitstream Installation Kit. However, the Bitstream Installation Kit produces font names that are cryptic at best, so Softcraft Fontware has the leg up for clarity in this regard. Softcraft Fontware also allows you to generate the font in one of several different character sets, an extremely useful option if your documents contain special characters or foreign languages. These characters may then be accessed by WordPerfect's compose feature.

Laser Fonts is the second program in this package, and worth almost the price of the package itself. Laser Fonts is Softcraft's installation program. The Bitstream Installation Kit makes and installs fonts in one step, but that is all it does. Softcraft takes the installation process several steps farther. Not only will it install fonts that you have made into the printer definition file, it will uninstall those fonts you no longer use and delete font definitions for which you do not have fonts. This reduces the size of the printer definition file dramatically, producing much faster responses in WordPerfect when you create or edit the printer resource file.

At first glance, it may alarm you to have font definitions deleted from the printer definition file, but as you acquire additional fonts, these definitions are added back into the .ALL file with all of the information intact. Another option allows you to generate outline and shadow versions of the font you are installing, essentially creating two more typefaces.

The third font manipulation program, Font Effects™, is one of those software programs that you will wonder how you lived without. This program will take any Hewlett-Packard compatible font and create a new font having special effects characteristics that you select. These effects may be as simple as adding a drop shadow to completely remaking the font with an almost infinite variety of special effects. A simple Dutch font may become a slanted outline font with horizontal lines inside the outlines, as shown in Figure 7-7. What you can do with a font with this package is limited only by your imagination and your sense of good taste. It is exactly for this reason that Font Effects includes a preview feature that will show you, on screen, what a particular effect will look like before you generate the font. Once you get past the hours of just playing with this program, you can get down to making some very fine looking fonts that will serve a variety of purposes, from drop caps to headlines.

The last program in the Word Processor Font Solution Pack is Laser Graphics. This program will shore up one of the real shortcomings of printing business graphics in the PIC format

SoftCraft
FONT EFFECTS

Figure 7-7. A series of Bitstream Dutch characters with special effects applied by Font Effects.

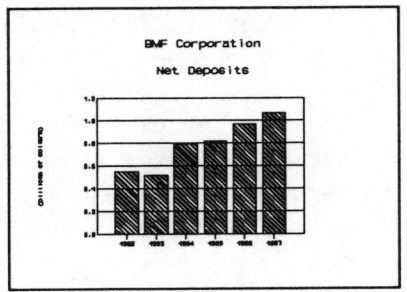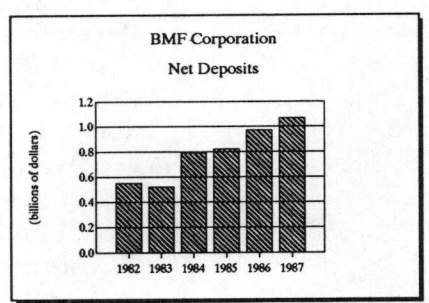

Figure 7-8. Two graphs printed in WordPerfect from the same PIC file. The left graph was printed by WordPerfect in the usual manner. The right graph was enhanced with Laser Graphics and printed as a printer command.

like those generated with Quattro, the "plainness" of these graphics when imported into WordPerfect. Consider the two examples of the graph we used in our sample newsletter in Figure 7-8. The left example was incorporated directly into a WordPerfect document and printed to a laser printer. Notice that the text that was originally a script font has been converted into a san serif font and that the graph has a generally uninspired appearance. Now look at the right graph. It was also incorporated into WordPerfect, but it was sent through Laser Graphics first to be enhanced. A true font was specified for the graph's text (this font must be one that we have already created) and the graph background was enhanced with a drop shadow. The graph was the put into a WordPerfect graphics frame, not a graph, but as a printer command. Let's look at this one a bit closer, not because we need to know how Laser Graphics works, but because it demonstrates one possible use of WordPerfect's printer command function.

If we have a file created in Quattro called PROFITS.PIC, we can run this file through Laser Graphics to create a file called PROFITS.400. The extension specifies the height of the graphic when printed. We then go into WordPerfect and create a graphics frame that is 4 inches high. But rather than loading a file into this frame, we go directly to the edit option. Since we have not loaded a file, we are placed in a blank text screen, not the normal graphics editing screen. As you know by now, most of WordPerfect's text editing features are available at this point, so press **Shift+F8, 4, 6, 2**. We are now in the Format: Printer Functions screen and being prompted for either a Command (option 1) or a Filename (option 2). If we select option 2 and enter PROFITS.400, we will send our "graphic" to the printer, not as a graphic image at all, but as a series of printer commands that will produce the image we started with using the actual fonts we specified in Laser Graphics. This is a good demonstration of Hewlett-Packard's PCL. As such, though, the effects you can achieve with Laser Graphics are limited to graphics printed on Hewlett-Packard laser printers. But the results, as you can see, are stunning.

Each of the four programs included in the Word Processor Font Solution Pack may be purchased separately, but you get a price break if you buy the software group for $595. Softcraft even throws in a Bitstream typeface package of your choice to sweeten the deal. And for serious desktop publishers that will find all four programs indispensable, it is a deal that can't be beat.

The Power System

The power system takes us to the very peak of desktop publishing with WordPerfect 5.0. With this system, you can take on virtually any publishing task and come out smelling like a rose. But performance has a price. You can expect to pay a minimum of $10,000 for one of these systems, and there is no upper limit if you happen to have money to burn. But if you happen to be one of the latter, you won't have it very long if you don't keep an eye on what you are spending. So as in putting together the previous system, cost will certainly be weighted heavily in this system.

Aside from all the power and flexibility this system will cost you, it will also be demanding of your work space. Make sure you have plenty of room in which to put all the equipment, because no matter how little you spend for your power desktop publishing system, it's going to take a lot of desktop. Before you spend a nickel on this system, plan your work area and be sure that everything will fit. Nothing will decrease productivity faster than having to crawl around and over things to get the job done.

The Power Computer

When it comes to power in a computer, there is a choice to be made as to the microprocessor you want to build your system around. The Intel 80386 microprocessor was the first to offer the processing speeds in excess of 12 Mhz. But several manufacturers are offering computers that contain the older Intel 80286 microprocessor that boasts speeds up to 20 Mhz. To further muddy the waters, Intel has introduced the 80386SX microprocessor. This microprocessor has a maximum rated speed of 16 Mhz, but as anyone who purchased an IBM AT will tell you, the rated speed of a microprocessor is often 20 to 30 below its maximum "safe" operating speed. So if trends hold true, by the time you read this, there will probably be computers with the 80386SX running smoothly along at 20 Mhz. And the cost of these new 80386SX machines should be about what 80286-based machines were when they were introduced.

Because of the rapidly changing landscape at the top of the performance heap, its difficult to pick one computer as being all things to all people. But there are two pretty safe bets: the Dell Model 310 and the ALR Flexcache Model 20386DT-R66. Both of these computers use the 80386 microprocessor cruising comfortably along at 20 Mhz. Each can be equipped with 8 megabytes of RAM and a math coprocessor. All come with one 5.25-inch or 3.5-inch disk drive and keyboard as standard equipment.

The Dell Model 310 is a dream machine that tops Dell's line of PCs. However, top of the line does not mean top of the budget. Costing thousands of dollars less than other machines that provide less performance, the Model 310 will zip you along at 20 Mhz with the entire 8 megabytes of RAM sitting comfortably on the motherboard, thus leaving your eight expansion slots free for other boards. Equipped with a 90 megabyte hard disk with an 18 millisecond access time, this computer costs a meager $4600 with the RAM and coprocessor options.

Advanced Logic Research is a company that was unheard of three years ago. But in those three short years, ALR has made a reputation for itself by offering top-notch computers at bottom drawer prices. The ALR Flexchache Model 20386DT-R66 is no exception. Also based on the 80386 microprocessor, this computer will stay right beside the Dell Model 310 with its 20 Mhz processing speed. The cost of this computer, which comes standard with a 66 megabyte hard disk having a 28 millisecond access time, will be $5400 after we add an additional 7 megabytes of RAM to its standard 1 megabyte and the 80387 math coprocessor.

The Power Display Group

To optimize our system for desktop publishing, we will select a monitor that is designed specifically for the task while providing the most flexibility for running other applications. The Genius^2 monitor/video adapter board combination from Micro

Display Systems provides just such a display group. The Genius^2 is a 19-inch monochrome monitor boasting an astounding 1280 by 1024 resolution that allows us to view two full pages side by side at an effective resolution of 100 DPI. The display can produce either black text on a white background or vise versa. It can also display four shades of gray to produce a reasonable display of gray-scaled illustrations. And the Genius^2 is directly supported by WordPerfect by way of the Setup feature.

To make this display group even more attractive, it is either directly supported or has drivers for over 130 of the most popular software packages available. And if you have software that does not support this display either by the software or by an MDS driver, the Genius^2 will emulate the CGA display standard. With CGA compatibility, there is virtually nothing that cannot be run with this display group. The price for this group is the clincher. For $2495 you will have the absolute ultimate in desktop publishing display groups.

The Power Peripherals

We will be using many of the same types of peripherals that we did in the standard system configuration, but we will take a big jump up in capabilities and, of course, price. We will still need a scanner, but for this system, we will opt for a scanner that will produce full 256 gray-shade files. The modem will transfer data files at 9600 baud across standard telephone lines.

The Scanner

It may not be immediately obvious why we would want a scanner capable of producing an image file with 256 levels of gray if there are no laser printers that can print gray-scaled images. And if the highest output device that we ever printed to was a laser printer, we would indeed consider other alternatives. But if you do desktop publishing long enough, there will come a time when laser printers will not provide the quality of output that is required for the task. So typesetters are the next logical step up. Typesetters can easily handle gray-scaled images to produce output that rivals traditional screening processes.

For our power system, we will use the Dest PC Scan 2020™. The PC Scan 2020 (Figure 7-9) is a flatbed scanner that can scan objects as well as pages and photographs to produce full 256 gray-level files. Scanning a full-page photograph will take approximately 4 minutes. The Publish Pak software included with this scanner runs under a version of Microsoft Windows to provide a scan resolution in 200, 240, and 300 DPI increments with scaling from 13 to 200 percent, depending on the resolution selected. Some editing functions such as cropping the image are included with Publish Pak. Output formats include both encapsulated PostScript and PCX, either of which is

Figure 7-9. The Dest PC Scan 2020 provides a 256 gray-level image file from scanned line drawings, photographs, and three-dimensional objects.

directly supported by WordPerfect. The PCX format will also allow our paint programs to edit the image as required.

The Power Modem

Transmitting files at 9600 baud has several benefits. First and foremost, this speed is four times faster than 2400 baud modems, meaning that you will incur one-fourth the telephone charges that you would if using the slower modem. Second, the on-line connect fees charged by many information services will be lower (though probably not one-fourth) than when connected at 1200 or 2400 baud.

The modem selected for the power system is the HST 9600 produced U.S. Robotics. This modem is an external unit that plugs into one of the communications (COM) ports in your computer. It is fully Hayes AT command set compatible, meaning you will have little difficulty configuring it to operate with your communications software. It will also fall back to 1200 or 2400 baud for compatibility with the maximum transmission rate of the modem on the other end of the connection. And at a list price of $799, it will pay for itself in short order if you do a lot of online communicating.

The Power Printer

As stated earlier, it is highly unlikely that your personal resources (financial and otherwise) will allow you to purchase one of the high resolution typesetters referred to in this book. So the next best thing is to buy a laser printer that can share files with typesetters, meaning a printer with support for the PostScript page description language. Aside from being able to produce exact duplicate proof copies of what will eventually be typeset, these printers normally have an extensive library of fonts built into the printer's memory, thus eliminating the expense and effort of purchasing and installing your own fonts. These fonts will take care of 95 percent of your publishing requirements.

PostScript font sizes are defined in real time when the job is sent to the printer, thereby avoiding the time consuming task of not only making the fonts in the proper size, but downloading them to the printer as well. But all fonts are not created equal, or rather the methods by which printers compose PostScript characters are not equal. The quality of the printed output varies greatly from one manufacturer to another. So just because a printer contains the PostScript language is not a guarantee that its output can stand up to its competitors.

For this system, we will require that our printer prints full-page graphics at 300 to 600 DPI, with a rated output of at least eight pages per minute. The page per minute rating (and this applies to all laser printers) is a measure of repetitively printing the same page, not different pages. For instance, our requirement of eight pages per minute implies that the printer be capable of printing eight copies of the same page in 1 minute. The actual printing time for eight unique pages will be higher.

There are two printers that meet these requirements and offer excellent output, the QMS-PS 810™ and the Varityper VT600™. The QMS-PS 810 (Figure 7-10) is a 300 DPI laser printer that not only has PostScript built in, but offers LaserJet+ and Diablo 630 emulation as well. It comes standard with 2 megabytes of memory and 35 resident fonts. These fonts can be scaled to produce characters as small as 4 points and each chararcter font contains complete international character sets. Letters are well formed and sharp, lines are crisp, and black areas print very black. For a competitive price of $5495, you will have a laser printer that beats the competition without breaking your budget.

The Varityper VT600 is the next best thing to owning a typesetter of your very own, without the space, technical complexities, and chemical processing requirements of these output devices. The VT600 provides astounding output at 600 DPI. In case your math is a little rusty, this is four times the print density of 300

The Complete System 255

Figure 7-10. The QMS-PS 810 is the top of the heap in 300 DPI laser printers.

DPI printers! It uses plain paper for prining text and graphics at a rate of 10 pages per minute. This printer has an extremely fast PostScript processor and also comes standard with 35 type fonts, but the fonts are stored on a built-in 20 megabyte hard disk. This quality does not come cheaply, though. At a price of $12000, the VT600 is the ultimate output device at the desktop level, but the results you see will put all of those 300 DPI laser printers to shame.

Each of these printers will accept serial or parallel input and are competitively priced within their markets. Of course, your individual requirements will determine which printer is right for you. But remember that the output of your desktop publishing system will be what readers ultimately use to gauge not only the capabilities of your system, but your capabilities as well. Therefore, the printer is the last place to be conservative on price. As the old saying goes, "you never get a second chance to make a first impression."

Power Software

Now that all of the hardware elements of the power system are in place, we need some power software to take full advantage of it. Again, we can break down the software required into the categories of bit-mapped graphics, vector graphics, and font management. Some will be carry-overs from the standard system because the highest priced software doesn't necessarily mean the best or most powerful software. We will also require some additional muscle in the way in which we manage all this software. An operating environment that extends the capabilities of the operating system will increase our productivity by getting the most performance possible from the software and the hardware.

Bit-Mapped Graphics

As in the standard system, bit-mapped graphics will be the crux of our image processing requirements. When we move up to power software, however, we will combine the versatility of the best bit-mapped graphics package available with a unique product that crosses the line between bit-mapped and vector drawings. The bit-mapped program is our old friend Publisher's Paintbrush. Its power software capabilities include support for editing the full-page 256 gray-level images that our scanner will produce. It also provides some of the best bit-mapped text creation capabilities available. The PCX file format that Publisher's Paintbrush produces has become an industry standard and as such, most other paint programs will produce files in this format. The widespread availability of programs supporting this format will broaden your flexibility.

Deciding which category Micrografx Designer™ belongs in is difficult. However, it has been included in the bit-mapped graphics category because it finds itself in the enviable position of being the first program to combine the flexibility of bit-mapped images with the quality of vector drawings. As such, this program seems to be pointing the direction of the future of graphics programs. Designer can import bit-mapped graphics through the Microsoft Windows Clipboard facility and produce a vector drawing of the image. This transformation is a completely manual process requiring patience on your part to trace over the image, but the future is bright for automating the task.

Of course, Designer is also a very capable vector drawing package, with all the tools you would expect for producing top-notch drawings available through one of the nicest user interfaces to be found anywhere. All these features make Designer an ideal companion to WordPerfect for power desktop publishing. While running under a version of the Microsoft Windows operating environment supplied with the program, Designer will go head-to-head with any vector drawing program running on the Macintosh today. And the output from Designer is completely compatible with WordPerfect's vector graphics formats and the results look stunning from either of our power printers. The list price for Micrographx Designer is $495, but the price is well worth the amazing things you can do with this package.

Power Vectors
When you discuss vector-based graphic applications for power users, there is one that comes immediately to mind: The AutoCAD® drawing system from Autodesk. This venerable program has maintained its market dominance, and for good reason. It has kept pace with user demands and technological advances. It is by far one of the easiest programs of its type to use and the support for the product by third-party vendors is unsurpassed. Drawings may be created as either two or three dimensional.

Three-dimensional drawings may be further enhanced with hidden line removal and, using AutoShade (also from Autodesk) the three-dimensional object may have shading added to produce a lifelike rendition of the drawing with variable perspectives, light sources, and reflectiveness. AutoCAD drawings may be plotted to a file rather than a plotter, resulting in an HPGL file that can be imported directly into WordPerfect.

AutoShade™ drawings can be saved as Encapsulated PostScript files to produce equally pleasing printed results. Priced at a hefty $2850 (AutoShade is an additional $495), AutoCAD is not for the faint of budget or the user who only dabbles in vector drawings. But if you plan to make a sizable part of your living by publishing CAD drawings within WordPerfect documents, you won't regret the purchase.

Communications Software

The communications software that we select for our power system is every bit as important as the modem we have. The software should take full advantage of the modem's features to provide the fastest file transfers possible. It should also be highly configurable to our communications requirements because each individual will have preferences about how the software should interact with the user as well as with the remote system. And because WordPerfect is available for a large number of different types of computers, the communications software should provide extensive support for terminal emulation.

A good script language is also essential in our selection of power communications software. A script file contains commands that are read by the communications software when the file is loaded and run. These commands may be as simple as a log-on sequence to an information service. Or the file may contain all the information required to dial up and connect with a remote site, get your mail, send and receive several files, and finally log off and hang up. And all of this may be done at night while you sleep and the telephone rates are lower. The power of this script language should be weighed in the purchasing decision at least as much as any other single feature.

The script language is almost a programming language in its own right, but you don't need to be a computer programmer to right one. However, the ease with which scripts can be written and changed is crucial to our selection process. The ability to transfer files in the background while we continue to use the computer for other tasks is also highly desirable. For instance, we may want to start a file transfer and then go back to WordPerfect to write a message to be posted before we log off. The file transfer would continue while we were in WordPerfect, thereby doubling our productivity.

Two communications software packages meet our criteria for power communications. The $295 Smartcom III from Hayes Microcomputer and Relay Gold by Relay Communications priced at $275. These programs represent the "cream of the crop" in communications software. Both are 100 percent Hayes AT command set compatible and both support communications at rates far beyond our 9600 baud.

Operating System Enhancements

Operating system enhancements are as varied in function as they are in numbers. Some offer menu shells for easy selection of application programs, others provide a form of "coprocessing" whereby two or more applications are loaded into memory simultaneously, and a few offer true concurrent operation of multiple applications. The difference between having a program loaded into memory and having that program available for processing is a huge step in terms of complexity. Programs that are merely loaded into memory are available for processing, but cannot continue active processing when swapped with another program also in memory. Therefore, if you are indexing a database, for instance, and place your database application in the "background" in order to do some work with WordPerfect, processing of the database is halted until the database application is brought to the "foreground."

The reason for this limitation dates back to the original design of the PC. The PC has several chips and internal software that controls how text and graphics are written to the screen. Most software developers, however, realized that this hardware and software created a bottleneck in the speed with which their applications would run. To increase the speed of their programs, they took to bypassing the computer's method of writing to the screen and chose to have their applications write directly to the video memory. Most popular applications today use this method, including WordPerfect. As a result, the application demands that the screen be available at all times when processing is being done.

Many software products have been developed to offer a solution to this product, but only two have met with widespread buyer acceptance: Microsoft Windows and DESQview® from Quarterdeck. Both of these products offer a true multitasking environment, but DESQview is the smaller, quicker, cheaper, and more adaptable of the two. All of the applications selected for our power computer (including WordPerfect) will function normally in the background mode, just a keystroke away from being the foreground application. The low price of $99 hides a program worth many more times that in increased productivity. Installation of the program is easy and with little computer knowledge you can have it up and running in short order. And once it is up and running, you'll wonder how you ever got along without it.

Windows is also an important product to be considered. If you plan to use Designer for creating vector drawings from bitmapped graphics, you will require Windows for its Clipboard capabilities. Presentation Manager (the user interface implemented by Windows) will also play an important role in future operating systems, including OS/2 (IBM's next operating system). Of course, whether you implement OS/2, Windows, or a version of DOS will be determined by your needs, the capabilities and limitations of each, and the acceptance of each by software developers and end users. Neither Windows nor DESQview represent a large investment. Provided you do not purchase software designed to run exclusively in one of these operating environments (Designer can run in a DESQview window, for instance), you can afford to be patient in your commitment to one of these operating environments.

Other Utilities

The term "other utilities" covers all those neat little programs that are indispensable but don't fit neatly into any category. Three of the more noteworthy of these include SideKick Plus™ from Borland International, Mace Utilities™ by Mace Software, and Disk Optimizer™ from SoftLogic Solutions. SideKick Plus provides a complete set of desktop organization tools (calculator, calendar, notebook, etc.) that remains in memory and can be immediately called up on screen with one keystroke. This program is an absolute must for making sense of the day-to-day chaos that we all must endure. The Mace Utilities program is a set of file management tools that can unerase files that are accidentally deleted, change the attributes of files, and many other useful tasks. Disk Optimizer is a program that takes a hard disk that has slowed to a crawl because parts of large files are stored all over the disk and puts the zip back in by reorganizing all the parts into contiguous files. The increase in a hard disk's access speed can be dramatically increased in a disk that contains a large number of fragmented files.

Appendix

Newsletter Source Files

This appendix contains the text of the news stories used for the example newletter in this book. If you want to follow along with the exercises, type each story in WordPerfect and save the file under the file name indicated. While you can learn a good deal about WordPerfect 5.0 by just reading each chapter, there is an old saying that learning is doing. So I recommend that you spend a few minutes to produce these files so as we go along putting our newsletter together, you will be able to work through the tutorial with us.

File Name: NEWS1.WP5

Deposits Top One Billion $$$

Hartford, CT

For the first time in the history of Barmecide Mutual Funding Corporation, customers' net deposits topped the $1 billion mark. President Franklin Minter said, "This is a milestone for our company, in terms of both our firm's growth and our customers' confidence." While avoiding speculation that stockholders would be receiving dividends for the first time since the company was founded in 1873, Mr. Minter did say that he expected a nice year-end bonus for himself and selected staff members. "It would only be fair. We have done a splendid job this year," said one staff member who asked not to be identified.

Employees have expressed delight that upper management has taken the lead in crediting themselves for the explosive growth of BMFC over the past four years. Said one, "For the first time, I am motivated to look toward the corner and hope they finally get what they have deserved for so long." Other employees were too shocked by the good news to offer any response. However, a party has been organized by a large group of employees to celebrate the occasion.

Tentatively schedule for Wednesday, March 13 at the Tusculoosa Bar & Dance Hall, all nonmanagement employees are encouraged to attend. There is no cover charge and the party will begin promptly when people begin to show up.

Congratulations, BMF Corporation and Mr. Minter, on a job well done!

File Name: NEWS2.WP5

Company Mourns Employee's Passing

Hackensack, NJ

Mr. William Beatty, corporate financial auditor for 16 years, passed away Thursday, April 20, at his home in New Jersey. He is survived by his wife, Helen, and three children, ages 7, 12, and 16. Funeral services are scheduled for Tuesday, April 25. Services will commence at 2:00 pm at the Samuel Morris Memorial Funeral Home.

Mrs. Beatty could not be contacted at press time, but the circumstances surrounding the death of Mr. Beatty have been described by Hackensack police as "suspicious." Mr. Beatty was killed in what appears to have been a car-bomb explosion. No personal effects were missing, prompting police to eliminate robbery as a motive. However, a briefcase containing certain financial records, thought to be in Mr. Beatty's possession, was not found at the scene.

All of us at BMF Corporation who worked with William mourn his passing. Donations to his survivors may be forwarded to Mr. Franklin Minter. Mr. Minter told **Insider Info** "It is my upper-most priority that the entire Beatty family be taken care of."

File Name: NEWS3.WP5

They Call This A Race?

The BMFC Runners Club held their annual "Spring Jump" run February 14 in Waterford. Distances of 2 and 5 kilometers were run starting at the Holy Street landfill. The races began with what sponsors hoped would become an annual event; a 10 meter tyke run for 1 to 3 year olds. However, a small oversight by the organizers of the event may force the tyke run to be canceled in future years. According to witnesses, the toddlers were well-behaved as they took their positions on the starting line. When the starter's pistol was fired, however, the children were scared by the sudden noise and ran in all directions. After several hours of frantic searching for their lost loved-ones, the New Jersey Highway Patrol was called in to assist parents in the search. About sundown the last lost child was located and waivers had been signed by all the parents concerned pledging not to file law suits against neither the sponsors nor BMF Corporation.

The senior division of this race was won by 63-year old Vince Norton. The results are being challenged, however, by 68-year old Ned Turner. Mr. Turner stated that he was leading Mr. Norton when he was pushed off the course by one of the scared children. The judges are considering his protest.

File Name: NEWS4.WP5

Management Course Offered

A management course tailored to the unique requirements of BMF Corporation employees is being offered by Waterford Junior College. Topics covered during the eight-week course include social conduct for upwardly mobile managers, getting the most from under-achievers, and creative bookkeeping techniques. Anyone interested in learning about workings of the inner circles at corporations such as BMF Corporation is encouraged to attend.

Class size is limited to the first 120 applicants, so early registration for this course is essential. The class times, dates, and meeting place will be announced after the class size is determined.

For more information, call your employee assistance representative or write directly to Waterford Junior College at 1400 W. DuMont Street, Waterford, NJ 01234.

File Name: NEWS5.TXT

Ms. Everett Collects Garbage

Ms. Susan Everett works in the Internal Auditor Section by day, but in her own time, Susan collects garbage. A loyal employee of BMFC for 24 years, Susan says that her addiction to collecting garbage began some 40 years ago when she went to the local dump site with her husband, the late Thomas Everett. There, among the piles of genuine rubbish, Susan discovered the treasures that now sit in every part of her home.

"All of these things were junk to somebody, but I love them," Susan says with a gleam in her eyes. The mainstay of her vast collection is a huge assortment of glass bottles in every color and shape. "Bottles are maybe my favorite, they're so pretty." Other items to be found include furniture, kitchen appliances, and things that defy description.

Susan also likes to collect items that are big. As a matter of fact, Susan says "the bigger, the better." The family station wagon has long since been replaced by a 2-ton pickup truck.

We at BMF Corporation always take time to salute the unique individuals that are our corporation. And Ms. Everett certainly qualifies as one of those unique individuals. Good luck, Susan, and happy hunting!

File Name: NEWS6.WP5

Computer Security Is Your Concern

When was the last time you thought about your computer after you had turned it off and gone home for the day? If you believe that your computer sits quietly in the dark awaiting your arrival the next morning, you may be in for a surprise.

What are you required to do before you have access to all the sensitive information stored inside your computer? It's doubtful that you (or anyone else) need to do anything more than flip the power switch before the data is readily available.

This fact was painfully demonstrated last month when extremely sensitive computer documents "fell" into the eager hands of federal investigators. The damage done has not yet been determined fully, but sources close to the situation say that the loss in fines against BMF Corporation due to the breach will be substantial.

Mr. Franklin Minter summed up BMF Corporation's position quite clearly. "If you want to keep your job, secure your data." It's just that simple. If you have data on your computer that could damage our corporation, put it on a disk and lock it up. A word to the wise is sufficient.

File Name: NAMELIST.DIF

Employee Update

Kelly Beck 12-23-88 Terminate	Thomas Mason 01-22-89 Retire
John Bernard 12-23-88 Terminate	Kurt Nielsen 12-12-88 Terminate
Stacy Collier 01-26-89 New Hire	Susan Quinn 01-13-89 New Hire
Gary Curtis 01-03-89 New Hire	Craig Russell 01-22-89 Retire
Patrick Donohue 01-17-89 Retire	Patrick Spain 12-16-88 Terminate
Douglas Kahn 12-12-88 Terminate	

File Name: GRAPH1.PIC

The following data was used to construct the GRAPH1.PIC graphic file.

1982   0.55

1983   0.52

1984   0.79

1985   0.82

1986   0.97

1987   1.07

File Name: GRAPH2.PIC

The following data was used to construct the GRAPH2.PIC graphic file.

1982   0.55

1983   0.52

1984   0.79

1985   0.82

1986   0.97

1987   1.07

Index

A

Adobe Illustrator 88	102
AFCs	86
alternate font	23
aspect ratio of graphics	
defined	154
retaining correct	153
automatic backup	161
automatic font change	159
See also AFCs	

B

Banner Style	
loading	146
baud rates	61
Block function	159
bridge software	104, 112
buffering, data	220

C

Canon printer engine	197
capture programs	104
capture software	
Grab Program	111
text	110
text and graphic	111
capture sofware	
graphic	111
character sets	80
clock speed	215
columns	
turning on	148
compose function	79, 97
consistency, document appearance	144
Convert Program	48
converting files	48

D

data transfer speed	219
density, printer	191
Designer	102, 256
DIF file format	51
display group	223
display resolution	215
dithering	107, 119
Document Description Language	195
document management	30
document processors	18
capabilities and limitations	19
definition	18
required functions	21
DOS text files	49

E

Edit Figure function	
to view codes	146
error detection and correction	238
escape sequences	83

F

Fast Save option	208
fat bit mode	105
file compare	31
file-by-file backup	225
font	
creation	64

273

Index

download with print job	71
initially present	71
font installation kits	
Bitstream Fontware	36
Laser Fonts	36
fonts	
bit-mapped	57
initially present	207
installation	57
outline	56
screen	223
special effects	246
Force Odd/Even	163
forcing new column	164
fragmented files	261
frame	
defined	24
page	152
frame editing	
error message	177
selecting a valid number	177
frame size and position	
automatic calculation of	151
frames	
horizontal position options	151
page	151
setting into columns	151

G

Generic text files	49
GIF file format	104
GRAPH1.PIC	
inserting in frame	152
graphic editing function	101
graphic line function	122
creating	164
gray levels	107

H

hard disk controller	218
Headlines style	
turning on	164, 167
using	157
HOTSHOT Graphics	111, 243
hyphenation	29
hyphenation zone	
defined	30

I

IBM AT	16
IBM PC	
introduction	8
open architecture	15
original capabilities	15
interface	
parallel	220
serial	219
Interpress	195

J

jaggies	100

K

kerning	
defined	28
information	81
keyboard definition	
creating	89
loading	144

L

LaserJet Series II	
capabilities	56
used for tutorial	55
leading, defined	28
line draw function	122
lines	
graphic	25

M

Macintosh computer	13
macro	
Pointing Hand	146
Pointing Hand, creating	142
mail order shopping	227
Master Document	
creating	147
expanding	148
generating tables and lists	31
Microsoft Word	18
minidocument	
in frames	157
mirror image backup	225
MNP error correction and detection	239
multitasking environments	260

N

National Publisher's Exchange	62
New Page Number function	173
Newsletter style	
creating	90
loading	146

O

Office Publisher, The	16
optical character reader	236

P

page composition software	
required support software	17
page composition systems	
faults	13
for minicomputers	11
for personal computers	12
page description language	195
page design	39
page layout process	39
PageMaker	16
paperless office	8
PCX file format	103
PostScript	195
Primary Merge file	53
printer control	207
printer control language	195
Printer Program	65, 73
printer resource file	67
printers	
controls in document processors	37
daisy wheel	8
dot matrix	8
Epson command set	191
laser	12
LaserJet Series II	55
Laserwriter	13
noise	194
read-only memory	197
printing file to disk	210
processing, foreground and background	259
Publisher's Paintbrush	105
publishing system software	
for personal computers	10

R

Ricoh printer engine	197
ruling lines	164

S

saving files	
automatic backup	161
in case of hardware/software failures	161
to allow experimentation	161
script language	258
Secondary Merge format	
in converting text	51
shortening columns	
by resetting bottom margin	174
with Ctrl+Return	174
soft fonts, defined	56
space filler, in columns	167, 171

style library 94
Styles
    collapsed and expanded 34
    creating 90
    in document processors 33
    loading 145
stylesheet
    See Styles
subdocument, expanding 183
subdocuments 148
substitute font 23
substitute fonts 88
SYSOPs 59

T

table of contents
    defining 184
    generating 181 - 183
    loading into frame 185
text
    as a graphic image 9
    ASCII compared to DOS 51
    flush right 159
    in frames 157
    justified 28
    proportionally spaced 25
text format commands
    in publishing system software 10
transfer protocol 62
turnkey systems 13
typeface installation 23
typefaces
    use of by document processors 22
typesetters
    Linotype 27
    Monotype 27

U

User-defined Box
    options 155
User-defined Box frame
    options 149

User-defined Box frames
    creating 149

V

vaccine programs 61
vectors 115
Ventura Publisher 16
vertical position
    for frames 168
VGIF program 104
video capture 102
Video Graphics Array (VGA) 234
view figure codes
    with Edit Figure 146
viewer programs 104

W

word spacing
    defined 29
WordPerfect
    support for color printing 194
WordPerfect 5.0 18
WYSIWYG display
    in document processors 35
    of text and graphics 11

X

XMODEM protocol 62